How To Tell
GOD From The DEVIL

A. Roy Eckardt

How To Tell
GOD From The DEVIL

On the Way to Comedy

Transaction Publishers
New Brunswick (U.S.A.) and London (U.K.)

Library of Congress Catalog Number: 94-4912
ISBN: 1-56000-179-8
Printed in the United States of America

Library of Congress Cataloging-in-Publication Data
Eckardt, A. (Arthur Roy), 1918–
    How to tell God from the Devil : on the way to comedy / A. Roy Eckardt.
        p.   cm.
    Includes bibliographical references and index.
    ISBN 1-56000-179-8 (hard)
    1. Theodicy.   2. God.   3. God (Judaism).   4. Devil.   5. Christianity and antisemitism.   6. Comic, The—Religious aspects—Christianity.   7. Comic, The—Religious aspects—Judaism.   8. Wit and humor—Religious aspects—Christianity.   9. Wit and humor—Religious aspects—Judaism.   10. Judaism—Doctrines.   I. Title.
BT160.E26   1994
231'.8—dc20   94-4912
                                                                          CIP

FOR
Alice Eliza
Paula, Kenny, and Jesse
Stacy, Steve, Elizabeth, and Stephanie

If within the old man there is not a young man,
then he is but one of the Devil's angels.
                    —Henry David Thoreau
(Thank you, Thoreau, for encouraging geriatric
comedy.)

The comic comes into being when society and the
individual, freed from the worry of self-preserva-
tion, begin to regard themselves as works of art.
                         —Henri Bergson
(*Merci, Monsieur,* for reminding us of the
aesthetics of comedy.)

Sour godliness is the Devil's religion.
                              —John Wesley
(Our divine is being rather prosaic; I allow him this
costly space only in observance of my Methodist
down-bringing.)

There are two equal and opposite errors into
which our race can fall about the devils. One is
to disbelieve in their existence. The other is to
believe, and to feel an excessive and unhealthy
interest in them. They themselves are equally
pleased by both errors and hail a materialist or a
magician with the same delight.
                              —C. S. Lewis
(The British have a knack for cautioning their American cousins, others too perhaps, to avoid extremes.)

It is a very serious thing to be a funny woman.
                    —Frances M. Whitaker
                         (1814–1852)
(Application: It is infinitely easy for funny men to
be boring.)

Real comedy can't be learned; it comes from a
need for justice.
                         —Elayne Boosler
(Here in a nutshell, gentle reader, is the problem
addressed by this book.)

Contents

Preface

I could call this book a mystery story, and, if purchasers did not look too carefully before buying, I could run off with some good sales. Alas, the pretense would be false, since "mystery" today has a special, popular connotation. It is the case, nevertheless, that all three of my "chief characters" are, as we shall see, mysteries.

A personal word, at once embarrassing and self-assuring: Here is a book wherein I have finally succeeded (I think) in presenting myself and my views in the way I should like family, friends, colleagues, and readers to remember me (dreams of glory). A great deal of my earlier work is, as the British like to say, redundant, or, as the Germans prefer to say, *ausgestorben*. But not *For Righteousness' Sake*. But not *Sitting in the Earth and Laughing*. But not....

No. That's it.

I dedicate this book to all members of my immediate family. With prejudice to none, but only love, I single out Alice Eliza, my wife and companion of more than fifty years. She appears a rather fragile little person, and so she is. But her place in my life is capacious, her *caritas* is massive, her presence is redeeming.

I think of human beings who have suffered and who suffer on the very day I write. To any of these who may wonder how the comedy I seek to represent or foster can escape trivialization and even sacrilege, I can simply say that it is my anguish that creates my humor. I intend this volume only to help make a little bearable our unbearable time, "after" the *Shoah*, "after" many other horrors, and "during" our individual and collective horrors of today. I try to work toward a more responsible moral place for myself and for the Christian community of which I am a part.

Many of the published sources I utilize are "primary," many as well are "secondary." I have always agreed with a teacher of mine, the late Gordon Allport of Harvard, that one is not to apologize for resorting to good secondary materials, provided one uses them with discretion and sustains them with creativity. Among other things, such sources help save the scholar from the hollow pretense that his own poor renderings of data are somehow entitled to the same hearing as are those of the experts. Thus, in chapter 6 of this book, since Heiko Oberman knows Martin Luther infinitely better than I do, I turn for aid to Oberman's rendering of Luther; but since I know Reinhold Niebuhr better than some other people do, I work via Niebuhr's own writings.

Speaking of sources, I may just add that biblical citations herein are from the New Revised Standard Version.

Finally, I extend many thanks to Laurence Mintz, my editor at Transaction Publishers, for his careful and helpful work.

A. ROY ECKARDT

1

Prologue

The Devil reveals the reality of our situation, the
fact that we can't really escape our earthly destiny.
—Ernest Becker

The late Abba Kovner used to show visitors at his kibbutz that the hut in which he composed his poems stood halfway between the children's playground and the cemetery. Is not this where we all do our work? We are propelled from the joy of childhood (i.e., those of us who are not, when little ones, hopelessly downtrodden and hungry) to the graveness of death; here is the story each of us shares. This story is particularly on my mind as I prepare this, one of my final books.

I

Many will lament, and properly so, the predominantly male cast of this work. I could ask readers to consult my *Black-Woman-Jew,* which sets forth the view that the question and the eventuality of human liberation are primarily the question and the eventuality of female liberation.[1] I could further plead that the sources I select for review and comment in this new book have been chosen, consciously at least, in a sex-blind way for their bearing upon our subject. Yet once all such pleas are offered up, the male bias and futility behind and within this volume will not have gone away. (Recently, I found myself attracted by the following lines— until I saw that they were written by a male uneasy about feminism: "I don't understand guys who say they're feminists. That's like the time Hubert Humphrey, running for president, told a black audience he was a soul brother."[2])

1

I might venture to insert that were it not so unwieldy, a more complete subtitle of the book would be *On the Way to Comedy, A Few New Twists and Turns Within the Christian Social Gospel.* In this connection I follow Harvey Cox's understanding of *politics* as something very broad and deep, the entire "sphere of human mastery and responsibility." I further agree with Cox, and with Paul Lehmann, when they suggest that God is a politician: "What God is doing in the world is politics, which means making and keeping life human." From this point of view, theology today ought to be "that reflection in action" whereby we try to find out "what this politician-God is up to" and seek to move in a like direction. "In the epoch of the secular city, politics replaces metaphysics as the language of theology." Of course, there is "no high court before which those who affirm God's reality and hiddenness can press their case against those who suspect, as Kafka did, that there is No One There at all."[3] If this is so with God, it is surely the case with the Devil. (Whether the Devil is also a politician remains for our reflection.)

Ordinarily I shy away from "how-to" books (other than technical ones). At best such endeavors manage only more or less superficial answers to questions whose gravity and complexity elude that kind of treatment. Yet here I am with a "how-to" creation of my own. My excuse is that I am grappling with a grave and complex human challenge, if only in provisional and heuristic ways, and that such an effort bears directly upon human living and dying.

This short study seeks to relate God, Devil, and Comedy. I could say "the myth of God, the myth of the Devil, and the myth of Comedy," but perhaps we ought to wait to see whether or how that eventuality can be made cogent. In a quite different frame of reference, Hippolyte Taine devised, a long time ago, the phrase "metaphysical poem."[4] Despite its oxymoronish cast—or maybe because of that—the expression might be applied to the present work.

We have witnessed in recent years a widespread effort to reconcile the incommensurateness of "transcendent" reality and "immanent" reality through the offering up of the construct of *myth.*[5] Myth fashions a marvelous, sometimes even magical, world of mediation between objective phenomena and pure fancy, between hard data and subjective invention. It expresses "truths" and "claims" that, in words favored by Reinhold Niebuhr, are to be taken "seriously though not literally."[6] An alternate yet rather related stance is that of *the comic,* which covets a like mediating role between the mystery of fact and the mystery of inter-pretation, thereby creating additional mysteries. The comic joins myth in nurturing the human imagination, yet at the same time it worries over the difficulties myth often gets into when trying to sustain its connection with real history, and then, in the end, it ventures a few words quite peculiar to itself.

The procedure I follow here can be simply, though not uncontroversially, stated (with a partial bow to Immanuel Kant): One preeminent, even historic instrument for distinguishing God and the Devil, or at least God and evil, is linked to theoretical (speculative) rea-son. It entails a markedly philosophic, sometimes a theologic, approach. Noteworthy is its creation of one or another implicitly or explicitly ra-tionalist (traditionalist, classical) theodicy. Rationalist, traditionalist theodicies endeavor to justify God before the fact of evil, to reconcile God and faith in the very face of evil, to attest to the justice of God despite evil.[7] In a word, theodicy strives to *argue*.

I do not say that this approach (reported upon at some length in chap-ters 2 and 3) is bereft of value, nor do I hold to an unbridgeable gulf between rationalist theodicy and an alternative, noticeably different, way, a turn toward resources within practical reason. I do suggest that the latter way is also worthy of being heard (chapters 5 and those that fol-low), with its greater allowance for or reliance upon the imaginative impulse. Theodicy as a whole is hardly lacking in creative imagination; I speak here in highly comparative terms. A peculiar resource for us may be found in the world of comedy, which is rather more childlike and joyful than is rationalist theodicy, with the latter's prevailing sober-ness. Perhaps lightheartedness ought to be taken more seriously.

I have inserted the adjective "rationalist" in front of the kind of theodicy primarily analyzed and assessed in this book because I am not referring to such a transrationalist theodicy as that of Wendy Farley in *Tragic Vision and the Divine Compassion: A Contemporary Theodicy.*[8] Despite the unqualified wording of her subtitle, Farley is able to tran-scend the traditional rationalist-theodicean stance in ways not incom-patible with the second part of the present study. I have in mind her insistence upon the divine compassion and divine justice. She is any-thing but a rationalist. Furthermore, for me, as we shall see, "the divine compassion" is coextensive with "the divine comedy." It is the case that the critique of theodicy we will eventually be making applies to all theodicies, including my own, insofar as such endeavors constitute human efforts to explain and cope with the reality of radical evil. However, as we shall also maintain, the relative convincingness of particular theodicies turns upon the degree to which they take the Devil into account, or at least a serviceably equivalent reality, as source and agent of radical evil. At this point, Wendy Farley's contribution is as problematic as any theodicy. As Jeffrey Burton Russell writes, "no theodicy that does not take the Devil fully into consideration is likely to be persuasive."[9] I propose a basic paradox for our ongoing reflection: Theodicy is least reasonable—indeed, least scientific or empiricist—when it denies the Devil, and even when it ignores him.

Were the category of theodicy to be ballooned out to encompass any and every reckoning with God in the face of evil, we should clearly have to include comedy within that endeavor. But I am suggesting a fundamental, if not wholly ironclad, distinction, at once methodological and existential, between theodicy as the utilization of human contemplation (theōriá) to deal with a life-and-death matter, and comedy, one application on the part of the practical reason to the same matter. We need little familiarity with comedy to be apprised of its essentially nonspeculative or transspeculative qualities—even if it is not possible to claim that its "practical," earthy, playful, or seemingly crazy bent is automatically more useful than "theory."

To "go beyond" theoretical/speculative reason is not to fall into irrationality or antirationality. The very term "practical *reason*" retains reason as its anchor. Surrogates of a comic vision are not required to be antiphilosophical. (The "philosophy of comedy" is, indeed, a highly reputable enterprise.)[10] All that these representatives need do, or what they can do, is to carry ahead the discussion of God/Devil by calling attention to resources that strictly theodicean analysis does not provide.

Hippolyte Taine's expression, a "metaphysical poem" (poetic metaphysics?), may thus be retained as allowing for the two sides of our dialectic: "metaphysical," i.e., the theoretical aspect, and "poem," i.e., the aspect of imaginative practicality.

I do not presume to boast any saving power for comedy/humor/laughter. I am only in search of ways to *tell* God from the Devil, not ways to vanquish the Devil. Differently put, I am not coveting one of God's major jobs. However, I should nowhere rule out the eventuality that laughter (divine as perhaps human) may do *something* to help rout the devilish forces, or at least to disconcert the Devil a little bit. In question form: Can anyone be counted upon to have a last laugh?

In olden times, when I was serving as editor of the *Journal of the American Academy of Religion,* I included as one rule on our stylesheet the noncapitalization of d-e-v-i-l. Since then, I have come to take the Devil rather more seriously than that—but also, I think, God, and also, I think, the grace of comedy.

Accordingly, the present inquiry is not an exercise upon the question of the existence of God as such, nor is it a disquisition upon the Devil as such, nor is it an analysis of the theme of comedy as such. Instead, I am limiting myself to relations. I want to consider how all of these concepts (realities?) might be connected. Taken together, the three seem to me to suggest a triangle, which, if not eternal, is at least historical and moral. The question is: How, if at all, may God-Devil-Comedy be linked?

II

Proceeding in reverse order, I venture a word upon the identity of each of our three variables.

1. I have already said a little about comedy. In coming to terms with comedy and the comic vision, I have grown to appreciate Edward L. Galligan's treatment of comedy as a constitutive, vital, and widely encompassing mode of the human imagination. Thus is comedy much more at home with images than with pure (?) ideas.[11] However, I concede, with E. B. White, that humor is essentially a mystery.[12] (If such is indeed the case for a fully human phenomenon like humor, is it not even more the case for the transcending identities of God and Devil? Gracious, we have no less than three most formidable mysteries on our hands!)

Mysteries do their best to elude definition. Yet we owe it to one another to make plain the varied linguistic and/or phenomenological ways we go about using our primary terms, however mysterious the realities or claims behind them.

I tend to place comedy and humor under the heading (my notion is indebted to the views of others) of a certain way or certain ways of celebrating the incongruous, the contradictory, the absurd.[13] John Morreall writes: "The essence of humor lies in the enjoyment of incongruity."[14] It is incongruity that makes humor and comedy possible. (Should you be moved to protest that this proposal merely substitutes one mystery for another, you are entirely right. For example, why should incongruity so often give rise to laughter? I don't think anyone knows.)

A closely parallel interpretation is that of Søren Kierkegaard: "Wherever there is life there is contradiction, and wherever there is contradiction, the comical is present."[15] But I should wish to balance this with an additional persuasion of Kierkegaard's, that a sense for the comic is a function of human suffering. I very much believe that this is so. In general, I tend to place the comic exercise within soulful and abiding responses to humankind's finitude, to—putting the matter in existentialist language—the incongruous human condition of "thrownness."[16] None of us asks to be born or to die. With every living creature, we are *thrown* into life, as into death. And do we ever wholly blot out the terrible thought that the happiest souls are those who have never been born? Albert Camus is right: "Man is not entirely to blame; it was not he who started history."[17]

To take the above position respecting the interpretation of humor is to assign the comic, in Peter Berger's wording, to "an objective dimension of man's reality, not just a subjective or psychological reaction to that reality."[18] In this last vital respect, the corpus of comedy teams up with both the Devil and God, as we are about to note.

2. Rollo May cautions against reifying the concept of the Devil, but he only means that this fault puts the Devil "in time and space." (With this qualification in mind, I should think the same caution applies to what we say of God.) May continues to explain that the Devil "in some strange form" is "essential to creativity."[19]

We are also the beneficiaries of a monumental, multivolume study of the Devil by the historian Jeffrey Burton Russell.[20] Russell treats the Devil empirically, historically, and phenomenologically. Simply expressed, the Devil is the personification of absolute evil, the essence of evil consisting in the deliberate "abuse of a sentient being, a being that can feel pain. It is the pain that matters." Evil is identified as "meaningless, senseless destruction. Evil destroys and does not build; it rips and it does not mend; it cuts and it does not bind. It strives always and everywhere to annihilate, to turn to nothing. To take all being and render it nothing is the heart of evil." Professor Russell confronts the Devil "in both of his fundamental roles, which though related, are distinct: he is the font and origin of all evil; and he is the very essence of evil."[21] (Russell's usage of "he" and "him" for the Devil is for purposes of convenience, and the same goes for God; he does not intend "to restrict either to the male sex."[22] I might interject that in our time of rightly affirming the dignity of women, we should be misguided to use "she" along with "he" when we refer to the Devil. That would be feminism gone wild. In this book, and for better or worse, I follow Russell's practice respecting the Devil, but not respecting God.)[23]

Radical evil is the Devil; the Devil is radical evil.

> The Devil is rooted in a perception of this radical evil. To suppose belief in the Devil to be outdated and superstitious is false. The question to ask about any idea is not whether it is outdated but whether it is true. The notion that new ideas are necessarily better than old ones is an unfounded and incoherent assumption, and no idea that fits into a coherent world view can properly be called superstitious. Those who believe in the Devil without fitting this belief into a world view may be superstitious, but those who have a coherent structure embracing the concept are not. Superstition is any belief held by any individual who has not fit that belief into a coherent world view. This definition varies from the usual dictionary definition of superstition as belief founded on ignorance. The dictionary definition does not work because one man's ignorance is another man's wisdom. [24]

It is not Russell's intention (nor is it mine) to amass metaphysical statements, claims, or judgments about the Devil, i.e., to vouchsafe what the Devil may "really" be beyond humankind's perceptions of the Devil. Russell does not speak of "the Devil *sub specie eternitatis* but...as perceived by the human mind." To be sure, in principle the Devil may or may not be more than the concept of the Devil. "The only reality we can know" is phenomena, mental constructs.[25] However, Russell consoles us that our knowledge is nonetheless "sure knowledge. The Devil is a real phenomenon; therefore the Devil is real."[26]

At the end of his volume *The Devil*, Russell asks the summary question, "What do I know about the Devil?" Here, in paraphrase, is his sevenfold answer:

1. I have directly experienced a force I perceive as evil, possessing unity and purpose, and coming from beyond me.
2. This experience is a common one among sane people in a number of cultures.
3. Arising as it does from out of my unconscious, I have to concede that the experience may not in fact be beyond me.
4. However, the experience has to be taken seriously, since the element of beyondness is constituent to the perception itself, and is quite widespread in the perceptions of other people.

5. Each individual interprets the experience within and through his personal and cultural preconceptions; hence, there is wide variety in the perceptions as reported.
6. My personal and cultural preconceptions have to be corrected to agree with the methodology I have chosen.[27]
7. The methodology I have selected manifests a definable development of historical tradition, asserting, as the latter minimally does, the reality of a principle of evil. For all my necessary reservations, I believe in the existence of a personification of evil, whatever it may be called.[28]

Russell concludes that the old belief that humankind is essentially good, and that evils can be overcome by "adjusting education, penal laws, welfare arrangements, city planning, and so on, has not proved its validity. Recognition of the basic existence of evil, and consequently of the need for strong efforts to integrate and overcome it, may be socially more useful and psychologically more true." Finally, if it is so that "a natural theology can be argued from the putative universal human experience of the good," surely "a natural diabology can be argued from the putative universal human experience of evil."[29]

I do not myself hold that a direct or unmediated "experience" of the Devil is necessary to the affirmation of the reality of the Devil, any more than a corresponding "experience" of God is necessary to the affirmation of God. I have never "directly experienced" either of these realities. At the same time, I do not rule out that certain kinds of dreams and visions may in some sense bring the Devil "near," just as certain other kinds of dreams and visions may, in a certain sense, bring God "near."

Overall, Jeffrey Russell's epistemology of the Devil is at once highly cautious—wisely phenomenological—but yet not at all agnostic. I ally myself with his view. That view accords essentially with the historically tried-and-true finding of the Devil as the archbeing of hatred, of enmity. In this connection, Harold M. Schulweis's description of evil is apropos: "The Gothic word 'evil' refers to the force in the universe that gives rise to wickedness, sin, misfortune, disaster. The presence of evil, its reality, makes a hole in the heart of the believer."[30] Schulweis's rendering further encourages me to be unwilling to settle for any less a concept than the Devil, indeed for no less a *reality* than the Devil.

To the above phenomenology-in-outline of the Devil, I add four small midrashim.

1. There is little argument over whether evil forces or powers are active in the world (with or without a source beyond the world). The life-and-death

issue instead is: How are these realities to be characterized and accounted for? For example, many interpreters will readily agree that Nazism was a demonic evil while yet expressing unwillingness to equate Nazism with "the work of the Devil."[31]

2. Is the wording "the Devil" a metaphor? In a certain respect, every one of our words is metaphorical, in view of the clear discrepancy between language as such and whatever it is that language is trying to identify, account for, or describe. But the many people who believe that there is a Devil would not concede that "the Devil" is no more than a metaphor. For them, the wording "the Devil" stands for *the Devil,* a real personification of real evil, just as "God" means the real personification of real good. (We shall later encounter Reinhold Niebuhr's usage of "symbol" to identify the Devil—as problematic a device as that of "metaphor.")[32]

3. Analysts of the Devil are confronted, minimally speaking, with a quadrilectic, a fourfold theoretical/existential dilemma: (1) To affirm the Devil may seem to convey the impression of opposing the Devil, since ostensibly the Devil could have operated more effectively were the Devil's reality denied. (2) To deny the Devil may seem to have the effect of aiding the Devil, since it gives him a free hand. Such literary greats as Dostoevsky and Baudelaire agree that the cleverest stratagem of the Devil is to convince us of his nonexistence.[33] Query: Can that same stratagem be resorted to by God? (3) To affirm the Devil may seem pro-Devil, since the Devil may be able to thrive on the publicity. (4) To deny the Devil may seem to oppose the Devil, on the (hopeful) ground that, by and large, people of today are too sophisticated to "believe in" the Devil, which belief is dubbed superstitious.[34]

4. In question form: Is there a plurality, a heterogeneity of evils, or is all evil to be traced to or contained within Evil (the Devil)? In the same way, is there a plurality, a heterogeneity of goods, or is all goodness to be traced to or contained within Good (God)? The second question under (4) takes us over into our third variable.

3. The ways people speak of God are legion. Perhaps Professor Russell will not object if, building conveniently upon the foregoing analysis, I simplemindedly allude to God[35] in a fashion that is diametrically opposed to Russell's explication of the Devil—to reverse Carl G. Jung's phrasing, God as (blessed) Shadow of the Devil. (Later in the book I resort further to the Jungian terminology.)[36] At minor literary peril, it is necessary to insert a disclaimer at this point, too essential to be remanded to an endnote. Although I am influenced by Jung's concept of the Shadow of God, I loathe Jung personally for his sympathies with Nazism and his antisemitism.[37] Is it possible to loathe someone who is dead? Or are we to follow the rule, *De mortuis nihil nisi bene* ("Speak only well of the dead")? I can speak well of Jung at one point: His own consorting with

the Devil may have helped teach him something about the Devil. But much more importantly, I should not want Jung to have the posthumous satisfaction of my failing to profit from significant conceptualization by him, just in order to keep my work "pure." (As an old friend, Arnold Nash, used to advise, the task of the Christian is to find the right sin to commit, and then to commit it, as against committing wrong sins.)[38]

In accordance with the procedure I have indicated, God may be looked upon as the personification of absolute good, the One who engages in construction eminently meaningful and sensible, who builds and does not destroy, who mends and binds, ever striving to create, to be blessed, and to sustain blessedness. God reaches out to inchoate being and renders it into something good. God may be dealt with in both God's fundamental roles—the font and origin of all good and, indeed, the very essence of good. And here too, still following a methodology that parallels Russell's, we need not intend final metaphysical judgments about God, i.e., we do not essay whom or what God "really" is beyond humanity's perceptions of God. Thus, in principle God may or may not be more than the concept of God. Yet if, as Professor Russell declares, the Devil is a real phenomenon, the same is surely the case with God. In this sense at least, the Devil and God are (blood?) siblings.

Russell's sevenfold response to the question of what he knows about the Devil can be readily applied to God: We may directly experience a force we perceive as good; this is a common experience among sane people in many cultures; we have to concede that the experience, arising from our unconscious, may not in fact be beyond us; the experience ought nevertheless to be taken seriously; we interpret our experience of God in highly varied ways, in keeping with individual and cultural predilections; these preconceptions must be corrected to accord with our chosen mothodologies; and these methodologies display definable developments of historical tradition, pointing to a principle and reality of good. These are among the grounds for one or another natural theology.

We have not yet framed a most poignant question: Is the Devil part of deity or somehow beyond deity? In the course of my exposition I hope to convey something of an answer to this question. For the present, here is Jeffrey Burton Russell's psychoanalytic-historical response to the query: "The study of the Devil indicates that historically, he is a manifestation of the divine, a part of the deity. *Sine diabolo nullus Deus.* Yet, morally, his work is completely and utterly to be rejected. The paradox can be resolved in only one way: evil will be absorbed and controlled when it is integrated, and it will be integrated when it is fully recognized and understood. Not by *repression,* which only increases the shadow in the unconscious, but by conscious *suppression* of the evil elements that we have recognized in ourselves, will that element of the divine we call the Devil be brought out of chaos and out of opposition into order and under control."[39]

My own description, as well, leaves wholly unsettled the competing alternatives of monism and dualism (chapter two), as it does also of the validity/invalidity of modified monism (chapter three), together with various other choices not here considered. The most I may venture for the present is to say that, overall, the Devil may be received as transcending the natural dimension. In this respect at least, the Devil makes his home somewhere in the same general neighborhood as God. Accordingly, while with Harvey Cox we may quite properly work to "disenchant" nature in every possible way,[40] this can have no effect whatever upon the reality of the Devil (any more than it can vanquish God). To sneak in one metaphysical presupposition, the Devil joins God in being essentially hidden.

To treat the Devil and God as polar opposites, without perforce claiming final metaphysical identifications of them, is of course not new. Michael Novak attests that, granted we do not know what God *is,* God "is at least more like human *acts* of honesty, courage, freedom and community than he is like anything else we know. When we experience such actions, we are more like God than in any other state we know."[41] In the same way, the Devil is more like human acts of lying, cowardice, servitude, and isolation than the Devil is like anything else we know. And to experience such actions, to engage in them, is to be more like the Devil than we are in any other state we know.

Notes

1. "Males are no damn good, with some exceptions"; this statement is not made presumptively, but comes only at the end of the book. Rephrased for the present study, it might read: "The devils of the world are mostly men." (A. Roy Eckardt, *Black-Woman-Jew* [Bloomington, Ind.: Indiana University Press, 1989], p. 186). See also, Mary McClintock Fulkerson, "Sexism as Original Sin: Developing a Theacentric Discourse," *Journal of the American Academy of Religion* 59 (1991): 653–75. Cf.: "Since girls suffer from emotional neglect, humiliation, and physical and sexual abuse at least as much, and probably more, than boys do, one

would expect psychoanalysts to deal with the discrepancy in male and female levels of violence. In fact it has received very little attention." (Myriam Miedziam, *Boys Will Be Boys* [New York: Doubleday, 1991]; cited in *Columbia: The Magazine of Columbia University* 17 [Fall 1991]: 23).

2. Roy Blount, Jr., as cited by Nancy A. Walker, *A Very Serious Thing* (Minneapolis: University of Minnesota Press, 1988), p. 165.

3. Harvey Cox, *The Secular City*, rev. ed. (New York: Macmillan, 1966), pp. 219, 223, and 227. None of this is to deny the essentiality of the divine hiddenness (p. 225).

4. "Religion by its nature is a metaphysical poem married to faith." (Hippolyte Taine, *L'Ancien Regime* [1876], as cited in Owen Chadwick, *The Secularization of the European Mind in the Nineteenth Century* [New York: Cambridge University Press, 1975], p. 209).

5. Consult Rollo May's essential psychological/psychotherapeutic study, *The Cry for Myth* (New York: W. W. Norton, 1991).

6. Reinhold Niebuhr distinguishes what he calls "permanent myths" from "pre-scientific myths," although he actually prefers the term "symbol" since it does not have the skeptical connotation of "myth." Permanent myths "are those which describe some meaning or reality, which is not subject to exact analysis but can nevertheless be verified in experience." (*The Self and the Dramas of History* [New York: Scribner, 1955], p. 97). For Paul Tillich, authentic myth can be considered an expression "of the depth of reason in symbolic form." (*Systematic Theology*, Vol. I [Chicago: University of Chicago Press, 1951], p. 81).

7. Consult David Birnbaum, *God and Evil* (Hoboken, N.J.: Ktav Publishing House, 1989), Part I.

8. Wendy Farley, *Tragic Vision and Divine Compassion* (Louisville, Ky.: Westminster/John Knox Press, 1990).

9. Jeffrey Burton Russell, *The Devil* (Ithaca, N.Y. and London: Cornell University Press, 1987), p. 228.

10. See, for example, Marie Collins Swabey, *Comic Laughter* (Hamden, Conn.: Archon Books, 1970).

11. Edward L. Galligan, *The Comic Vision in Literature* (Athens, Ga.: University of Georgia Press, 1984), p. x.

12. E. B. White, *The Second Tree from the Corner* (New York: Harper & Row, 1989), p. 173; also A. Roy Eckardt, *Sitting in the Earth and Laughing* (New Brunswick, N.J. and London: Transaction Publishers, 1992), p. xvi.

13. Incongruity does not always make for comedy; a great deal of it serves tragedy. (See Swabey, *Comic Laughter*, pp. 3-5, 16, and 28).

14. John Morreall, *Taking Laughter Seriously* (Albany, N.Y.: State University of New York Press, 1983), p. 47.

15. Kierkegaard continues: "The tragic and the comic are the same, in so far as both are based on contradiction; *but the tragic is the suffering contradiction, the comical, the painless contradiction.*" (Søren Kierkegaard, *Concluding Unscientific Postscript* [Princeton: Princeton University Press, 1941], p. 459).

16. Eckardt, *Sitting in the Earth*, p. 204.

17. Albert Camus, *The Rebel* (New York: Vintage, 1956), p. 297. That human beings have no say in their creation raises the question of the licitness of suicide. But, cf. Norman Podhoretz: "God wants us to live," whereas the Devil wants us to choose death. "Suicide is thus the supreme act of obeisance to the Devil." ("Speak of the Devil," *Commentary* 51 [April 1971]: 6).

18. Peter Berger, *A Rumor of Angels* (Garden City, N.Y.: Doubleday, 1969), p. 90.
19. May, *Cry for Myth*, pp. 272–73.
20. Russell's work extends to five volumes: *The Devil* (cited above); *Lucifer* (Ithaca, N.Y. and London: Cornell University Press, 1986); *Mephistopheles* (Ithaca, N.Y. and London: Cornell University Press, 1990); *The Prince of Darkness* (Ithaca, N.Y. and London: Cornell University Press, 1992); and *Satan* (Ithaca, N.Y. and London: Cornell University Press, 1987).
21. Russell, *Devil*, pp. 11, 17, 23, 26, 31, and 35.
22. Ibid., p. 34.
23. In Hebraic thinking, the feminine element of the myth of the serpent or dragon is not carried over to the Devil. (Ibid., p. 217). Chalk up one point for Judaism vis-à-vis the sterling cause of feminism.
24. Russell, *Lucifer*, p. 22.
25. "The only thing that is immediately and directly experienced is thought, so that all that can be said with certainty is that *thought exists*"—contra the (brazen) *cogito ergo sum* of Descartes. However, "this lack of certainty does not mean that we must retreat into solipsism. It is possible to seek, and to find, knowledge that is less than absolute." (Russell, *Devil*, p. 258; see also pp. 259–60). In this connection, I support the Kantian assumption that while concepts without perception are empty, perceptions without concepts are blind.
26. Ibid., pp. 42–3. On this matter, consult two powerful analyses by Henry A. Murray, "Dead to the World: The Passions of Herman Melville" and "The Personality and Career of Satan" in Murray, *Endeavors in Psychology*, ed. Edwin S. Shneidman (New York: Harper & Row, 1981).
27. Russell's methodology rests upon the *history of concepts*, because that approach "offers the best way of understanding" such a concept as the Devil, which "is not firmly rooted in physical nature and therefore not open to scientific method." (Russell, *Devil*, p. 259; see also *Lucifer*, p. 23). As far as the theological enterprise is concerned, "the history of concepts provides the theologian with the only coherent picture of the Devil that is demonstrably consistent with historical reality. Historical theologians may personally assent to the historical tradition or reject it, but they cannot meaningfully define the Devil in terms foreign to it." (Russel, *Devil*, p. 25).
28. Russell, *Devil*, pp. 259–60.
29. Ibid., p. 260.
30. Harold M. Schulweis, *Evil and the Morality of God* (Cincinnati, Oh.: Hebrew Union College Press, 1984), p. i.
31. The psychoanalyst Henry A. Murray speaks of the "total incarnation" of the Devil "in the person of Adolf Hitler." (Murray, *Endeavors in Psychology*, p. 530).
32. As Alan P. Lightman points out, metaphor is of critical use in science. Indeed, it carries "a greater burden than metaphors in literature or history or art. Metaphors in modern science must do more than color their principal objects; they must build their reality from scratch." ("Magic on the Mind: Physicists' Use of Metaphor," *The American Scholar* [Winter 1989]: 97–101).
33. Russell, *Prince of Darkness*, p. 254.
34. Cf. Heiko A. Oberman: In the course of the nineteenth century, "superstition fell victim to sophistication" and "so did the awareness of Satan's threat." (*Luther* [New York: Doubleday Image Books, 1992], p. 88). Cf. also the senior devil in *The Screwtape Letters* of C. S. Lewis: "When the humans disbelieve in our existence we lose all the pleasing results of direct terrorism and we make no magi-

cians. On the other hand, when they believe in us, we cannot make them materialists and sceptics. At least, not yet." (*The Screwtape Letters* [London: Collins Fount, 1977], p. 39). This classic work of Lewis's offers "counsel" from the senior devil Screwtape to a junior devil, his nephew Wormwood, on how to corrupt humankind.

35. It is interesting that ordinarily we speak of "God" without assigning a definite article, yet we say "the Devil." Jeffrey Russell is aware of this terminological complication: "The Judeo-Christian Yahweh is to be considered historically as one manifestation of the High God. To minimize this difficulty, I use the term 'the God' for the High God—the divine principle—and 'god' for the lesser gods. I avoid 'God' owing to its inevitable associations with Yahweh. I use the term 'the Devil,' as opposed to Satan, to designate the personification of evil found in a variety of cultures." (*Devil*, pp. 33-4). I do not dissent from the need for clarification that Russell discerns even though, for me, Yahweh (God) is the High God.

36. In contrast to the Freudian belief that the Devil and God are merely personifications of repressed, unconscious drives, Jung interprets them as omnipresent realities of the psyche as such. In raising certain elements of the unconscious to a collective unconscious, Jung sees them as transcending the individual psyche. The Devil reflects an autonomous, timeless, universal collective unconscious. Consult Russell, *Prince of Darkness*, pp. 242-48. A Jungian analyst, June Singer, identifies the collective unconscious "as an extension of the personal unconscious to its wider and broader base, encompassing contents" held in common by the family, social group, tribe and nation, race, and eventually all humanity. "The wonder of the collective unconscious is that it is all these, all the legend and history of the human race, with its demons and its gentle saints, its mysteries and its wisdom, all within each of us—a microcosm within the macrocosm." (*Boundaries of the Soul* [Garden City, N.Y.: Doubleday Anchor Books, 1977], pp. 95-6).

37. Jung wrote: "One cannot of course accept that Freud or Adler is a generally valid representative of European mankind. The Jew as a relative nomad has never created, and presumably never will create, a cultural form of his own, for all his instincts and talent are dependent on a more or less civilized host people.

[It] has been a great mistake of medical psychology to apply Jewish categories, which are not even valid for Jews, to Christian Germans and Slavs. In this way the most precious secret of Teutonic man, the deep-rooted, creative awareness of his soul, has been explained away as a banal, infantile sump, while my warning voice, over the decades, was suspected of anti-Semitism.... Has the mighty phenomenon of National Socialism, at which the whole world gazes in astonishment, taught them to know better?" (From Jung's *Zentralblatt für Psychotherapie* (1934), as quoted in Paul Johnson, *A History of the Jews* [New York: Harper & Row, 1987], p. 474).

38. In the Gospel of Luke, Jesus provides some interesting counsel to his disciples: "Make friends for yourselves by means of dishonest wealth, so that when it is gone they may welcome you into the eternal homes." (16:9).

39. Russell, *Devil*, pp. 31-2.

40. Cox, *Secular City*, pp. 15-21.

41. Michael Novak, "Planetary Theology," *Christianity and Crisis* (22 Mar. 1971): 44.

Part I

Rationalist Theodicy and Its Nemesis

2

Monists vis-à-vis Dualists

Monists: God Is and the Devil is Not

Many forms of religious faith disallow, at least in effect, any space for the Devil. Thus, in pure guise philosophic-religious monism contends (I again cite Professor Russell) that "apparent evil is part of a greater good that lies beyond the power of poor mortals to perceive." Insisting upon "the totality" of the power of God, monism tends to remand evil to an erroneous "formulation of the human mind too limited to grasp the nature" of the divine.[1]

When given theological voice, monism is exemplified in monotheism, the avowal that authentic divinity entails one God and the power of that God, in place of any other supposed gods and despite all contrary appearances of evil or onslaughts by evil. In the Jewish and the Christian traditions the primary relation God has with the Devil is to be the Devil's sworn opponent, the divine foe of cosmic, worldly, and moral evil. More positively put, God is pledged to honor justice and righteousness.

Is this to suggest a modicum of dualism? Perhaps so, yet God is also construed, ultimately, as victor over evil.

Let us look at exemplary thinkers.

For David Birnbaum, as he explains in *God and Evil: A Jewish Perspective,* the Devil, indeed the very idea of the Devil, is anathema. In contrast to Jeffrey Burton Russell, who assimilates evil within the category of the Devil, Birnbaum drops the Devil entirely from the cosmic and world scene. Categorically, Birnbaum declines "to take the route of attributing evil to 'Satanic forces,'" a path that, for him, implies "a source other than the Divine" but yet, he insists, fails to explain "the origins of the Satanic."[2] Evil, while surely evident, is to be reckoned with in quite another way.

17

Birnbaum's argumentation is somewhat disjointed and repetitive, but its thrust is clear. True, of all philosophic challenges to theistic faith, "none is more serious than that posed by evil. For theistic faith posits God to be omnipotent and omni-good." The major challenge is: "Why does not omnipotent, omnimerciful God intervene to counter gross evil?" Notwithstanding, for Birnbaum God's power and thereby God's reputation remain intact. Furthermore, however much it is so that the divine essence remains inscrutable, the living relation between the divine and humankind is not to be relegated to something unfathomable. And the divine-human interaction must remain morally intelligible.[3]

Positively speaking, David Birnbaum offers us a contemporary extension of the kabbalistic motif that "Divine contraction was/is necessary for the very existence of the world." He cites with consent Adin Steinsaltz's judgment that "the world becomes possible only through the special act of Divine withdrawal or contraction (*tsimtsum*). Such Divine non-Being or concealment is thus the elementary condition for the existence of that which is finite."[4]

The all-decisive consideration is human freedom. If man is fully to achieve his potential of privacy, responsibility, and selfhood, the elements of divine contraction become a necessity. "The Deity, who is omnipotent and just, assumes an increased state of contracted omniscience and omnipresence, to allow man to quest for his own limitless possibilities." This is how God's Providence (care and concern for humanity) is manifest.[5] *It is the divine contraction that perforce occasions evil.* "With the creation of potential for good, which is required for man to be able to reach his spiritual potential, potential for evil indirectly, but nevertheless inexorably, came into existence as a consequence." At this point Birnbaum acknowledges his discipleship of Moses Maimonides.[6]

Occasionally I am given to wonder whether absolute monism is possible. At times David Birnbaum himself sounds dualistic: "Good and evil form a duality. Creating potential for good, by definition, creates the inverse potential for evil along with it. Good only exists with its duality, evil. In order to create potential for good, potential for evil was, by definition, created. God's omnipotence or nonomnipotence is not the issue. It is rather a question of definition. By definition, good comes packaged with concomitant evil." However, the dualism is only apparent. For beyond his (rather questionable) refuge in "definition," Birnbaum contends for the objective effect that creation, including humankind's potential for freedom, must have upon God. "Since gross evil does exist," we have to adjudge that "real-time omniscience is not a steady-state situation." The same is true with the divine omnipotence. Birnbaum goes so far as to say that divine "self-contraction is solely for the purpose of granting man the necessary freedom to achieve his potential." Any such achievement is incompatible with "a God who intervenes when peril threatens." Indeed, the only way that redemption can be attained is "from a base of freedom," and freedom "implies an environment of ascendant evil."[7]

Here is David Birnbaum's summary statement:

> We have attempted to make the case that potential/knowledge/evil/good/freedom/ privacy/human dignity/Providence/Divine consciousness are all interlocked with each other in a cosmic dynamic geometric relationship, with man as the protagonist; that as man ascends in knowledge, and implicitly in his demand for greater freedom, the Divine Face of *Rachamim* (Mercy) is preempted by the Divine core of Potential.[8]

Over on the Christian side, H. Richard Niebuhr is a forceful exponent of what he calls "radical monotheism." As with David Birnbaum, the Devil is conspicuously absent.

In an earlier study Niebuhr's apprehension of evil is somewhat reminiscent of Jeffrey Burton Russell's: "Events can be evil only as they occur in the history of selves, as they are related to persons who cause them or who suffer their effects." As well, "evil imaginations of the [human] heart" bring evil consequences to human communities. But "the why and wherefore of evil in this context is a mystery."[9]

Evidently, the destruction of one or another uninhabited galaxy is not to be considered integrally evil. (But is not such destruction a diminution of "being," as per Niebuhr's reasoning below?)

In a subsequent study H. Richard Niebuhr puts forward a theology of radical monotheism—for all his reservation that noone has ever actually yearned "for radical faith in the One God." In harmony with the Augustinian principle that whatever is, is good—a principle echoed as well in David Birnbaum—Niebuhr discusses a "center of value" that is nothing less than "being itself" or "the realm of being."

> For radical monotheism the value-center is neither closed society nor the principle of such a society but the principle of being itself; its reference is to no one reality among the many but to One beyond all the many, whence all the many derive their being, and by participation in which they exist. As faith, it is reliance on the source

of all being for the significance of the self and of all that exists. It is the assurance that because I am, I am valued, and because you are, you are beloved, and because whatever is, is has being, therefore it is worthy of love. It is the confidence that whatever is, is good, because it exists as one thing among the many which all have their origin and their being, in the One—the principle of being which is also the principle of value. In Him we live and move and have our being not only as existent but as worthy of existence and worthy in existence. It is not a relation to any finite, natural, or supernatural value-center that confers value on self and some of its companions in being, but it is value relation to the One to whom all being is related. Monotheism is less than radical if it makes a distinction between the principle of being and the principle of value; so that while all being is acknowledged as absolutely dependent for existence on the One, only some beings are valued as having worth for it; or if, speaking in religious language, the Creator and the God of grace are not identified.

Apprehended as "faith loyalty," radical monotheism "is directed toward the principle and the realm of being as the cause for the sake of which it lives. The universal human loyalty made possible by radical monotheism expresses itself as "reverence for being."

And such loyalty gives form to morality since all moral laws and ends receive their form, though not their immediate content, from the form of faith reliance and faith loyalty. Love of the neighbor is required in every morality formed by a faith; but in polytheistic faith the neighbor is defined as the one who is near me in my interest group, *when* he is near me in that passing association. In henotheistic social faith, my neighbor is my fellow in the closed society. Hence, in both instances the counterpart of the law of neighbor-love is the requirement to hate the enemy. But in radical monotheism my neighbor is my companion in being; though he is my enemy in some less than universal context, the requirement is to love him....

Radical monotheism dethrones all absolutes short of the principle of being itself. At the same time it reverences every relative existent. Its two great mottoes are: "I am the Lord thy God; thou shalt have no other gods before me"] and "Whatever is, is good."[10]

hence theistic! not monotheistic — monotheistic is,
"I am, there are no others."

In a later work, H. Richard Niebuhr expounds upon suffering, sin, and death. Everyone "is aware of the extent to which the characters of people he has known have been given their particular forms by the sufferings through which they have passed." Suffering "cuts athwart our purposive movements." It "is in the response to suffering that many and perhaps all men, individually and in their groups, define themselves, take a character, develop their ethos." Aware as he is of the anxiousness of human anxiety and the guiltiness of human guilt, Niebuhr knows that "I experience my guilt not as a relation to the law or to an ideal, but to my companions." Again, it does appear that death and its rule over our history "leads us to develop our defensive measures of *Thou shalt nots* and that isolates us from each other.... Idealism and respect for the law of reason may protest, but man continues to do what seems to him fitting [amidst his] history of guilt and fear of loss of himself." Deep in our minds there remains a "great overarching myth," the "interpretative pattern of the metahistory, within which all our histories and biographies are enacted," a myth that keeps alive an "almost unconquerable picture...of everlasting winter lying on the frozen wastes of existence...or, otherwise, of all-destroying fire raging before and after the brief interval...of life upon our planet or in our galaxy." There persists "the image of myself as coming to that future when there is no more future. It is that understanding of the society, into whose actions I fit my actions, as bound with all the tragic empires of history toward the eschaton, beyond which there is no healing of diseases, no resurrection."[11]

At the communal level, our story is one "of conflict and war and uneasy truces that hold off anarchy awhile. As flesh lusts against spirit and spirit against flesh within the self, so community lusts against community, nation against nation, church against state and state against church, religion against religion." At times, H. Richard Niebuhr almost verges upon a doctrine of the Devil—as when he focuses upon the determining forces of nature, the determining powers of the social world, and the determining complexes of emotions within us. Could these determinants be representing the "principalities and powers and the rulers of the darkness of this world " of which the New Testament writers speak? The system of nature is surely powerful and it is entirely "heedless of our concerns"; the systems of society, called by such names as industrialism, capitalism, and nationalism, manifest great and fateful hegemony over us; and our own "complexes of emotions" so largely dictate how we accept and react to our fellow humans. Yet, while there are "powers not identifiable with the willed influences of human groups or individuals," powers that "exercise dominion over us at least in [the] sense that we adjust our actions to them," these nevertheless are "not all evil powers, not devils," even if we, along with Walter Rauschenbusch, may be tempted to call some of them "superpersonal forces of evil."[12]

We may also allude to H. Richard Niebuhr's most recently appearing study, a posthumous work made possible by his son's devoted effort and his editing of several manuscripts: *Faith on Earth: An Inquiry Into the Structure of Human Faith.* Early on Niebuhr acknowledges that acute internal conflicts must beset the mind and heart of the believer that are due to adverse experiences "indicative of everything else than the presence of beneficent solicitude at the center of existence"—experiences that pose the sober question of whether we are able to *trust* reality or are instead forced to *distrust* it. Certain it is, however, that we are deprived of any way to "understand our believing and unbelieving, our trusting and distrusting, our keeping faith and our faithlessness, our relations of faith to men and the gods or God, by attempting to get outside of the dialogical situation in which our breaches of faith as well as our errors of understanding occur."[13]

Our believing and disbelieving of human companions is not alone "a parable of our believing and disbelieving God but is intimately connected with it." We reveal a certain immaturity when we make God the object of our trust and distrust while all the while evading the question of our own fidelity to God. Nonetheless, this God, this Transcendent Being, this Unconditioned, this One is "the inescapable, the radical source of self-existence." Yet the tragedy remains that our natural faith (natural religion) embodies itself in negative and not positive form, "not as trust but as distrust," a distrust that manifests itself "in hostility, fear, and isolation.... Sometimes defiance marks the human attitude in man's encounter with the ultimate antagonist; more frequently the sense of antagonism appears in the form of human fear before the powerful enemy and perhaps still more frequently the effort is made to put all thought of the Other out of the mind while the self devotes itself to the little struggles and victories of life." The "natural religion of fear is no less an expansion of distrust of the Transcendent than is the natural religion of defiance. If defiance says, 'I am against God,' fear says, 'God is against me.'"[14]

I believe it is easier to endure a universe indifferent to us, that could not care less about us, than a universe that is hostile to us, that is out to do us in. (Paul Ramsey used to insist, I think with justice and free from guile, that there is no such thing as dignity in dying.)

By calling attention to the foregoing passages, I have sought to make room for Niebuhr's extraordinary judgment that humankind's "natural religion" (antagonism to, fear of, distrust of the Transcendent) is treating God as though God were, in effect, the Devil. Yet, any conviction of the Devil does not finally materialize because, for Niebuhr, the primary explanation of the treatment of God as antagonist is not humanity's victimization by destructive evil but rather human sinfulness: "This distrust in God, this belief that he will not keep his promises, presupposes a desire or a will to break faith, since one does not suspect another of promise breaking if one has had no experience of it in oneself." Indeed, all human loyalty is marked by "the corrupted form of broken promises," and all human trust appears "in the perverse form of the great suspicion that we are being deceived."[15]

Finally, Niebuhr carries over from his other writings a conceptualization of God as Enemy.[16] Thus, in *The Responsible Self* we read:

> The natural mind is enmity to God; or to our natural mind the One intention in all intentions is animosity. In our wretchedness we see ourselves surrounded by animosity. We live and move and have our being in a realm that is not nothingness but that is ruled by destructive power, which brings us and all we love to nothing. The maker is the slayer; the affirmer is the denier; the creator is the destroyer; the lifegiver is the death-dealer.... [The] One beyond the many is the enemy.... The One power present in all powers is enemy. The maker is destroyer. In sin man lives before God—unknown as God, unknown as good, unrecognized as loveworthy and loving.... [We understand] that there is an ultimate power...but that it is against us, desiring the death not only of the transgressor but also of the righteous, not only of the vicious but also of the virtuous. Hence all our righteousness in loyalty to finite societies or causes has been infected with anxiety, defensiveness, and hidden rebellion against the One.[17]

However much the point of view of H. Richard Niebuhr admits of massive personal, systemic, perhaps even demonic forces, one finds no essential Devil in his thinking. In light of the contrary history of Christianity—whether Orthodox, Roman, or Protestant—this absence may appear either as strangely ironic or as a blessed advance, depending upon our own outlook respecting the reality/nonreality of the Devil. Niebuhr's recognition of God as Enemy may operate functionally the way ideologies of the Devil serve, but the fact is that Niebuhr's overall point of view acts to negate unalloyed or unabashed deviltry. If God as Enemy appears to function as Devil, this is the case only provisionally and only insofar as the destructive power of human sin (distrust) is not as yet broken. Once that break occurs, the Enemy becomes the Friend.

Again, while hints are evident in Niebuhr of what we shall allude to below as "modified dualism" (="modified monism"), any "dualism" is here highly inhibited, even attacked, by a, finally, "radical monotheism."[18] For once we attest that it is God who bears ultimate responsibility for "all things"—the cardinal monist assertion—we are kept from placing essential blame for gross evil upon some being or force other than God. (Yet does this not mean that God must carry the final blame-worthiness? For is not the very "freedom" to do evil traceable ultimately to God?)

My assessment of monism in general is reserved for chapter 4, along with responses to dualism (only in passing) and to modified monism. For now, the question may at least be raised and remembered for later discussion: Can we ever rest easy with accounting for and dealing with gross and radical evil by limiting ourselves to one or more of the following culprits—God; humankind; a congeries of natural, social, and emotional determinants?

Dualists: God Is and So Is the Devil

In the measure that one or another of the religious faiths act to limit the power of God—through such variables as randomness, chaos, matter, free will, and evil—such faith is moving away from monism. Jeffrey Burton Russell presents dualism as the positing of "two opposite principles of good and evil" and then "attributing evil to the will of [the] malign spirit." Thus does evil not just "happen"; it is the direct consequence of an immanent, destructive purpose or purposes. While the two principles "need not be (though they usually are) antipathetic," they are entirely independent and most often of separate origin. "Each of the principles is absolute in itself," even if "neither has absolute or omnipotent power." The essential point is that absolute and radical evil *is* being held to exist. As Professor Russell comments, "dualism does seem to offer an explanation of the world as we really observe it, a world in which the mixing of impulses to good and impulses to evil is not readily explicable. Much would in fact become understandable if there were a force drawing us to evil as well as one beckoning us to good." Dualism finds considerable support in the way we experience good and evil. And not only is dualism coherent with our own "perceptions of the world," it "for the first time limns a figure clearly recognizable as diabolical."[19] To resort to Paul Tillich's terminology, there appears to be "a split in the creative ground of being."[20]

It was in Persia (today's Iran) shortly before 600 B.C.E. that a prophet named Zarathustra (Zoroaster) provided the foundations of the first thoroughly dualist faith through his affirmation that radical evil is not at all a manifestation of the divine, a part of deity, but instead proceeds from a wholly disparate, antagonistic reality. There are two spiritual principles: "Ahura Mazda, the God, lord of goodness and of light," and "Angra Mainyu ('Destructive or Tormenting Spirit'), lord of evil and darkness. Ahura Mazda has in his complete freedom chosen the good, and Angra Mainyu has in his complete freedom chosen the evil." We may adjudge that "the two spirits are opposites," but they are as well twins, a "coincidence of opposites" (Nicholas of Cusa).[21] Here was "a revolutionary step" in the life story of the Devil, "for it posited, for the first time, an absolute principle of evil,...the first clearly defined Devil." What Zarathustra did was to wrench "from the unity of the God a portion of his power in order to preserve his perfect goodness." God's goodness was saved—at the price of his omnipotence. One of the main inspirations of Zarathustra's dualism was the conflict between the truth and the lie; for him, Angra Mainyu, lord of evil, personified the lie (Druj).[22] (We shall return to the essential matter of "the lie" and lying.)

To make mention of the classical world, a dualist outlook sprang up in Greece in the sixth century B.C.E. Iranian dualism knew nothing of any good spirit and evil matter dichotomy, whereas in the myth of the Orphic tradition humankind was assigned a dual nature: spiritual and material, corresponding to the good, divine soul and the evil, Titanic body that imprisoned the soul. This variation within dualism was to have great influence upon Gnosticism and Christianity, and upon medieval thinking in general. The outcome was eclectic: The Orphic and Iranian dualisms were merged, and "the idea that the body and the flesh are the work of cosmic evil became implanted in Jewish and Christian minds"— although much more within Christianity than within Judaism. The conflict of body and soul, with the material world as the source of evil, could eventuate in the notion of the Devil as "lord of this world." To the Pythagoreans, the soul is a prisoner of the body (*sōma sēma*). It is true that many Greek philosophers remained monists, regarding evil as an undifferentiated aspect of the One (Parmenides) and as lying in human error and weakness (Socrates, Stoics, Cynics, even Sophists), but with Plato and the Platonists the ideal or spiritual world—the world of Ideas— emerged as at once more real and superior to the material world. Paradoxically, the Platonic persuasion of evil as non-Being, with its influence upon Augustine and Aquinas, helped underwrite the Christian and Jewish monism to which we have already made reference. Yet the concept of the Devil "owes much, if not directly to Plato, to the permutations of his thought" in the Platonists, for whom evil entails "the resistance of matter to the divine will."[23]

With special reference to Plotinus (205?-270?), Jeffrey Burton Russell sums up some of the confusions that

> have blurred the development of the concept of the Devil. On the one hand, evil does not exist, and thus there can be no principle of evil. Some theologians argue that evil, being nonexistent, does not constitute a real problem and, because evil is not real, the Devil cannot exist. This is the consequence of Plotinus's ontological monism. But if a value scale is used, then the opposite of absolute good is indeed absolute evil. A principle of evil does exist, and such a principle can be personified by the Devil. In a system such as that of Plotinus, the status of the principle of evil is unclear. On the one hand, it is the lowest order of being or lacks being altogether. Ontologically it scarcely exists. But when the moral element is introduced, it is possible to conceive of a being of high ontological status making a choice for evil. [We humans, while fashioned in the very image of God, make that choice all the time—A.R.E.] This idea, though an implicit possibility in Plotinus, was never an explicit option for him, but it eventually became part of Christian tradition.[24]

The Devil could become the principle of *moral* evil. All in all, Greek dualism proved to be "of enormous importance" in the forming of the Jewish and the Christian conceptions of the Devil.[25]

On the question of dualist influences and Hebraic/Jewish thought, no Devil (Hebrew, *satan*)[26] had as yet appeared in the preexilic period. But gradually the idea developed—with Iranian influence, most likely, respecting apocalyptic and Qumran literature[27] and perhaps also the Hebrew Bible—that a malignant spirit was the instigator of evil. Hebraic and Jewish dualism remained limited, in accordance with the increasing dominance of the rabbis. It is the case that during and after the sufferings of exile, there was a kind of twinning of God into a good and an evil principle. But the twinning remained incomplete; "always some sense was retained of the underlying integrity and oneness of the God." Hebraic/Jewish thought refused to say that evil as well as good stems from the divine nature. In late Jewish apocalyptic, as at Qumran, the Lord and the Devil, the Prince of Darkness, come to "stand each at the head of a heavenly host girded for the final conflict at the end of the world." Tension remained between an essential monotheism and a nagging dualism. With that, no matter how theologians and prophets twisted and turned, they could not wholly extricate their good God from evil,[28] any more than we can do so today. Even the Prince of Darkness is the creature of God. This tension carried over into the Jewish-Christian era. It will endure through tomorrow.

To express the situation psychomorally, ambivalence toward God is never wholly lacking in Judaism and in Christianity. Yet perhaps one hint of how to tell God from the Devil here surfaces, a fairly truistic but also imperfect one: God is usually loved and hated; the Devil is usually, though not always, only hated. Differently put, if just one of God's sides is annihilative, the Devil, not unlike a Moebius strip, can boast only the one side: unrelieved destructiveness.

To refer more specifically to original Christianity, its "concern with the Evil One was great from the outset." A conflict between good and evil "stands at the center" of the New Testament. That is to say, the Devil "occupies a central position" therein "as the chief enemy of the Lord"—though also, there is no point in denying, a creature of God. Satan retains under his jurisdiction "*all* opposition to the Lord." We witness here the infiltrating of dualism within a fundamentally monotheistic structure of belief, just as happened with Hebraic/Jewish persuasion. The diabology/demonology of the New Testament was, indeed, substantively adapted from Hellenistic Judaism: "The opposition between Yahweh and Satan becomes the opposition between Christ and Satan." In this regard, demon possession is a common means "Satan uses to obstruct the Kingdom of God.... By exorcising the demons, and by curing diseases sent by them, Jesus makes war upon the kingdom of Satan," in this way announcing that a new eon has come. Jesus says, "If it is by the spirit of God that I cast out demons, then the kingdom of God has come to you" (Matt. 12:28). It is implied that the coming of God's Kingdom in its wonderful fullness will mean the going of the Devil in his terrible emptiness.[29]

Although the origin of Satan is not considered in the New Testament,[30] it is a central thesis of Christian Scripture that "the powers of darkness under the generalship of the Devil are at war with the power of light." "The whole world lies under the power of the evil one" (1 John 5:19). The Devil murders, lies, punishes, causes death, sorcery, and idolatry, tempts to sin, brings disease, and blocks the teaching of God's Kingdom. The Devil *almost* becomes "a principle of cosmic evil independent of the good Lord."[31]

In his exposition of the Devil in the New Testament, Jeffrey Burton Russell goes as far as to maintain that

Christianity is in fact a semidualist religion. On the one hand, it rejects the full dualism that asserts the opposition of two eternal cosmic principles. But it has also generally rejected the monist complacency of [a] hidden harmony. The tension between monism and dualism has led to inconsistencies in Christian theodicy. But the tension is also creative. Creativity arises whenever meaning strains against the bounds of form, when novelty strains against the strictures of tradition. Water is drinkable only when held in a container. Precisely in its willingness to confront the problem of evil without recourse to the simpler solutions of either dualism or monism, Christianity advanced the notion of the Devil creatively.[32]

On this interpretation, it is a moot point whether a Christianity that admits of the Devil is better treated at this juncture or in the next chapter where we encounter modified monism. At the very least, I suggest that Christians who claim to adhere to a "Bible-centered" faith but who "abandon" the Devil are left with much to ponder. For "the whole point of the New Testament" is "the saving mission of Christ" in "opposition to the power of the Devil." Antimodernist Christians often go into shock over denials of the Bible as the Word of God, God Godself, the Virgin Birth, the divinity of Christ, the Trinity, the sinfulness of humanity, and so on—yet they can calmly, and free from all trepidation, deny or ignore the Devil. What is going on here? Who is responsible for this prejudice against the Devil and the Devil alone? Were I the Devil, I would feel downright insulted. I would resolve to get back at these practitioners of bias. If it is so that a sophisticated era has no time for the Devil, fine. But why does the same era still have time for the other dogmas on the above list? Harvey Cox argues that in a secularized era, God has not been murdered; God has been neutered.[33] It would appear that the Devil has met a like or even greater fate: the Devil is dead.[34]

Nevertheless, and in summary:

> The chief characteristics of the Devil at the time of the New Testament were these: (1) he was the personification of evil; (2) he did physical harm to people by attacking their bodies or by possessing them; (3) he tested people, tempting them to sin in order to destroy them or to recruit them in his struggle against the Lord; (4) he accused and punished sinners; (5) he was the head of a host of evil spirits, fallen angels, or demons; (6) he had assimilated most of the evil qualities of ancient destructive nature spirits or ghosts; (7) he was the ruler of this world of matter and bodies until such time as the Lord's own kingdom would come; (8) until that final time he would be in constant warfare against the good Lord; (9) he would be defeated by the good Lord at the end of the world.[35]

The later medieval Christian era saw the Devil come into the Devil's own glory. True, the church treated many forms of dualism as heretical—e.g., the Bogomils within the Byzantine Empire, and later the Cathars further west.[36] Tertullian (c160–c230) had insisted that evil is neither the work of God nor of an evil principle, but stems from human sin alone. Gregory the Great (Pope Gregory from 590–604), like the fathers of the Council of Braga (563), construed God as the source of all being. Evil cannot exist: it is privation. Satan's will to evil drives him out of reality into nothingness. Faced with the awful choice that either evil does not exist or it is a part of God, Gregory (and much of Christian tradition, including Dante and the later scholastics) opted for the non-Being of evil. John of Damascus (675?–750?) strongly attacked dualism for its allegedly fundamental illogic, following as he did the patristic notion that evil is the privation of good.[37]

Nevertheless, in the Christian Middle Ages the Devil prospered notably. In anticipation of chapter 4, I submit that the debate over whether the Devil *is* something or is instead the privation of good could hardly lie further from the real world. ("Cancer is an evil because it causes suffering; to define *evil* in such a way that cancer is not 'evil' does not alleviate the problem of evil, since it leaves us with the cancer and the suffering it causes.")[38] The truth is that in a medieval frame of reference we behold a Satan supposedly without "being" who yet succeeds very well in "being" and in "being" many things for himself. Thus, Gregory the Great's assurance of the non-Being of evil did not keep him from a vivid belief in diabolical temptation, according to which the soldiers of Jesus Christ find themselves arrayed in battle against the powers of darkness. Should these Christians drop their guard for but a moment, the forces of evil would take them captive. All human sin is indeed the work of the Devil. Along a similar line, there developed an ideology of "war in heaven." Many medieval authorities exegeted Revelation 12 to say that following Satan's sin a conflict broke out in the heavenly places, with the just angels under Archangel Michael's direction working together to drive out the Devil and other apostate angels. It was standard medieval conviction to regard the Devil, who had been among the highest of all angels, as a fallen angel due to his own sin. "War in heaven" ideology became definitive in later theology and literature, including most notably John Milton's *Paradise Lost*.[39] In the early fourteenth century, Dante Alighieri, greatest of the medieval poets and lay theologians, wrote his celebrated *Comedy*, wherein the cosmos, envisioned in accordance with a strictly moral design, is a battlefield between God and Lucifer,[40] Christ and Satan, the ascent toward Good versus the descent toward Evil.[41]

Ironically, Christian heresy itself contributed to a concentration upon things devilish, through, e.g., the insistence that heretics were servants of Satan. Thus, Cathar dualism, insisting as it did upon the enormous power of the Devil, "increased the widespread terror of his ability to interfere with terrible effectiveness always and everywhere." Differences between the church and the Cathars respecting dualism have themselves "been oversimplified. The debate was not between two extremes but rather where on the spectrum between dualism and monism the truth lay. Orthodox Christianity is itself a quasidualist religion—in the place it has traditionally given the Devil, in its tendencies to reject the world, and in its efforts to relieve God of the responsibility of evil."[42]

The Fourth Lateran Council (1215) epitomized the church's reaction to dualism, affirming in its very first canon that the one good God made all things *ex nihilo*. The goodness of creation extended to the Devil's own life. Yet by his own free will, the Devil sinned, and the human race became sinful by yielding (freely) to the Tempter.[43] However, the eschatology involved here could not be more ironic. The church's very struggle against dualism was consummated in a dualism all its own. For the assembled church authorities of 1215, at the final resurrection evil souls will be sent to suffer the Devil's torment; good souls will enjoy eternity with Christ.

Central to the medieval church's diabology was its symbiosis of Jew/Devil, a policy of immense moral (i.e., immoral) significance for the future, through creating an atmosphere that ensured the hells of Auschwitz-Birkenau, Belzek, Chelmno, Maidanek, Sobibor, and Treblinka. Jews were teamed up with heretics, witches, Muslims, pagans, sinners, sorcerers, and other "limbs of Satan" as prominent helpmates of the Devil.[44] But Christian antisemitism boasted a unique historical-theological-moral rationale that, in the perspective of history, makes other forms of Christian hatred seem, by contrast, like child's play. Distinctively, the symbiosis of Jew/Devil boasts New Testament authorization: "You [Jews] are from your father the devil, and you choose to do your father's business" (John 8:44). And "the Jews" (not "Jews" but "*the* Jews") were singularly guilty of two monstrous, related crimes: they murdered "our Lord,"[45] and they abidingly and hardheartedly spurn the very faith in Jesus Christ that could save them from their sin. How may this dual transgression ever be accounted for other than via the Jews' ongoing pact with the Evil One, a pact for which they even now retain full culpability?[46]

The demonization of Jews assumed many guises: the Antichrist will be a Jew from the tribe of Dan; the Jews sacrifice Christian children to the Devil (ritual murder); the Jews desecrate the Eucharist and holy Christian images; the Jews poison Christian wells; the Jews carry the Devil's own physical characteristics (hooked noses, bestial horns, and tails); the Jews are "full of sorcery"; and so on.[47]

Jeffrey Burton Russell enters a most provocative, though, I believe, debatable, judgment:

> To what extent was Christian diabology responsible for the vicious anti-Semitism of the late Middle Ages, Renaissance, and Reformation? It seems to have borne bitter fruit. Yet if no idea of the Devil had existed, the course of anti-Semitism would probably have been little different. First of all, it had as many social as religious causes. [I do not agree that this is so.—A.R.E.]
>
> Second, the religious causes consisted of ancient barriers between Jews and Christians, each group excluding the other from its community. Without a Devil, Christians would still have excluded Jews, blamed them for the crucifixion, and regarded them as sinners cut off from the mystical body of Christ.... Diabology was a handy weapon, but it was just that: a weapon, not the cause, of anti-Semitism.... Christianity's theological tradition bears much responsibility for anti-Semitism but diabology is not the chief culprit.[48]

I think that Russell here underestimates the Devil, which is a little strange because he avoids this everywhere else in his work. In chapter 1, we discussed Russell's allowance for, or at least nondenial of, the objective reality of the Devil. To be true to our shared phenomenological approach, we do well to entertain the eventuality that antisemitism is not a mere human and Christian weapon but constitutes the Devil's own special weapon. To suggest a parallelism: Just as Israel is a chosen people of God, so too the antisemites are a chosen people of the Devil. The Devil may be received as Chief Antisemite.

Joshua Trachtenberg closes his classic study, *The Devil and the Jews: The Medieval Conception of the Jew and Its Relation to Modern Antisemitism*—which first appeared during the latter days of Nazism—with these words:

> The Christian religion is in disfavor today among certain leading antisemitic circles whose consuming aim is to destroy all Christian values; among others hatred of the Jew is preached in the name of a hypocritical and false Christianity. Whatever their attitude toward the teaching and the church of Jesus, this one offshoot of medieval Christian fanaticism, antisemitism, makes them kin. The magic of words has transmuted a pernicious medieval superstition into an even more debasing and corrosive modern superstition. Antisemitism today is "scientific"; it would disdain to include in the contemporaneous lexicon of Jewish crime such outmoded items as

satanism and sorcery (though these notions, in all their literalness, have by no means disappeared). To the modern antisemite, of whatever persuasion, the Jew has become the international communist or the international banker, or better, both. But his aim still is to destroy Christendom, to conquer the world and enslave it to his own—and the word is inescapable—devilish ends. Still the "demonic" Jew....[49]

The trailing ellipsis is not mine but Trachtenberg's. Here is one midrash upon his most apt words: We are reminded of a (diabolical) colossal instance of "mistaken identity": For "the Jew" substitute "the Devil." One ploy of the Devil is to set up the Jew as his alter ego. What shrewder choice could the Devil make than to hit upon such a sworn enemy of the Devil?

I return to the issue of antisemitism and the Devil toward the end of chapter 3.

Notes

1. Jeffrey Burton Russell, *The Devil* (Ithaca, N.Y. and London: Cornell University Press, 1987), pp. 32, 145.
2. David Birnbaum, *God and Evil* (Hoboken, N.J.: Ktav Publishing House, 1989), p. 213.
3. Ibid., pp. 10, 14, 36-7, 45, and 194.
4. Ibid., p. 127.
5. Birnbaum acknowledges that "to insist on classic individual Providence for the Jewish children" of the Holocaust simply implies "a God-turned-satanic controlling the cosmos." Yet he goes on evidently to agree with Arthur A. Cohen that the Holocaust is a "perfected figuration of the demonic." (Ibid., pp. 147, 235). Presumably, the demonic is here held to differ from the Devil.
6. Ibid., pp. 54, 62, 94, 114, 141, 146, and 215.
7. Ibid., pp. 95, 103, 115, 135, and 161.
8. Ibid., p. 165.
9. H. Richard Niebuhr, *The Meaning of Revelation* (New York: Macmillan, 1941), pp. 92, 99.
10. H. Richard Niebuhr, *Radical Monotheism and Western Culture* (New York: Harper & Bros., 1960), pp. 31-4 and 37.
11. H. Richard Niebuhr, *The Responsible Self,* ed. Richard R. Niebuhr and James M. Gustafson (San Francisco: Harper & Row, 1978), pp. 59-60, 100, and 106.
12. Ibid., pp. 138-39.
13. Epistemologically, Niebuhr adheres to a "subject-object duality as the unavoidable situation in which we must carry on all of our thinking and which we cannot transcend." (H. Richard Niebuhr, *Faith on Earth,* ed. Richard R. Niebuhr [New Haven, Conn. and London: Yale University Press, 1989], pp. 3, 30).
14. Ibid., pp. 44, 50, 65, 67, 68, and 75.
15. Ibid., pp. 72, 79, and 82.
16. We may interject that in *The Screwtape Letters* of C. S. Lewis (London: Collins Fount, 1977), God is "the Enemy" all right—but exclusively the enemy of the Devil.

17. Niebuhr, *Responsible Self,* pp. 140–42.
18. Radical monotheism is central to Islam.
19. Jeffrey Burton Russell, *The Prince of Darkness* (Ithaca, N.Y. and London: Cornell University Press, 1992), p. 19; Russell, *Devil,* pp. 32, 98–99, and 101.
20. Paul Tillich, *Systematic Theology,* Vol. III (Chicago: University of Chicago Press, 1963), p. 142.
21. In the sixteenth century Martin Luther was to draw from the mystics the idea of God as a coincidence of opposites: wrath/love, repudiation/grace, law/mercy (Russell, *Prince of Darkness,* p. 171).
22. Russell, *Devil,* pp. 98, 99, 101–2, and 106–7; in general, pp. 98–121. Russell is careful to distinguish the teachings of Zarathustra from subsequent Zoroastrianism (or Mazdaism), which boasts four major strands: (1) Zarathustra's teachings; (2) the teachings of Mazdaism proper; (3) the teachings of Zarvanism, a heresy from Mazdaism; and (4) the teachings of the Magi, which eventuated in Mithraism. (Ibid., p. 104ff.). See also Russell, *Prince of Darkness,* pp. 17–24.
23. Russell, *Devil,* pp. 137–39, 142, 144–46, 148–49, 160, and 167.
24. Ibid., p. 166.
25. Ibid., pp. 168–69.
26. "As the Devil has many names in different religions, so he has many names within the Judeo-Christian tradition itself." (Ibid., p. 189).
27. See Russell, *Prince of Darkness,* pp. 39–42.
28. Our reference here to the Hebrew Bible is highly attenuated; much more will be said of relevance to that literature in conjunction with our review of Jon D. Levenson's *Creation and the Persistence of Evil* in Chapter 3. Consult Russell, *Devil,* Chapter 5—"Hebrew Personifications of Evil." (Ibid., pp. 174, 176, 183, 205, 211–12, 214, and 218–20).
29. Consult Michael Green, *I Believe in Satan's Downfall* (London: Hodder & Stoughton, 1988).
30. "The Devil is prince of a host of evil spiritual powers, who may be viewed as fallen angels or as demons. The distinction between the two, already hazy in Judaism, becomes even hazier in the New Testament." (Russell, *Devil,* p. 236; see also pp. 234–37, 247–49, and 252). The New Testament identifies evildoers as followers or sons of the Devil. (Ibid., p. 239; John 8:44; Acts 13:10; 2 Thess. 2:3–9; 1 John 3:8; 12 Rev. 2:9 and 3:9). On the future of the Devil, see Russell, *Devil,* pp. 242–45, 255.
31. The Hebraic and Christian traditions, "though implicitly dualistic, explicitly insisted that Satan was not an independent principle coeval with the God of light, but rather a creature of the good Lord, and, like the rest of the Lord's creation, originally good. It was therefore necessary to assume an initial fall of Satan from grace, that fall resulting from his free decision to reject the will of the creator." (Ibid., p. 256).
32. Ibid., pp. 221, 227, 228, 229–31, 237, 240, 247, and 249; Russell, *Prince of Darkness,* p. 52.
33. Harvey Cox, *Religion in the Secular City* (New York: Simon and Schuster, 1984), p. 201.
34. However, a Gallup Poll of 1991 found that half of the American people believe in a personal Devil. And "the majority of Americans" believe that the Bible is either the literal or the inspired Word of God. (*Christian Information,* Vancouver Island, B.C., August 1991).
35. Russell, *Devil,* pp. 249, 256; see also Russell, *Prince of Darkness,* pp. 48–51.

36. Jeffrey Burton Russell, *Lucifer* (Ithaca, N.Y. and London: Cornell University Press, 1986), pp. 44-9, 185-190, and 315-16; see also Russell, *Prince of Darkness,* Chapter 5—"Satan and Heresy" and Chapter 6—"Dualism and the Desert."

37. Russell, *Prince of Darkness,* p. 69; *Lucifer,* pp. 37-8, 95-6, and 187.

38. Ibid., p. 196.

39. Ibid., pp. 94, 100, and 202.

40. The medieval tradition as a whole assumes the unity of Satan and Lucifer, treating them as names of a single Devil, the personification of evil. (Ibid., p. 11).

41. Ibid., p. 216; in general, pp. 216-33; Russell, *Prince of Darkness,* p. 142; in general, pp. 140-46; Dante Alighieri, *The Divine Comedy of Dante Alighieri,* 3 vols., ed. and trans. Allen Mandelbaum (New York: Bantam Books, 1982, 1984, 1986). "Divine" does not appear in Dante's original title. "Comedy" connoted a happy ending.

42. Russell, *Lucifer,* pp. 299, 185.

43. Ibid., p. 189.

44. Ibid., pp. 79, 83-4, and 299.

45. Today, of course, responsible scholarship, including much Christian scholarship, acknowledges the crucifixion of Jesus as a strictly Roman business. Yet many contemporary Christians and church bodies keep alive traditional charges against "the Jews."

46. At the heart of the witch craze was the "knowledge" that witches signed pacts with Satan. The craze had its roots in medieval times and reached its zenith in the sixteenth and seventeenth centuries. (Russell, *Lucifer,* p. 81; Russell, *Prince of Darkness,* p. 165). On the famous Salem witch trials, consult Paul Boyer and Stephen Nissenbaum, *Salem Possessed* (Cambridge, Mass.: Harvard University Press, 1974); in a broader frame of reference, Kai T. Erikson, *Wayward Puritans* (New York: John Wiley, 1966) and John Demos, *Entertaining Satan* (New York: Oxford University Press, 1982).

47. Russell, *Lucifer,* pp. 84, 192. Still among the best studies of Christian antisemitism in the Middle Ages is Joshua Trachtenberg, *The Devil and the Jews* (1943; reprint ed., Cleveland, Oh. and New York: Meridian Books, 1961). Consult also Joel Carmichael, *The Satanizing of the Jews* (New York: Fromm International, 1992).

48. Russell, *Lucifer,* pp. 192-93. Russell's spelling "anti-Semitism" is unfortunate. The correct term is "antisemitism." James Parkes, the British expert on the phenomenon involved, used to speak of "anti-Semitism" as "pseudo-scientific mumbo jumbo," which implies an actual quality called "Semitism." The word "anti-semitism' is "not a scientific word, and it is entitled to neither a hyphen nor a capital." (James Parkes, personal conversations).

49. Trachtenberg, *Devil and Jews,* pp. 219-20. On the Devil and the fortunes of dualism subsequent to the high Middle Ages, consult, among many available works, Carmichael, *Satanizing the Jews,* chapters 4-8; Lewis, *Screwtape Letters*; Heiko Oberman, *Luther* (New York: Doubleday Image Books, 1992); Jeffrey Burton Russell, *Mephistopheles* (Ithaca, N.Y. and London: Cornell University Press, 1990), including full bibliography; Russell, *Prince of Darkness,* chapters 10-17; and Frederick Sontag, *The God of Evil* (New York: Harper & Row, 1970).

3

Modified Monism: A Middle Way?

The problem for monism is that radical evil stays rife; the problem for dualism is determining the fate of goodness.

I adopt the term "modified monism" to represent theodicies that are dissatisfied, implicitly or explicitly, with either pure monism or pure dualism. Hence, the phrasing "modified dualism" would do just as well as "modified monism." We have already made reference to semidualist elements within Christianity. In modified monism every effort is made to address evil with unqualified seriousness and to make full allowance for its destructive reality while yet not abandoning the faith (the hope) that goodness remains ultimate or at least will "one day" emerge victorious. Once we limit ourselves strictly to the working description of modified monism contained in the previous sentence, we are enabled to place such reputedly monotheistic faiths as Judaism and Christianity under the heading of modified monism.

There is the analytical danger that this middle way will become a kind of catchall. However, the third alternative, polytheism, is clearly required in any complete phenomenology.[1] Accordingly, while the ongoing dominance of the one God in Judaism and Christianity makes it impossible to categorize either of those religions as dualist, continuing Jewish and Christian recognition and emphasis upon evil poses the question of whether either faith is or can be unreservedly or unambiguously described as monist. In Isaiah 45:7, Yahweh says, "I make weal and create woe."[2] Again, Jewish and Christian religious experience has made a place not only for angels but also for demons, and the fact is that angels and demons "occupy a middle ground between polytheistic monism [the gods as manifestations of the God] and an extreme monotheism that denies the existence of more than one god." Since the essential principle of Hebraic religion was monotheism, a principle that Chris-.

tianity came along to affirm, it was necessary to stop short "of positing two separate principles" and attributing to each of them a personality. This had the consequence of leaving the Devil "in an anomalous position. On the one hand, he was author of evil, and his existence relieved the Lord of direct responsibility for many of the evils of the world. On the other hand, he was not an independent principle but the creature and even the servant of the Lord. This anomaly led to an implicit tension between monism and dualism." Jeffrey Burton Russell proposes that monotheism "is not incompatible with a modified form of dualism that posits a spiritual ruler of evil who is inferior to the spirit of good." Russell generalizes, not uncontroversially (cf., e.g., the radical Christian monotheism of H. Richard Niebuhr) that "such is the Christian tradition."[3]

We may, in any case, adjudge that the Devil, as identified overall in Judaism and in Christianity, finds places to live both in the second part of chapter two above and now in the present chapter. Like our more affluent sister/brother humans, the Devil is able to afford more than one domicile.

I

Paul Tillich's ontologized Christianity, wherein God is to be apprehended as "ground of being," furnishes a counterpart to H. Richard Niebuhr's enterprise of identifying God with "the realm of being."

Tillich goes so far as to make the claim that "God does not exist," but by this he means that God must never be reduced to just one more being beside other (finite) beings. On this basis, Tillich continues, God is "being-itself beyond essence and existence. Therefore, to argue that God exists is to deny him." The term "ground" applied to God serves to indicate that "the ground of revelation is neither a cause that keeps itself at a distance from the revelatory effect nor a substance which effuses itself into the effect, but rather the mystery which appears in revelation and which remains a mystery in its appearance." This latter judgment is significant in linking "ground of being" and "mystery" respecting God. Furthermore, God is no mere static substance. A dynamic element in God makes possible "the divine creativity, God's participation in history, his outgoing character." There is a "not yet" within the life of God (balanced, however, by an "already"). To say that God is being itself is to include "both rest and becoming, both the static and the dynamic elements.... The divine life inescapably unites possibility and fulfillment."[5]

As is the case with H. Richard Niebuhr, Paul Tillich refrains from speaking of the Devil—and not because such speech would bind the Devil to appear. For, Tillich assures us, "Satan, the principle of the negative, has no independent reality."[6] However, a point of partial divergence between Niebuhr and Tillich, and the reason I locate Tillich within the company of modified monists despite his identifying of God and Being, is Tillich's repeated allusion to "the demonic" and "demonic structures" (as against Niebuhr). The "demonic" is of course tied etymologically to "demon" and "demonry."[6]

In one place Tillich makes the Devil sound like Niebuhr's God-as-Enemy: The face of the divine "takes on demonic traits" for those who are aware of their "estrangement from God." Yet overall the demonic is, for Tillich, "the elevation of something conditional to unconditional significance," to ultimacy, "the claim of something finite to infinity"—a form of behavior and pretension that humankind is very good at, in and through its varied sins of self-idolatry and god-idolatry. (Whenever the Christian church claims "to represent in its structure the Spiritual Community unambiguously" we have an instance of the demonic "in the realm of the holy." Every religion embodies a struggle between the divine and the demonic.) Contemporary human experience of "disruption, conflict, self-destruction, meaninglessness, and despair" has "given theology a new understanding of the demonic-tragic structures of individual and social life." In one context Tillich equates "demonic powers" with "structures of destruction" and the "demonic realm," an equation that could imply, more than in a delimitative way, human endeavor and blameworthiness. A demonic structure is even capable of driving humanity "to confuse natural self-affirmation with destructive self-elevation"; "the self-destructive structures of existence" seek, if never with total success, to plunge humankind "into complete annihilation." The demonic's essential characteristic is exactly a "split within being itself": Being versus non-Being.[7]

I believe that at the human level and in the culture of today, much of the question of the demonic must devolve around the issue of the conscious self versus the unconscious (Unconscious?). The "secular psychology of the unconscious has rediscovered the reality of the demonic in everyone."[8] Did we see fit to conclude that the unconscious dimension somehow transcends (rather than simply fills out) the human realm as such, we would have a basis here for affirming the demonic as transhuman. Tillich contends that toward the close of the Middle Ages "the demonic prevailed over against the divine in terms of anxiety."[9] This could be a description of certain dominating structures of our own epoch. However, in the end, Tillich's reasoning is reminiscent of H. Richard Niebuhr's, as of David Birnbaum's, when Tillich states categorically:

> Evil is nonbeing. When this statement is made, whether by Plotinus, Augustine, or myself, the charge is made that this means that sin is not taken seriously, that sin is nothing. The sound of the word "non-being" conveys the impression to some that sin is imaginary, not real. [Yes, how can "nonbeing" be anything but "not real"?— A.R.E.] However, a distortion of something which has being is as real as the undistorted state of that being, only it is not ontologically real. [How can something be "real" and not "ontologically real"? At best, such a "something" would be "unreally real," whatever that might mean.—A.R.E.] If sin were ontologically real, this would mean that there is a creative principle of evil, as in Manichaeism; but this is what the Christian doctrine of creation denies. Augustine said, "*Esse qua esse bonum est,*" being as being is good. Evil is the distortion of the good creation.[10]

The above apologia will probably not change the minds of those for whom the Devil is real. A distinctive and, I think, unresolved problem with Tillich's ontologizing of Christianity (as of Augustine's) is how to make evil as "real" coherent with "non-Being." In his exposition of "Evil in the Classical World" Jeffrey Burton Russell speaks more than once of that world's confusion between the ontological dimension and the moral dimension.[11] We may find ourselves up against a similar case here— although I do not know of anyone who has ever wholly escaped the miasma involved.

Withal, Paul Tillich's theology is at most a form of modified monism. It is not materially dualistic.[12]

II

Another figure who falls within the rubric of modified monism is the biblical and rabbinic scholar Jon D. Levenson in *Creation and the Persistence of Evil,*[13] a nonkabbalistic exposition of Judaism, contrasting markedly with the approach of David Birnbaum.

Levenson faults Yehezkel Kaufmann for failing to allow for real challenges to God's absolute sovereignty within the Hebrew Bible. Scholars generally agree today that *creatio ex nihilo,* the teaching that God fashioned the physical world out of nothing, does not correctly describe the biblical viewpoint. However, the influence of that misinterpretation is still present. "The fragility of the created order and its *vulnerability to chaos*" continues to be played down. The truth is that the Bible qualifies God's sovereignty via the "jarring juxtaposition" of a state of affairs that could even "lead one to believe that YHWH is now a *deus otiosus,* unable to equal his feats of yore." Levenson's subtitle, *The Jewish Drama of Divine Omnipotence,* slightly obscures his position; as his reasoning develops, it is clear that by so-called divine omnipotence he means no more than (1) a superior power within the bounds of the present dispensation, and (2) a hoped-for, unqualified power only within an indefinite tomorrow. In one place he refers to God as "potentially omnipotent," a much happier way to phrase his actual position.[14]

In large measure, Genesis 1:1–2:3 poses "the question of how to neutralize the powerful and ongoing threat of chaos." In that passage, as in Psalm 82, the deity's expressed mastery of creation is anything but primordial. It is not the mastery of an "unchallenged sovereign ruling from all eternity in splendid solitude." On the contrary, the demise of "the dark forces" opposed to God "lies in the uncertain future" (cf. as well Ps. 74:12–17). The very fact that prophet and psalmist see fit to summon God to act against evil or recalcitrant forces (cf., e.g., Isa. 51:9; Ps. 74:10–11) underscores the point.

> To call upon the arm of YHWH to awake as in "days of old" is to acknowledge that the adversarial forces were not annihilated in perpetuity in primordial times. Rising anew, they have escaped their appointed bounds and thus flung a challenge at their divine vanquisher. As was the case in Noah's flood, so here too creation has been reversed, only this time in defiance of God, not in obedience to his just will. In both instances the positive order of things associated with creation is not held to be *intrinsically* irreversible, as if the elements that threaten it, human evil or the sea dragon, have been definitively eradicated. The continuance of the positive order is possible only because of a special act of God....[15]

Jon Levenson develops his thesis of the postcreation persistence of evil with the aid of largely biblically oriented essays upon such themes as the survival of chaos despite the victory of God; the futurity and presence of a cosmogonic victory;[16] the vitality of destructiveness amidst the fragility of creation; the neutralizing of chaos in and through cult;[17] the two idioms of biblical monotheism: covenant and combat; and a particular dialectic, the autonomy of humanity over against God vis-à-vis the heteronomy of God over against humanity.[18] A paraphrase of passages in Levenson's summary chapter 4 will encapsulate his argumentation:

> At most, the biblical creation accounts offer an environment conducive to human habitation in that it is made relatively secure against threats of chaos and anarchy. The mastery achieved by YHWH is at many times fragile, often "a memory and a hope rather than a current reality"—in short, "a confession of faith." For, alas, the forces of chaos that were captured and domesticated at creation still survive. An eschatological combat myth, while rare in the Hebrew Bible, abides and grows in Jewish apocalyptic materials and is present in the *aggadah* of Talmudic rabbis. Obstacles that YHWH must surmount include idolatrous worldly powers (Gog), antisemitic peoples (Amalek), and the urge toward evil that lives "deep in the ambivalent human heart." Indeed, the perpetuation of the eschatological combat myth in postbiblical Judaism helps argue against the notion that the myth is only vestigial to the Bible. Were evil traceable to human culpability alone, the myth could fade away. But it did not fade away; here enters the specter of the divine responsibility for suffering, but also a dare to God to act anew as "the magisterial world-orderer that the old myth celebrates." The central affirmation of an abiding apocalyptic is that the suprahistorical disequilibrium that ensures historical evil cries out for suprahistorical correction. And since "evil did not originate with history, neither will it disappear altogether *in* history, but rather *beyond* it, at the inauguration of the coming world." From the general theological perspective involved here, YHWH remains a semiotiose deity, but yet one who can still be aroused to respond to the urgings of his cultic community and effect, with that community, new victories.[19]

Levenson's interpretation of Judaism positions him against a shallow optimism that dismisses or overlooks malign onslaughts against the human community. There are "cosmic forces of the utmost malignancy." At the same time, his rendering of Hebraic thinking guards him against cynicism and pessimism: While "the failure of God is openly acknowledged: no smug faith here, no flight into an otherworldly ideal," yet God is also to be "*reproached* for his failure, told that it is neither inevitable nor excusable: no limited God here, no God stymied by invincible evil, no faithless resignation before the relentlessness of circumstance." The truth abides that Judaism "is not optimistic but *redemptive,* and the creation of humanity with [its] powerful, innate and persistent will to evil is part of [the] vision of redemption, not part of its description of present reality." Once all this is said, such a passage as Genesis 1:26–27 endures to do precisely what Claus Westermann "says is impossible: it appoints the entire human race as God's royal stand-in."[20]

When we apply Levenson's dialectic to the issue of optimism/pessimism, no unmitigated dualism is permitted. However, the forms of opposition to an "omnipotent," i.e., relatively superior, God that he delineates (with primary concentration upon the Hebrew Bible, but in part as reflected within postbiblical materials) suggests a certain functional equivalency of the Devil. At times his reportage extends to the name and power of Satan himself. Levenson reminds us of a lesson we are coming to learn: *The more God is exculpated, the more evil is divinized.*[21] Again, insofar as the "demonic" is describable as the opponent of (or at least as opposition to) God, we find in Levenson—though he does not utilize the concept "demonic"—a certain parallel to Paul Tillich's modified monism. The struggle against radical evil remains unfinished.

III

To exemplify further modifiedly monistic theodicies, let us consider a more weightily philosophic approach, that of Frederick Sontag. A potentially fresh procedure is suggested via the full title of his work, *The God of Evil: An Argument from the Existence of the Devil.*[22] For the distinctiveness of his outlook is made evident through his assertion that atheism may offer the ground we need for reconstructing our thinking about God. "If the force of evil is the main source of atheism, the God that atheism can lead us to will have to be a 'God of Evil.'" The needed view will locate the forces of evil somewhere within God's nature itself. This immediately brings up the question, I am prompted to suggest, of the nature of the link between atheism and the Devil.[23] Sontag's advocated usage for "Devil" is: "a symbol for the negative and destructive forces loose in the world," or, less variously, a "center for destruction." Perhaps a hint of an answer to the question of the link between atheism and the Devil is found within Sontag's remark at the outset that "it is not easy to find a God in atheism and evil."[24] Does God comprise the link? If not, Sontag would have done better to choose such a title as *The Devil of Evil.* Also, certain distinctions vouchsafed by Jeffrey Burton Russell are still on my mind, such that the further query arises: Does the link in question extend only to the *concept* of God, or is it meant to encompass the *reality* of God?[25]

Having acknowledged that at the root of the persisting tendency that is moving so many people away from God and toward atheism lies certain "permanent and forceful features of our world and existence (e.g., evil)," Sontag aims at a new *via negativa*: Can we "form a possible concept of God from the very sources of the argument against him"? But he wishes to go beyond concept to reality: Any God we may find to exist "must be such as to account for the existence of the arguments against him, since he placed them in the world in deciding to create it as he did."[26]

The instance of question-begging here is a whopping one: Where has Sontag established, or even attested, that God made the world? However, once a *creatio* by God is presupposed—a giant step—we can accept Sontag's subsequent reasoning, "If any concept of God [we can even allow, "if any God"—A.R.E.] is incapable of accounting for the factors that argue against him," it is not God that is being described, "since the forces leading toward atheism are very real and would have to have been created willingly and knowingly by any God worthy of his name." What kind of God would do such a thing and why? Sontag does not hold that the powers of evil threatening us exist of necessity.[27] But he does find them to be fully permitted by God.

Sontag is accepting of a massive presupposition: "Any God could have designed a world in which his presence would be unavoidably obvious." Again, God did not need to choose "to conceal himself"—even though "the chief ground of atheism" lies in his hiddenness.[28] I find a twofold difficulty at this point. On the one hand, God is being handled very anthropomorphically. On the other hand, and contradictorily, God is being treated as a being who can do anything (a view that Sontag elsewhere avoids). Many of humanity's divinities would seem to fail to have the potentiality Sontag implies for them.

So far, we have clarified the import of the title *The God of Evil*: a God who allows evil to question God. In alternate terminology, what can the negative tell us about the positive?

Severe experiences of evil are able to induce catastrophic emotional disturbances that threaten simple acceptance of a "good God." While such experiences may not issue in the complete denial of God, they perforce raise serious questions about the kind of God there is. This is how there arises, then, "the argument from the existence of the Devil": Is a theory of God possible "that can accept into itself" a negative argument? "What kind of God can we construct who might allow such brutal destruction to exist in a world when he could have ruled it out?"—a God who even permits undeserved suffering. In this latter connection, Sontag fully grants the excessiveness of evil: "We are dealing with a God who felt perfectly capable of electing a more destructive world than was necessary in order to achieve his purpose."[29]

Once the legitimacy of atheism is acknowledged, the God we are able to have must be a God "not dependent upon men to exercise sufficient control to accomplish his purpose. If he were man-dependent, he would seem to have chosen a very risky path in concealing himself." Further, he is a God who is "not concerned to make his intentions continually obvious"; he is "above anxious concern over whether men acknowledge his presence and his intent." And on the question of what might be God's purpose in revealing himself through evil as well as through good, God seems prepared to have humankind curse him. He does not lie awake because sufferers are screaming at him. "Clearly he does not intend to intervene very often to prevent needless suffering or to put an end to pain." In addition, God "can afford the luxury of not coercing others to adopt his views"; evidently it "does not upset him to be misunderstood." Yet a God constructed from arguments rejecting his existence can at least answer "why we have this particular form of a world rather than some other." But it is still "strange that God should both allow such wanton destructive power and permit it to weigh more heavily than good." This is definitely not a world wherein we are "rewarded according to our goodness or punished only if we are evil." God is a complex God who has, evidently, hidden himself behind evil; "he is to be discovered there or not at all."[30]

Disassociating himself from Jean-Paul Sartre's existentialist rejection of God, Sontag moves on to an argument for God built upon existentialism's own constitutive tendency to atheism. The analysis centers around questions of nothingness-anguish-God: "God can only be understood by passing through nothingness. He who knows no anguish cannot know God.... [Only] through the natural tendency to atheism is Being revealed.... Existentially it is possible to escape from anguish, and the world can be accepted at face value—except where God is concerned. Then negativity, nothingness, and anguish cannot be avoided, and a God will be found through them" or he will simply not be found.[31]

For Sontag, while "the first impact of a powerful malignant force leads to a denial of God," the second impact can be an acknowledgment "of what it is that holds evil in check so that its destruction and betrayal, though extensive, at least are not complete." Furthermore, there are definite similarities between God and humankind: the possession and use of power and will (though of differing strengths),[32] participation in suffering, a knowing responsibility for decisions, the facing of contingency, an acceptance of possibility, a lack of necessity, the enjoyment of simple pleasures and common events, and the quality of emotion.[33] Along with humanity, God is confronted by threatening forces. But God can be exempt from actual destruction because his relation to non-Being and evil is unique. *"The flaws that lead to man's downfall must find their sources in God's nature or else go unexplained.* The same tendencies in man, those in which nonbeing both reveals and threatens his existence, must be present at the root of the divine nature. This possibility of imbalance and loss all too often overwhelms man," but "in God it may be prevented from causing destruction." Any "concept of God must contain within itself the source of evil in a positive and not a negative sense, because the mass of men feel evil to be stronger than simply a negation of good." A God "who allows more chaos than is necessary and who remains never fully open to us" is nevertheless "a God to whom man may relate," though "never in such a way that the relationship cannot fade and be lost at any moment." In this regard, human beings have a perfect right to argue with God. Yet God can purify "both himself and us by his ability to be present in the lowest, since to find God in the unexpected depths of Being's horrors is a much more realistic experience than to find him in a peaceful silence and solitude."[34]

The search for human freedom joins the problem of evil to form the two most likely causes of atheism in the modern world.[35] Here is one convenient summarization by Sontag respecting the reality of evil as it impinges, at least partially, upon the question of freedom:

> In the face of the power of atheism, our method has been to gather the forces of evil into one center. This we have personified as the Devil in contrast to God, although our aim was to construct a concept of God. To do this we allowed ourselves to be guided by the necessity to include these negative forces in our account. The only possible answer to atheism is to take all the forces that drive toward it and see if there is a God who could accept these into his own nature. In its starkest form, evil means the destruction of what has a right to exist, but in its milder form it involves a draining or a crippling of the power of existence. Some of this comes about through natural forces. However, God must bear the responsibility for unleashing those wild powers upon us indiscriminately. He alone can account for setting the limits on our power and knowledge just exactly where they are. The odds assigned to us in this struggle are not impossible, but they are certainly not the most favorable either.

Freedom fails to accomplish its delicate task of working its way between opposing forces unless and until "it understands how nonbeing underlies Being and how facing the Devil can lead to God."[36]

As with other figures we are discussing, an assessment of Sontag is postponed to the next chapter.

IV

I close this chapter by recapitulating something I have written elsewhere, but including a number of previously unpublished additions and continuing reflections.

At a minimum, reference to my own expressed viewpoint does two things. First, it connects with and develops further my brief conversation with Jeffrey Burton Russell at the end of chapter 2, where I venture to link the Devil particularly and vocationally with antisemitism, suggesting that just as Israel is a chosen people of God so the antisemites can be treated as a chosen people of the Devil. Second, and a more telling point: To allude to an *Anschauung* I have formed upon the Devil serves to avoid insulating myself against the overall critique to be offered in Part II of this book. If in saying this, I introduce a note of incongruity or surprise, all well and good, since here is one way in which the road to comedy can be caught sight of. If criticism ordinarily intends that the laugh be on others, a more catholic and responsible criticism will enable the laugh to be on oneself as well. Authentic humor applies to the comic himself, or to the would-be comic. Insofar as comedy may have a critical function in the presence of highly somber theodicies, there is no moral excuse for exempting one's own theodicean reflections from the assessment. However, since I have no literary need at all to introduce my own particular ruminations upon the Devil, the self-mockery intimated may seem a bit masochistic. But I should prefer to say: a bit mischievous.

What I am going to report differs from various reputable theodicies in being infinitely more partial and fragmentary. I have not propounded any justification of God before the fact of evil; I am merely speaking of what is, for me, one of the (singular) ways in which radical evil can operate in the actual world in which we live, an accounting that, to be sure, has some bearing upon the question of God. My view may have theodicean implications, but I offer nothing of an integral or complete theodicy. Furthermore, to take the Devil seriously does nothing in or of itself to resolve the problems that any and all theodicies are up against.

It was the so-called Yom Kippur War, way back in 1973, that quickened my interest in the subject of the Devil, although I had thought some about the matter before that year. I wrote a piece titled "The Devil and Yom Kippur."[37] The following paragraphs are adapted from, but also revise and go beyond, that brief exposition, an essay that may raise more questions than it helps to answer. For better or for worse, here is my little spiel:

For many people "God" constitutes an imperative symbol for a wholly unique power of righteousness and creativity. Beyond this, there are certain people who testify to the electing power and role of God. More concretely, some of these people attest to God's special choice of Israel. In addition, human beings themselves engage in electing activities—for example, of presidents, prime ministers, and senators. All this raises the question of whether the Devil may also be possessed of electing capabilities. "Devil" is an imperative symbol for a wholly unique power of evil and destructiveness, a special agent of radical evil—the Devil as Shadow of God. (Incidentally, I find fascinating the custom in British parliamentary politics that speaks of "shadow ministers." In a Jungian frame of reference, who is [more] the Devil, the incumbent or the "loyal opposition"? Or both?)

One possible accompaniment of the Devil's uniqueness is his capacity to originate and concentrate upon unqualifiedly and totally unique evil. But is there a form of evil in this world that is wholly unique? I believe there is: the evil known as antisemitism. Before elaborating upon that assertion, I will fill out the symmetry: God elects the Jewish people to life (*haim*); the Devil (as, for example, in the German Nazi) uniquely elects the Jewish people to death. The Divine Visage is pursued by its Shadow.

While the Reign of God is held to encompass all humankind, yet the chosen people of God are sustained. So too, while the Devil covets a universal kingdom, his "faithful remnant," his special witnesses are likewise sustained, through the millennia and across all boundaries. There are absolutely no restrictions upon membership in the religion of antisemitism. All are welcome to its ranks. It is the world's one universal faith—one faithfully reflective of the Shadow.

Were the phenomenon of antisemitism localized in time or in place, the credibility of introducing the Devil into the scene would doubtless falter. But in truth we have no parallels to antisemitism. Antisemitism is not a matter of "human prejudice" in any general sense. Various forms of prejudice manifest themselves as accompaniments of historical transience and spatial contingency. By contrast, whether we speak of time or of place, of temporal enduringness or of geopolitical pervasiveness, no prejudice comes near antisemitism.

In the past thousand years one of every two Jews was murdered. In the twentieth century two of every five Jews were murdered. In the past fifty years one of every three Jews was murdered.[38]

In "The Devil and Yom Kippur" I adduce a number of historical and contemporary exemplifications and justifications of the claim that antisemitism boasts a uniquely universal character; many other such data are listed in my study *Black-Woman-Jew*. The latter list is frighteningly tiresome in its length, extending over no less than three pages.[39] Come to think of it, *tiresomeness* is the whole point.

Thus may the elucidation or disclosure of the Devil be demanded etiologically and existentially because the hatred of Jews is anything but a matter of evil as such. It is *this* evil, an evil wholly incomparable and suffusedly incredible, an evil so unbelievable that it does not even require the presence of Jews. "Devil" and "antisemitism" can be apprehended as a type of dialectical or twinning parthenogenesis: Antisemitism is born of the Devil, and the Devil is born out of antisemitism. Incredibility is normally the opposite of credibility, but it is not necessarily the opponent of truth. To speak of the life and destiny of the Jewish people as unbelievable receives its rationale from the affirmation of an unbelievably unique God; to speak of the life and destiny of the antisemites receives its rationale from testimony to an unbelievably unique Devil. Were the divine election of Israel duplicable in other elections, we should have to settle for "games of the gods" or some other mundane, repetitive accounting. In the same way, were the ongoing persecution of Jews duplicable in other persecutions, we should have to settle for "carryings-on of evil powers or demons" or some equally mundane, repetitive explanation. But there is nothing like antisemitism. Accordingly, it is reasonable to speak of the Devil's special presence within, and his jurisdiction over, that particular phenomenon.

If this envisionment respecting the Devil makes some kind of sense, then has the Shadow of God, the terrible Shadow of God, the most terrible Shadow of God taken on peculiar shape. For Israel never did *ask* to be "chosen"; I state this with the same intended ethical connotation as: no human being ever asked to be born. It is God—*the* God (in Jeffrey Russell's preferred wording)[40]—who is said to elect Israel, thereby potentializing, indeed actualizing, the horrible equation Antisemite=Amalek[41]=Devil. In Jon Levenson's wording, for rabbinic thought "Amalek is the hypostatization of God's authorship of a world in which Jewry suffers for being themselves [as against for their *doing* or *failing to do* something—A.R.E.] and of his willingness to allow genocidal anti-Semites to survive to strike again."[42]

The watchword of all Amalekites is, "Come let us wipe them out from the nations so that the name of Israel will not be remembered" (Ps. 83:4). That antisemitism is tied to Jewish "being" rather than to Jewish "doing" points up the way in which election by the Devil is the other side (the Shadow?) of election by God. Irving Greenberg shows how idol worship in our world necessitates antisemitism:

> Jewish existence constitutes a witness that the Messiah and/or the final perfection is not yet here. If it were here, the Jews would be one with humanity, that is, would disappear. Premature messianists in whatever form, are angered by the persistence of the Jew who thereby gives the lie to their presumptions. Idolatry is tempted to make the Jews disappear and thereby clear the way for its own uncontested dominance.
>
> The twentieth century has made the matter even clearer. *Whosoever would be God must destroy the Jews totally.* As long as one Jew is alive, the Jewish denial of all but God remains. The twentieth century has unleashed such gigantic and total power that the temptation to become God is overwhelming; therefore, a plan to murder every last Jew became conceivable—and doable.[43]

The thesis may be entertained, with aid from both the history of Europe and the psychology of depth, that for all their enormous differences, Nazism and Christianity share a certain need to liquidate the Jew: the Nazi (and his confreres) in the service of the idolatry of race, the Christian because the Jewish presence testifies, in and of itself, that authentic faith in God is not the spiritual monopoly of an (idolatrous) church.

I shall try to be more concrete. One familiar and viable way of living with the spiritual finding that God is at once judge and font of mercy is through the assurance that God afflicts the comfortable and comforts the afflicted. We may suggest that, by contrast, the Devil afflicts the afflicted and comforts the comfortable. Accordingly, a main difference between God and the Devil is that while God grieves over the suffering of God's people, the Devil delights in that suffering. This brings us to the War of Yom Kippur.

In the community in Pennsylvania where I work there has lived a man who for years on end—he does not seem to be around anymore—wrote to local newspapers expressing virulent hostility to Israel. But he never did so except under one very exacting condition. By actual count, the letters would appear immediately after the Jewish people underwent specific suffering at the hands of their enemies. Naturally, the 1973 attack upon Israel was to witness one more castigation of Jews by this man. Again, a certain Christian clergyman utilized the Yom Kippur War to identify Israel as a criminal community, a racist state like Nazi Germany, a manufactory of human waste, dedicated to "crimes against humanity." And on the identical occasion another Christian, a Protestant theologian, employed the Devil's *kairos* to put forward the thesis that Israel is simply not worth all the trouble she causes the world; she ought to be dismembered for the sake of international justice. All these "prophets," together with unnumbered others, live by the Devil's manual of instructions: "You are permitted to hold your peace only until the Jews are attacked; then, you must do something. But never attack the attacker, you must attack the Jewish victim; you are to do so while the Jew is 'down.' For the Jew is never really 'down'; his alleged tribulations are part and parcel of his secret arsenal for conquering the world." The Jewish world-conspiracy never ends.

God may be viewed as judging God's people in their sins; the Devil judges "the Jews" when others sin against them. The fittingness of the hypostatization or symbolization of Amalek enters here; cf. Deut. 25:17: Amalek "attacked you on the way, when you were faint and weary." Were God to afflict the comfortless, God would transfigure Godself into, or retreat into, the Shadow of God. (Some Jews of the Holocaust and other times have grievously pondered whether God had done exactly that and thereby become the Evil One.) Were the Devil to afflict the comfortable, he would become as the integral God (fat chance). A primary working distinction between God and the Devil is not so much that God does what is right while the Devil does what is wrong, but rather that God does what is right at the right time, whereas the Devil supplants the mercy that the times are calling for with remorseless, destructive vituperation and judgment. (What is being said here has nothing to do with any absurd "finding" that Jews can do no wrong. They are as unrighteous—and righteous—as the rest of us.)

I offer one other comment on behalf of concreteness. Antisemites in several countries "deny" that the Holocaust ever took place; the "event" is a lie invented by the worldwide Jewish conspiracy. I use quotation marks for "deny" because I have no doubt whatever that these people do not in fact believe that there was no Holocaust. Such "historical revisionism" has been rightly called the cutting edge of today's antisemitic movement.[44] In a preliminary exposition of the Devil in chapter 1 of this book, I list a multifaceted dilemma we face respecting the affirmation/denial of the Devil. The second variation upon the dilemma reads that the denial of the Devil may function as pro-Devil, on the reasoning that the Devil can operate more effectively in the absence of any recognition of him. It makes sense to identify the "claim" that the Holocaust never happened as a diabolical stratagem—a denial of the Devil's work, in the service of the Devil. The truth that the Holocaust is the only major historical happening to be "denied" in this way further points up the singularity and incomparability of antisemitism.[45] The "revisionist denial" of the Holocaust has been denominated, appropriately, as the effort to murder Jews a second time. The same people murdered twice: Of whom else can this be said?

Finally, a word may be in order respecting the singular "discovery" on the part of an earlier Christian world that the Jew is in league with the Devil and indeed partakes of the Devil's being. (The Christian collective unconscious respecting Jews has been and remains fertile ground for carrying out satanic programs.) We may reflect that this disguise, in fact fabricated by the Devil himself, is a perfectly stunning tour de force. For at a single stroke the Devil equips himself to get out from under the charge that he is the secret author of antisemitism. He can now make clear to everyone that, after all, it was the real Devil (the Jew) who "made him do it." On this ploy, the true and only cause of antisemitism remains the Jew.

Fortunately, the knife cuts two ways: That the Jews are equated with the Devil serves to remind us—of course, only rationally speaking—that antisemitism is indeed the Devil's special work, his favorite cause. For only the Devil could produce the demonic stratagem of maintaining the Jew as his singular family relation. Thus, John in 8:44—wherein "the Jews" have the Devil as their father—can only be traced to the Devil. For who but the true father could ever know his own son?[46]

As Joel Carmichael makes clear in his important historical analysis, *The Satanizing of the Jews,*[47] the mystical antisemitism of the Christian church and others had and has nothing in fact to do with Jews.[48] We may offer the parallel point that there is one sense, and one sense alone, in which the satanizing of Jews cannot be reduced to the work of Christian mysticizers + German Nazis + (many) Americans + (some) Arabs + various other humans, and so on. While all of these people are to be charged with being fully responsible and culpable representatives of *Judenfeindschaft,* the indeterminate demonry they compound and exacerbate is no more than glimpsed in and through their efforts, as in a glass darkly. As we have noted, antisemitism in its essence transcends bounds of time and place. Its force is infinite. Its true father is the Devil; the human antisemites are no more than his flunkies.

I include one or two midrashim upon the foregoing interpretation. One pragmatic, "good" consequence of the persuasion that the Devil is the true father of antisemitism—not that the present exposition is in any way pragmaticist—is this viewpoint's support for the truth that "changes" in Jewish behavior or belief are irrelevant and indeed powerless respecting the fate or future of antisemitism. Antisemitism is exclusively the problem of the antisemite.[49]

Again, one winsome feature of Frederick Sontag's monograph *The God of Evil* is his postscript, "Never Trust a God over Thirty." He proposes that we think of God as eternally youthful—a God who maintains the flexible virtues, vitality, and freedom of the young, while yet being immune to "the quixotic changes and instabilities" that accompany these characteristics in humanity.[50] I ended the original piece "The Devil and Yom Kippur" with an allegation that the nemesis of the Devil, Chief of the antisemites, is that he has grown dreadfully old. I now limit myself to five quick examples from among thousands available. In 387, John of Chrysostom could say that the synagogue is a place of prostitution and that the Jews are possessed of demons. In 1215, the Fourth Lateran Council, and later Innocent III, could decree that Jews wear "a badge of shame" on their clothing. In 1543, Martin Luther could demand that since the Jews are revealed as murderers, usurers, and "full of every vice," their synagogues are to be set afire (cf. *Kristallnacht,* 9–10 November 1938) and their homes destroyed. Just after the Holocaust, a representative of the Near East Christian Council could write that the Palestinian Jewish leadership is "spreading a spirit of intolerance and narrow jingoism" scarcely distinguishable from "the Nazi race doctrine." And soon thereafter a former president of the Union Theological Seminary in New York could assail the "resurgence of fanatical Jewish nationalism," Israel's "parasitic economic basis," and "the aggressiveness of the new state" with its "covetous eyes" on Arab lands.

We have heard it all before, and it has grown infinitely tiresome. The voices of the antisemites go to compose a cosmic broken record. The Devil has long since run out of ideas. He has become a crashing bore.

There is some comfort in this state of affairs. His youthful Adversary puts him to shame:

> Do not remember the former things
>   or consider the things of old.
> I am about to do a new thing;
>   now it springs forth, do you not
>   perceive it? (Isa. 43:18-19)

> The steadfast love of the Lord never ceases,
>   His mercies never come to an end;
> they are new every morning (Lam. 3:22-23)

Behind the Shadow of God, the equation Antisemite=Amalek= Devil arranges itself with relentless, even fateful force. We may not emerge from its darkness into the light until, in accordance with Yevtushenko's dream,

> the last antisemite on the earth
> is buried for ever.

> Then at last will
> the International ring out.[51]

Notes

1. An exhaustive phenomenology must of course allow for polytheism, which we are not treating.
2. This verse stands out amidst general biblical silence upon the origins of evil.
3. Jeffrey Burton Russell, *The Devil* (Ithaca, N.Y. and London: Cornell University Press, 1987), pp. 98, 105, 250, and 251.
4. Paul Tillich, *Systematic Theology,* Vol. I (Chicago: University of Chicago Press, 1951), pp. 156, 205, 246, and 247.
5. Paul Tillich, *Systematic Theology,* Vol. II (Chicago: University of Chicago Press, 1957), p. 171. But, cf. Tillich elsewhere: "The demonic, anti-divine principle, which nevertheless participates in the power of the divine, appears in the dramatic centers of the biblical story." (*The Courage To Be,* [New Haven: Yale University Press, 1952], p. 34).
6. On the etymology here, consult Russell, *Devil,* p. 142; cf. pp. 174, 189-91. On the New Testament and names of the Devil, see pp. 228-29.

7. Tillich, *Systematic Theology,* Vol. II, pp. 27, 51, 77, 164, and 167; Vol. I, pp. 49, 140, and 285; Vol. III (Chicago: University of Chicago Press, 1963), pp. 102, 244, and 337. Tillich holds that the doctrine of "double predestination" violates "both the divine love and the divine power." Ontologically speaking, "eternal condemnation is a contradiction in terms. It establishes an eternal split within being-itself. The demonic, whose characteristic is exactly this split, has then reached coeternity with God; then non-being has entered the very heart of being and of love." (*Systematic Theology,* Vol. I, p. 285). Thus is the teaching of double predestination to be traced to demonic inspiration.

8. Ibid., Vol. III, p. 207.

9. Paul Tillich, *A History of Christian Thought,* ed. Carl E. Braaten (New York: Simon and Schuster, 1968), p. 148.

10. Ibid., pp. 53-4. See also Tillich, *Political Expectations,* ed. James Luther Adams (New York: Harper & Row, 1971), pp. 66-88, passim.

11. Russell, *Devil,* Chap. 4.

12. In *The Interpretation of History* (New York: Scribner, 1936), Tillich includes a lengthy analysis of the demonic (pp. 77-122). The materials go back to 1926 (in the German original). In the exposition here, I have primarily relied upon Tillich's writings from a considerably later time. Like his later reflection, the 1926 materials are somewhat unclear upon the issue of the objective versus the nonobjective character of the demonic, as in the (abstract) "basic meaning" he assigns to it: "the unity of form-creating and form-destroying strength." Again, "form of being and inexhaustibility of being belong together. Their unity in the depth of essential nature is the divine, their separation in existence, the relatively independent eruption of the 'abyss' in things, is the demonic." Still further, demonry at the social level "is the reign of a super-individual, sacred form which supports life, which at the same time contains the force of destruction in such a way that the destructive power is essentially connected with its creative power." (Ibid., pp. 81, 84, 91; see further, pp. 85-93: "The existence of the demonic"). By placing Tillich's thought under the heading of modified monism, as against the other possibility of nonqualified monism, I have sought to give all due allowance to his insistence upon the "actuality" or "reality" of the demonic, even though his overall analysis of the subject remains, I think, ambiguous. Thus, to be contrasted with the citations just given from *The Interpretation of History,* we find such illustrative passages as these in the same source: "The affirmation of the demonic has nothing to do with a mythological or metaphysical affirmation of a world of spirits. [The dwelling of the demonic] is the subconscious level of the human soul." (pp. 85, 89). Fortunately, we are given one wholly unambiguous declaration by Tillich that can be explained succinctly as: There is *no* objective Devil (Satan). The 'Satanic' (destruction without any creation) contrasts with the demonic in that it "has no actual existence." (Tillich, *Interpretation of History,* p. 80).

13. Jon D. Levenson, *Creation and the Persistence of Evil* (San Francisco: Harper & Row, 1988).

14. Ibid., pp. xiii, 4, 26, and 41.

15. Ibid., pp. xiv, 6-7, 11-12, 18, and 20.

16. "Cosmogony is not fully grasped until it has been related to the microcosm and to the rites that took place there and were thought to allow human participation in the divine ordering of the world." (Ibid., p. 91).

17. "The reality that the Sabbath represents God's unchallenged and uncompromised mastery, blessing, and hallowing is consistently and irreversibly available only in

the world-to-come. Until then, it is known only in the tantalizing experience of the Sabbath." (Ibid., p. 123).

18. Levenson makes full allowance for the one biblical text in which Leviathan is held to be created by God. (Ibid., Chap. 5—"Creation Without Opposition: Psalm 104"). In this chapter he also reveals how and where Genesis 1 belongs in the trajectory from the ancient combat myth to the creation theology of the Abrahamic faiths. (Ibid, p. 53).

19. Ibid., pp. 47-50.

20. Ibid., pp. 24-5, 39, 44, and 116.

21. Ibid., pp. 44-6, 136. On humankind's Evil Impulse, see especially pp. 45-6.

22. Frederick Sontag, *The God of Evil* (New York: Harper & Row, 1970).

23. Against the implication of his title and subtitle, Sontag has more to say about atheism as such than he does about the Devil and evil. This could accord with his philosophic bent. However, his rendering of atheism tends to concentrate upon concerted opposition to God—largely on the ground of destructive evil—rather than upon the practical "atheism" that is widespread today and simply exhibits little or no care for things religious. It seems to me that the "atheism" of unnumbered contemporaries is prevailingly a matter of disinterest as against aggressive a-theism. God has simply lost importance.

24. Ibid., pp. ix, x, 3, 4, and 30.

25. In one place Sontag accedes that "the only way to deal with God seems to be by examining concepts about him." (Ibid., p. 54).

26. Ibid., pp. 1-2.

27. Ibid., pp. 2, 153.

28. Ibid., pp. 16, 19-20. The three citations just referred to are contained in a chapter called "A God in Hiding." Is not this phrase a tautology? Does not "godness" imply "hiddenness"? Much happier is Sontag's acknowledgment, "even if we use all the phenomena of the world as a base, God can never be seen directly from them." (Ibid., p. 17).

29. Ibid., pp. 12, 13, 18, and 26.

30. Ibid., pp. 21-2, 24, 26, 38, 39, 40, and 42. On the complexity of God, see also pp. 48-9. On the effort to argue to God from the future, see especially pp. 50-2.

31. Ibid., Chap. 6—"The Existential God." The quoted words are from pp. 78, 81, 82. Sontag gets into difficulties, at least of a logical variety, when he makes freedom ontologically anterior to Being. I submit that nothing can be ontologically prior to Being, because ontological reality *means* Being as such (as Being means ontological reality as such). Again, Sontag, in orthodox existentialist fashion, i.e., existence-ism, would have existence preceding essence "for God too." (Ibid, p. 83; cf. *existere*, to emerge). I think we must say that, on the contrary, essence (*essentia*, Being) *is* existence; theologically construed, neither is prior to the other. That is to say, what God is (essence) *is* as God lives (existence)—contra humankind, wherein essence and existence come apart. Again, to Sontag, "becoming" is necessarily prior to "being"; becoming is "the basic category for the understanding of both Being and God." Further, "since atheism asserts the nonexistence of God, any view which builds upon its insights will have to give primacy to Nonbeing." (Ibid, pp. 138-39, 146). Sontag occasionally falls into a reification fallacy, as when he tries to make non-Being transcend actual Being and speaks of the "power and extent" of non-Being (pp. 156, 161)—a difficulty we have noted in passing in the case of Tillich and Augustine. I suggest that there can "be" no transcendence in non-Being because there is no non-Being to do any transcend-

ing or to do anything else. Non-Being has only logical reality and no ontological reality. But when Sontag comes to equate non-Being with nonrealization and nonrealization-as-yet (pp. 146ff.), his understanding of non-Being is made somewhat more plausible.

32. God's power is possessed of "absolute sufficiency." (Ibid., p. 143). On will and God, see especially pp. 152-53.

33. To Sontag, personality, in humankind and in God, entails "will, power, and knowledge in effective combination." And once we "accept the crucial role of personality in all selection for existence or destruction," it becomes necessary to "personify the forces of evil in the Devil." However, freedom "is not an attribute in itself"; it is "the description of how all [personality] structures function together." (Ibid., pp. 157-59).

34. Ibid., pp. 111, 123-24, 128-30, 132-33, 139, and 144. Further to God's participation in suffering, consult ibid., Chap. 10—"The Insights of the Vulgar." Happily, Sontag does not fall prey to the theological ideology according to which the phenomenon of human freedom removes divine responsibility for the evils that humankind brings. Yet humankind remains culpable for its evils (p. 151); I certainly agree with that.

35. It is to be noted that while such worthies as Nietzsche and Sartre can reject God in the name of freedom, others can celebrate God as the needed author and even guarantor of humankind's freedom. This would seem to suggest that the category of freedom as such may not constitute a very useful referee pro/contra God.

36. Ibid., pp. 145, 150, 165.

37. A. Roy Eckardt, "The Devil and Yom Kippur," *Midstream* 20 (Aug./Sept. 1974): 67-75; republished in Frank Ephraim Talmage, ed., *Disputation and Dialogue* (New York: Ktav, 1975), pp. 229-39. See also A. Roy Eckardt, *Your People, My People* (New York: Quadrangle/New York Times Book Co., 1974), Chap. 7; and Alice L. and A. Roy Eckardt, *Long Night's Journey Into Day* (Detroit: Wayne State University Press; Oxford: Pergamon Press, 1988), pp. 59-67.

38. Consult Simon Wiesenthal, *Every Day Remembrance Day* (Philadelphia: American Interfaith Institute, 1992).

39. A. Roy Eckardt, *Black-Woman-Jew* (Bloomington: Indiana University Press, 1989), pp. 133-35.

40. See Chap. 1, n. 36.

41. See Chap. 3, p. 40; Levenson, *Creation and the Persistence of Evil*, p. 49.

42. Ibid., p. 45.

43. Irving Greenberg, *The Jewish Way* (New York: Summit Books, 1988), p. 232, italics in original.

44. So, for example, several Jewish groups in Canada point out; see "Top court quashes Zunder's conviction," *The Globe and Mail* (Toronto), 28 Aug. 1992, p. 1.

45. Cf. Emil L. Fackenheim: "There has been a resurrection of the devil's logic. In effect, the present right-wing version of the devil's logic states that Hitler never murdered any Jews—and that he should have finished the job." ("Philosophical Reflections on Antisemitism," in *The Jewish Thought of Emil Fackenheim*, ed. Michael L. Morgan [Detroit: Wayne State University Press, 1987], p. 281).

46. Jesus of Nazareth is supposed to have made the accusation mentioned. This is historically out of the question; Jesus was himself a faithful Jew.

47. Joel Carmichael, *The Satanizing of the Jews* (New York: Fromm International, 1992). In linking Jew and Devil the Christian church inflicted upon itself and the world a confusion of subjects that is, in and of itself, diabolic. In and through the

Jew/Devil identification, the church has done unique obeisance to the Devil. See also William Nicholls's comprehensive historical study, *Christian Antisemitism: A History of Hate* (Northvale, N.J. and London: Jason Aronson, 1993).

48. One reason why the protestation, "some of my best friends are Jews," is so revealing is its embodiment of the antisemitic premise that evil Jewishness is not exhausted in single human beings. Along the same line, were the State of Israel not "there," it would be necessary to invent such a state.

49. In the category of favorite devilish tricks: If you blame victims long enough, they will come to blame themselves. Self-hatred among Jews is a sign of the success of the Devil.

50. Sontag, *God of Evil,* pp. 168, 170.

51. Yevgeny Alexandrovich Yevtushenko, "Babiy Yar."

4

The Neverending Crisis of Rationalist Theodicy

*What are we to make of a creation in which the
routine activity is for organisms to be tearing
others apart, everyone reaching out to incorporate
others who are edible to him?*

—*Ernest Becker*[1]

*The phenomenon of human suffering continues to
bleed through the explanations that attempt to
account for it.*

—*Wendy Farley*[2]

The fat is now in the fire. A rather reputable company of monists, dualists, and modified monists has passed before us; they are next up for review. And, perhaps a little oddly, by venturing into their company the writer of this book subjects himself to the same kind of judgment.

The theodicies we have reviewed are of undoubted aid in the theoretical (linguistic, conceptual, in general intellectualist) analysis of the twin phenomena of radical evil/radical good. Yet there are problems. The evaluative commentary to follow will move from the general to the specific—first, a brief overall critique, and, second, some responses to individual figures and viewpoints.

I

Is the Devil an excrescence, or is a theodicy that disallows or ignores the Devil the real excrescence? Equally, or perhaps even more, to the point—is the associating of God with *some* sort of place in the kingdom of evil a moral trespass, or is the inability to recognize and concede that place the real moral trespass?

A weighty and comprehensive difficulty faced by different rationalist theodicies is linked to the question of the divine responsibility (*Verantwortlichkeit*), more precisely, the divine blameworthiness (*Tadelnswürdigkeit*) and culpability (*Strafbarkeit, Schuld*).

A decisive ontological/moral consideration asserts itself. It involves what might be called the primordial problem of the divine determinism/ determination. In question form: Could there be some crucial respect in which God had no choice but to create the cosmos and this world? Analogically, we may recall an observation in the *Pirke Aboth*, "not of thy will wast thou formed." That observation is directed to humankind, but the point can readily be elevated and applied to God. The same parallel may be drawn respecting the remark of Albert Camus, cited in the prologue that begins this book, "Man is not entirely to blame; it was not he who started history." Is it of God's will that the creation has taken place? Or was the act somehow forced upon God—at the hands of Necessity or some comparable Surd? Must we conclude that God is "not entirely to blame," indeed not to blame at all, since it was not really God who "started the history" of this planet?

Were the latter conclusion (determinism visited *upon* the divine) the proper one, the burden of God's culpability for evil (as for anything else) would dissipate. But once the creation is tied to God's will (determination *by* the divine), the question of God's accountability for evil (as for everything else) comes very much to the fore. And it refuses to go away.

The alternative of God's self-determination in the creation is central within the Jewish, Christian, and Muslim traditions; thus does the issue of divine culpability become inescapable for us.

So-called natural evils cannot be excluded from divine responsibility. As I write this chapter, parts of the American South have been devastated by what may be the worst natural catastrophe in the country's history to date, Hurricane Andrew. It is interesting that such innocent sounding names should be assigned to what ought to be called "acts of God"—at this point the wording on insurance policies and other such documents is much more honest—or perhaps "acts of the Devil." That the latter denomination is forbidden carries its own sociotheologic commentary upon our culture. Be that as it may, the current practice of applying human names to hurricanes when human beings bear absolutely no responsibility for such catastrophes is insulting to humanity.

I have to make a concession and offer a confession: The theoretical reason cannot here be excluded; it is now engaging itself in a kind of moral judgment (in company, of course, with the practical reason). However, the fact of God's responsibility for the world produces in turn a massive dilemma for our speculative reason once that variety of reasoning involves itself in theodicy: What can it ever mean *reasonably* to "justify" God before the fact of evil? Theodicy is seen to be problematic in and of itself.

If God has the power to destroy the Devil (radical evil) and wishes the Devil destroyed, what could God possibly be waiting for? Why delay the coming victory until, say, the "end of the world"? An alternate version of the same question reads: Why is there *so much* evil? Why is evil so excessive?[3]

The special moral-theological problems of different versions of rational (also transrational?) theodicy all follow from the foregoing state of affairs:

Should we opt for the monist alternative, we seem to have no choice but to make God immanently responsible for radical evil.

Should we take the dualist path, God may appear to be let off the hook, but no more than deciduously. For we are quickly brought to inquire: What is God doing to fight radical evil? And how can we count upon God to win out? Is there any hope for hope?

And should we follow the way of modified monism (modified or qualified dualism), are we not beset now by the *one* and now by the *other* difficulty: God's continuing responsibility for evil (the problem facing monism) *and* the enigma of what God is doing or can do about evil (the problem facing dualism)?

In keeping with prevailing assumptions within the contemporary Western religious tradition, the alternative of unqualified or radical dualism can probably and agreeably be released from the present assessment. Such is my procedure or assumption. We are still left with formidable ontological/moral issues created by both monism and modified monism. This is not to say that plagues of exactly equal quality are to be visited upon these other two houses. The monist argument or theodicy may be distinguished as a special kind of cop-out—to be sure, an inadvertent one. It fails to address the foundations and force of evil in evil's total, excessive horror. This monist view, at least by default, does acknowledge God's culpability or presence at the point of evil—not a small contribution. Unqualified monism also serves to point the way to one or another modification of itself. True, insofar as God carries *ultimate* responsibility for radical evil, it becomes *ultimately* impossible to separate God from the Devil. However, it is the modified monist who works stubbornly and with much anguish to rescue and retain that very distinction. And she does so other than through such an (abortive) method as splitting Being and non-Being (see the critique of H. Richard Niebuhr later in this chapter). The modified monist toils desperately to keep some kind of space between God and the Devil, if only through so fragile a conceptualization of evil as Shadow of God.

II

Let us be more concrete now and review and assess the more pertinent data from chapters 2 and 3, as these were led up to in chapter 1.

For a theodicean apologist like David Birnbaum, the evil of evil gets "justified" in and through such considerations as the divine freedom, God's purposes and goals, and most especially through the gift of freedom to human beings, without which they could never realize their highest potential. Radical evil is never a calculating vice of God; the nature of the divine/human relationship is what *occasions* evil (though, it is true, also makes it inevitable).

The trouble here is a dual one: (1) Philosophically, no independent rationale or even excuse is being furnished for the claim that the full realization of human potential is contingent upon the intercession of freedom. If God is *in essentia* omnipotent, as Birnbaum and others maintain—I do not—God would appear to be capable of arranging a universe in which human freedom is totally realized while gross evil remains totally absent. It is interesting that Birnbaum should concede that the divine allowance for the potential pain that is gratuitous, arbitrary, and not distributed equally is "unfortunate," though he finds this "apparently necessary to the cosmic order."[4] To identify something as "unfortunate" is to hint at the possibility of something fortunate. To make evil necessary in order that there be unalloyed human freedom is, I suggest, an instance of apriorism, an erroneous anthropomorphic notion, and hardly a *sine qua non* for the presence of a fully divine, all-transcending God.

(2) Morally, Birnbaum's argument does nothing to *free* God, or even to neutralize God, from ultimate blameworthiness respecting the evil that relentlessly binds itself to the God who is finally responsible for all things.[5] To "occasion" evil is nonetheless to be fully culpable for evil. In a monist (monotheist) frame of reference any claim that evil "has to be there" is completely powerless to offset the responsibility of God respecting the presence of evil. To make God's ends depend upon the creation of a world such as ours is rather superstitious. But the issue before us is not in the first instance one of how to "explain" evil. The major issue is a moral one. To argue, as Birnbaum does, that evil "has to exist" as a counterpart to good or as a means to God's ends is to fashion a superfluity. *For no one ever forced God to create a world, and no one ever forced God to create this world.* I find myself forever repeating a single sentence of Eliezer Berkovits—but only because I think it irrefutable: "God is responsible for having created a world in which man is free to make history."[6]

As for H. Richard Niebuhr's version of monism or "radical monotheism," three comments can be made: (1) I offer a word upon the final part of Niebuhr's conceptualization as reproduced in chapter 2 of this book: God as Enemy. We have noted that for Niebuhr, once the power of human sin is broken the Enemy becomes the Friend. More specifically, by means of the grace that is mediated through the Christian gospel a "great reconciliation" with the divine Enemy takes place. I have written elsewhere that the latter persuasion has to be received dialectically, due to an anguishing truth:

> While it is so that the Enemy becomes the Friend, the human being is still compelled to mourn that the Friend appears to remain as Enemy. To proceed otherwise would be to fall into a Polyanna complex of spiritual complacency, unrealism, and sentimentality. The *metanoia* of God from Enemy to Friend simply does not wholly eradicate God as Enemy (any more than it disposes of God as Void).[7] The question and the promise of the divine *metanoia* are no more than those of the direction God is going and yearns to go, the question of God's own life story. [The] Christian identification of God as Friend does not eliminate the truth that this One continues to give *some kind of consent*—if God is indeed *the* universal One—to disease and rape, to war and typhoon, to anxiety and hunger, to meaninglessness and despair, to destruction and death. Thus [do we remain] compelled to move, not alone from Void to Enemy to Friend, but also from Friend to Enemy to Void.[8]

(2) H. Richard Niebuhr's Augustinian hypothesis that whatever is, is good implies a twinning: whatever is not, is evil; or whatever "is" evil,

is not. Evil is taken gently by the hand and walked back into the cradle of non-Being. It may well be that such radical monotheists as Niebuhr are driven to this intolerable resolve by a praiseworthy anxiety to avoid the blasphemy of making God evil. Yet, when all is said and done, the reducing of evil to non-Being scarcely comprises a serious effort to look into the face of evil. And it hardly supplies a convincing or helpful way to tell God from the Devil. The effect instead is to trivialize evil and even to explain it away. This tendency is part of a condition that many theodicies share, a proclivity simply to restate the problem they are ostensibly seeking to address. (The charge last mentioned is perhaps most applicable to unqualified dualism, which, so it is often alleged, only perpetuates rather than resolves the question of evil's menace.)

In contrast to an attempted reduction of evil to non-Being, the heart of evil is, as Professor Russell has declared,"to take all being and render it nothing": not to turn being into evil but to make being into nothing. These few words of Russell's help to demonstrate, linguistically/empirically, that it is out of the question to equate evil with non-Being. Evil *is* being—the being that takes other being and beings and turns them into nothing.

In describing the early Christian theological argument that evil is non-Being, Jeffrey Russell utilizes the analogy of holes in Swiss cheese when describing evil in the cosmos.[9] We may be made to think of one historical development of the concept "hole" that is almost too horrible to contemplate. The Nazis *threw* living children into holes, into non-Being. The holes were noncheese all right—and they were also of the Devil. So much for evil as "merely the absence of good."

(3) The difficulty in H. Richard Niebuhr's "radical monotheism" that we have noted—namely, to negate the Devil in this way hardly makes the Devil disappear—falls primarily under the rubric of the theoretical reason. Niebuhr redeems himself with aid from the practical reason, a stress upon the praxis of God in weighty contrast to a philosophic concentration upon "being itself" or "the realm of being." While Niebuhr stays completely away from the resource of Christian comedy,[10] he dwells with much effectiveness upon the historical and historic divine action. What counts is what God *does*. We return to this opportunity in chapter 8.

III

In chapter 3, where modified monism is discussed, four figures are allotted space: Paul Tillich, Jon D. Levenson, Frederick Sontag, and myself. Within the frame of reference of the theoretical reason, and given its limitations, I find myself somewhat less critical of modified monism than I am of unqualified monism (and of unqualified dualism).

I wish that Tillich were clearer and more decisive regarding his view of the objective quality versus the nonobjective quality of the demonic. Again, I totally dissociate myself from Tillich's equating of evil with non-Being. That Tillich was my teacher could account for my lack of additional criticisms of him, but then H. Richard Niebuhr was also my teacher, and I have enumerated the basic problems that I have with Niebuhr's viewpoint. So I don't imagine this is the explanation. My views upon the Devil are hardly traceable to Tillich and his influence. Neither am I critical of Levenson's exposition, and he is a stranger to me. I do believe that Levenson underestimates or plays down the activeness of the biblical God (cf. his stress upon *deus otiosus*). But Levenson's accounting of the Tanak's general *Anschauung* of God and evil is quite accurately representative of Scripture, and I am in accord with this.

In the matter of Frederick Sontag's position, and to some extent of my own, the critical atmosphere becomes more intense.

Sontag's point of view is distinctive, not so much for his version of modified monism as for his method. He readily meets the criterion of modified monism: an affirmation of one good God who, for various reasons acceptable to Godself, nevertheless permits evil in the world, including excessive evil, more evil than is necessary. But, unfortunately, Sontag's method carries within itself the seeds of an alternative that diametrically opposes his own argument.

The problem with Sontag's method comes about with the agreed truth that justifications for atheism are equally justifications for the Devil. Thus, his finding that, for all the legitimacy of atheism, it is God who is *there* is an arbitrary one, an option mirroring personal preference rather than philosophic cogency or convincingness. Of course, nothing is wrong with personal predilection as such. But a problem arises when subjective preference is presented in the guise of authentic philosophic procedure.

The fact is that upon the identical line of reasoning put forward by Sontag, we can emerge, not with a more or less good God, but instead with a more or less evil Devil, a Devil who, for all the legitimacy of theism as for various reasons known and acceptable to Devilself, nevertheless permits good in the world, including excessive good, perhaps more good than is necessary, but yet a goodness that is severely held in check.

With the above substitution on the table, we are enabled to recast and reapply certain materials set forth by Sontag as reported in chapter 3, e.g.: If the force of good is the main source of theism, the Devil that theism can lead us to will have to be a "Devil of Good." The Devil we reach must be a Devil "not dependent upon men to exercise sufficient control to accomplish his purpose. If he were man-dependent, he would seem to have chosen a very risky path in concealing himself." Again, he is a Devil "not concerned to make his intentions continually obvious"; he is "above anxious concern over whether men acknowledge his presence and his intent." And upon the question of what might be the Devil's purpose in revealing himself through good as well as through evil, he seems prepared to allow humankind to bless him. Clearly, he does not intend to intervene very often to prevent needless happiness or to put an end to enjoyment—including even blessings that are undeserved. It does not upset the Devil to be misunderstood. And a Devil constructed from arguments rejecting his existence can easily answer the question of why there is this particular world rather than some other. Finally, should the objection be raised, "Why opt for the Devil over God?," we may reply, in Sontag's own (self-condemning) words, that wanton destructive power weighs "more heavily than good."

And so it is that a title opposite to Sontag's could be just as sensibly, or more sensibly, fabricated, *The Devil of Good: An Argument from the Existence of God*—a Devil who allows goodness to question him. From a perspective wholly within the bounds of Sontag's own procedure and argumentation, there appears to be no basis for his allotting of ontological and moral precedence to God rather than to the Devil.

To come finally to my own partial and fragmentary viewpoint, as included in the last section of Chapter 3, I do join Frederick Sontag in approaching questions of God and evil from the "side" of the Devil. Some of my expressed sentiments may seem to smack of dualism, though I don't mean them in quite that way. Also, despite my announced opposition to rationalist (or empiricist) theodicy as such, I have had the temerity to propound one theodicean or quasitheodicean way to tell God from the Devil, an unabashedly historical way: God elects Israel to life; the Devil sentences Israel to death.

Three critical comments upon my stance may be enumerated, two of them mine and one from another scholar: (1) To disseminate the reputed truth of antisemitism as wholly unique may only contribute to a compounding of moral evil in the real world, to a metastasizing of antisemitism itself. Ever on the prowl for ammunition, the antisemite may readily seize upon the announced prevalence and uniqueness of opposition to Jews as merely telling proof that the Jewish people are indeed inherently evil—else, why the universality of this opposition? I am unsure of how to deal with this state of affairs, other than to urge discernment of it as a further discrete case of the Devil's cleverness.

(2) The immediate occasion of my piece "The Devil and Yom Kippur" was a given historical instance of the afflicting of the Jewish people when they are themselves under affliction. But surely this characteristic is found, at least in ancillary fashion, beyond the praxis of antisemitic demonry. The Kingdom of Satan thrives upon human helplessness and grief no matter where it is found. On the very day I write this chapter, Serbian gunners deliberately attacked a funeral party that included a score of orphans from Sarajevo who were burying children killed in a previous Serbian attack.[11] This sort of variation within the Devil's program can easily recruit and boast devotees other than antisemites.[12] However, we must beware of the Devil's own trap, which, in the name of talking up the Devil's culpability, would remove blameworthiness and guilt from these particular Serbians.

(3) Walter Harrelson has raised a serious question regarding my embryonic endeavors to link together the dimension of comedy and the issue of the Devil, and more especially my ostensibly "mischievous" approach to that subject. As Harrelson writes, "monotheism requires that we dispense with devil or angels in any sense other than as creatures of God with certain distinctive functions that differentiate them from human beings. And Eckardt's resort to the Devil to account for certain diabolic features of human life seems to me unnecessary and misleading. [James Parkes used to make a comparable criticism. —A.R.E.] Eckardt points out that resort to comedy is tricky. But so also is resort to mischievousness. Play is fine, but notions of Devil and deviltry are really not at all humorous, and they may not even be instructive in fact."[13]

Perhaps the second part of *How To Tell God From the Devil* will throw a little light upon this issue. In the meantime, I may be permitted two responses: (a) Highly problematic in my reflections upon the Devil, as perhaps in parallel expositions by others, is their unrelieved solemnity, perhaps sometimes bordering upon morbidity. (b) We may be reminded, with the present study as a resource, that some convinced mono-theists do not delimit the Devil in quite the way that Professor Harrelson suggests.

IV

A conclusion to which we seem to be led thus far is that evil is too formidable and monstrous for any human accounting or explanation to be capable of justifying God. This suggests that either we are immured within an unresolvable, painful enigma—not separable from the Devil's own work?—or we may just be enabled to find that God takes the matter into God's hands. On the latter alternative, it is possible to emerge from, i.e., to be brought out of, the Shadow of God. But that is a question of grace, and I shall later try to give voice to it.

Notes

1. Ernest Becker, *The Denial of Death* (New York: Free Press, 1973), p. 282.
2. Wendy Farley, *Tragic Vision and Divine Compassion* (Louisville: Westminster/ John Knox Press, 1990), p. 19.
3. Jeffrey Burton Russell, *The Devil* (Ithaca, N.Y. and London: Cornell University Press, 1987), p. 205.
4. David Birnbaum, *God and Evil* (Hoboken: Ktav, 1989), pp. 156, 145.
5. As Frederick Sontag rightly points out, "responsibility for the order created is first on God's shoulders and then on man's. This produces an anguish over free-dom for both." (*The God of Evil* [New York: Harper & Row, 1970], p. 84).
6. Eliezer Berkovits, "The Hiding God of History," in Yisrael Gutman and Livia Rothkirchen, eds., *The Catastrophe of European Jewry* (Jerusalem: Yad Vashem, 1976), p. 704. Cf. Sontag: "Nothing compels God to act. [His] power makes him immune to forced action under duress." (*God of Evil,* pp. 84, 148-49). But when Berkovits adjudges that the Holocaust did not involve a question of God but wholly one of man, his implied dismissal of the Devil is far from convincing.
7. Niebuhr cites approvingly Alfred North Whitehead's affirmation that religious faith is, to quote Whitehead, "transition from God the void to God the enemy, and from God the enemy to God the companion." (Cited in H. Richard Niebuhr, *Radical Monotheism and Western Culture* [New York: Harper & Bros., 1960], pp. 123-24).
8. A. Roy Eckardt, *No Longer Aliens, No Longer Strangers* (Atlanta: Scholars Press, 1994), pp. 33-4.
9. Russell, *Devil,* p. 205.
10. Here H. Richard Niebuhr contrasts with his brother Reinhold; see the latter's influential essay, "Humour and Faith," in *Discerning the Signs of the Times* (New York: Scribner, 1946), pp. 111-31.
11. *New York Times,* 5 August 1992. People who engage in the looting of property of those who are afflicted by one or another disaster are also special agents of the Devil.

12. Cf. James Cone: "If God is good, why did God permit millions of blacks to be stolen from Africa and enslaved in a strange land?" (Cited in A. Roy Eckardt, *Black-Woman-Jew* [Bloomington: Indiana University Press, 1989], p. 24).
13. Walter Harrelson, "Reflections on A. Roy Eckardt's Theological Writings," afterword in A. Roy Eckardt, *Collecting Myself,* ed. Alice L. Eckardt (Atlanta: Scholars Press, 1993), p. 446.

Part II

Under Construction

5

Excursus: The Laughter of Zen

A primary meaning of "excursus" is "digression," a deviation from a main subject. As we will see, there is a sense in which the comic strain within the Zen *Weltanschauung* is religioculturally deviationist. (Zen must not be reduced to the comedy of Zen; but the comedy of Zen is in harmony with Zen as a whole.)[1] This chapter does not comprise a change of subject; I simply want it to help us in a somewhat difficult transition from the intense, theoretical argumentativeness of Part I to the relatively different, practical claims, needs, and attitudes of Part II. Apart from its other possible values or truth, Zen marshalls great shock value. However, I stay with the word "excursus" because I am not putting forward the laughter of Zen as any positive resource in meeting the question of this book. I merely wish to get one foot out from under the heavy blanket of intellectualism. Perhaps the chapter comes down to a psychological gambit—let us say, the strategic equivalent of three self-replenishing martinis—which is strictly prefatory to Part II. Stated differently, but not in un-Zen fashion: Zen's usefulness "this side" of Nirvana and solely to the present, selfish literary effort is tied to its uselessness. (Am I selling myself—or Zen—short? From the vantage point of Zen itself, the worry is probably gratuitous, for Zen masters themselves never shrink from such declarations as "all the attainments of the Buddha are really nonattainments" [Bodhidharma, d. circa 536]; "attaining Buddhahood must be regarded as an illness" [Niu-t'ou]; indeed, that the Buddha himself is "a wiping-stick of dry dung" [Yun-men, 862–949].)[2]

We may surmise that if God is truly God, God is scarcely sitting on the edge of the holy seat waiting to be "justified." An unknowing awareness (now *there* is an oxymoron; one that is, however, carefully chosen) of this state of affairs may lie somewhere out in the mists behind the comic/cosmic vision of Zen. To be sure, Zen could not care less about theodicy with all its rationalist-empiricist maneuverings, it clarifications, its clarifications of clarifications, and its clarifications of clarifications of clarifications. (Shall I go on?) But this evasion of theodicy is primarily due to the fact that Zen is nontheistic. Comedic Zen retains a related but much larger antagonist, the theoretical or speculative reason as such; this is what gives Zen its primary pertinence to our study. If there is, ultimately speaking, a subtle but strong intellectual undercurrent to Zen, this is yet associated, paradoxically, with its human struggle—replete with gales of laughter—against the unhelpful intellectualism that, sadly, can take captive the very quiddity of philosophic effort. The possible "service" of Zen to us is at the same time put into question by its joyous/stubborn obliviousness to any such thing as the Devil. I think it is clear by now that I agree with Professor Russell (as cited near the beginning of this book): "No theodicy that does not take the Devil fully into consideration is likely to be persuasive." May not a similar judgment be made respecting such an antitheodicy as Zen?—as long as the viewpoint involved sustains *some* kind of bearing upon the question of evil, which Zen surely does.

A suggestion to which we are led thus far is that for the purposes of this book, Zen may have something to give us, yet we do well not to expect too much of it: a comic spirit, *sí*; the Devil, *no*; and, of course, God, *no*.[3] But the same triad can be phrased more sympathetically: If Zen is self-limited theologically and diabologically, it has much to offer comically, perhaps even cosmically so.

I

It is time, or past time, to try to describe more definitely what this Zen-thing is and does. My term "Zen-thing" is neither frivolous nor derogatory. I intend it as a youthful way to take the laughter of Zen with the seriousness it merits, while at the same time intimating something of Zen's playfulness. I could say "Zen-phenomenon," but that would not sit very well with Zennists in their battle against intellectualist jargon.

We may call for help upon *The Laughing Buddha: Zen and the Comic Spirit* by Conrad Hyers, an American classic. I have to pass over many of the riches of Hyers's exposition. The identification "American classic" is made, not simply to be descriptive, but to the end of acknowledging and respecting the dismay and indignation of Zennists over the many Western books on Zen.[4]

Insofar as Zen wishes to shock, let us give way at the outset to added shockingness:

> A monk who saw Yao-shan (758–834) meditating asked: "In this motionless position what are you thinking?" "Thinking that which is beyond thinking." "How do you go about thinking that which is beyond thinking?" "By an act of not-thinking."[5]

> Upon viewing a funeral procession for one of his monks, Master Chao-chou (778–897) exclaimed: "What a long train of dead bodies follows in the wake of a single living person!"

> In response to a monk's inquiry respecting the present abode of the Buddha, one master is said to have answered: "The Buddha is in the outhouse."

> Master Ling-ch'ui (ninth century) asserted that explanations of fundamental matters are "like drawing legs on a painted snake."

> And Lin-chi (d. 867) attested that *bodhi* (Enlightenment) and Nirvana (the "blowing out") "are a stake to which donkeys are fastened."[6]

Among the distinctive features of Zen is the "singular and delightful at-homeness of the comic in Zen, and of Zen in the comic.... In a unique sense, the house of Zen is the house of laughter." Zen and the comic spirit of Zen arose "out of the collision of the lofty spiritualism of Indian Buddhism and the earthiness of Oriental humanism and naturalism." Zen brings to the fore one of the major aspects of Taoism. It is not impossible to interpret Zen "as that point in the movement of Buddhism from India to China and Japan in which humor comes to be most fully developed and self-consciously employed as an integral part of both a pedagogical method and an enlightened outlook—that is, both as one of the stratagems for realizing enlightenment and as one of the consequences for enlightenment." The uses of humor in Zen, and the general Zen spirit and perspective, "share in the comic inclination to move toward reducing tensions, overcoming conflicts, and including opposites in some larger unity. In so doing Zen reflects both the traditional Indian Buddhist critique of [epistemological/ontological] dualism and the Chinese vision of a harmony of opposites, as in the complementarity of the yang/yin cosmology." But the meaning and the thrust of Zen are not easy to express, due to its "radically intuitive, experiential, and wordless character"; also due to its iconoclastic temper.[7]

It may be freely admitted that "relative to the fundamental problem of suffering (*dukkha*), laughter seems to represent the hollow, superficial, and finally empty levity of momentary delight (*sukha*), foolishly evading or ignoring the deeper issues of life and death." Again, "there are kinds of laughter that indulge in the elevation of one person or group

over another, as in the case of racist or sexist or ethnic jokes." It is
further the case that laughter can be all kinds of dubious things: "sadis-
tic, demented, nervous, morbid, crude, teasing, taunting, cynical, bitter.
Humor may be a way of evading truth and avoiding responsibility....
Certainly, therefore, laughter, smiling, and joking are not necessarily
reliable indices of the comic spirit, nor are all kinds of nonsense, absurdity, and playfulness necessarily informed by the comic perspective."[8]

These caveats of Conrad Hyers are a good warning, not only respecting our consideration of Zen but as *Stellvertreter* for comedy in
this book.

On the constructive side, we are advised that "in no other tradition
could the entire syndrome of laughter, humor, comedy, and 'clowning'
be said to be more visible and pronounced than in Zen, where the comic
spirit has been duly rescued from those miscellaneous and peripheral
moments to which it is so commonly assigned and restricted." Zen speaks
to "the ultraseriousness and anxiety, and consequently the fanaticism
and dogmatism, which frequently accompany the intensities of religious
conviction and commitment"— as well as, we may add, the comparable
exploits and vagaries of so-called secular thinking and behavior. What
unites various "lighter manifestations" of the human spirit

> is a lightheartedness and playfulness that refuses to absolutize or to take anything
> with an inflexible and unqualified seriousness—especially one's self and one's
> situation. In its highest Zen form, it is the refusal, born of the freedom and perspec-
> tive which in Buddhism is known as enlightenment *[bodhi]*, to be contained within
> and defined by the vicious circle of grasping and clinging, and that resists the
> temptation to enter the bondage of attachment to anything, however consequential
> or sacred. At this point the "other side" of the comic and "this side" of seriousness
> and sacrality become one in the freedom of he who has gone beyond holy and
> unholy, sense and nonsense, having and not-having, self and other.[9]

In successive essays Conrad Hyers delineates this overall perspective. In "The Smile of Truth" we read that Kasyapa, disciple of Gautama
the Buddha, smiled a "smile of understanding," "the signature of the
sudden realization of the 'point,' and the joyful approval of its significance.... It is the glad reception of the moment of insight which has
taken the world by surprise, a moment of seeing with the freshness and
immediacy of the little child, full of amazement and wonder—a 'holy
yea' [Nietzsche] which is capable of transforming even specks of dust
into stars and frogs into Buddha. It is this smile, historically authentic or
not, which is the beginning and the end of Zen."[10]

Hyers attends to the issue of whether seriousness or gaity, or both, comprise the essence of Zen; it is not necessary to our purpose to pursue that argument in detail. Hyers himself is content with a balance, a kind of middle way.

> When intimations of sublime serenity and imperturbable tranquility are anticipated, we may in fact be confronted with the raucousness of a laughter that seems to shake the very foundation of the world.... Zen is not only the tradition of the overwhelming ferociousness of Bodhidarma, who seems to pounce like a great Bengal tiger out of every ink-sketch to break the arms and legs of unsuspecting monks, or like a celebrated Chinese dragon summarily to devour all traces of ego, desire, and attachment. It is also the tradition of the jolly Pu-tai, spurning cloistered confinement, dancing with innocent abandon, and playing with children in the streets, or of the clamorous laughter and mad buffoonery of the monastery fools, Han-shan and Shih-te. Here, too, one discovers that ego, desire, and attachment have a way of getting themselves broken and devoured in the realization of some great Cosmic Joke, and in the greatness of a Cosmic Laughter, which reveals itself in the strange holiness and wisdom of these Holy Fools.[11]

In "Zen Masters and Clown Figures" we are reminded that "it is almost as if one were watching an ancient Oriental version of the slapstick characters in a Marx brothers film, with the wisecracking Groucho, the tune-playing Chico, and the wordless Harpo. But, as in all profound comedy, one soon discovers that the object of laughter is really oneself in the larger predicament and folly of humanity.... The realization of an authentic liberation...is attested by humor; and the symbol of that liberation is the paradoxical figure of the clown." In the clown-figure "the exalted is humbled, and the humbled is exalted; opposites are united and distances softened." Again, there can be no confusion here with libertarianism; license "has nothing to do with the rigors and sensitivities of Zen" but "is no more than a regression to childish irresponsibility and self-indulgence." The Wisdom of Fools is able to perceive the "true nature of folly."[12]

In "Laughing at the Buddhas and Abusing the Patriarchs" emphasis falls upon the iconoclastic character of Zen humor. True liberation calls for the overturning of all idols. "Anything, however holy, is potentially an idol; therefore anything is a legitimate object of laughter"—not excepting the Buddhas themselves together with the patriarchs. The Zen practice of profaning the sacred—in various delightful ways—is thus "unparalleled in the history of religion and religious art." In "The Buddha and the Bullfrog" it is attested that Zen means "a spiritual democratization of things in which the categories of importance versus unimportance, value and valuelessness, profundity and triviality, wisdom and simplicity, beauty and ugliness, good and evil, sacred and profane, no longer apply.... The mystical *coincidentia oppositorum* is symbolically achieved in the motley figure and the *punctum indifferens* of the clown-fool. His is an amorphousness and an ambiguity that represents an order of being and knowing that lies before and beyond all duality and hierarchy, in the region of freedom and innocence and playful spontaneity attained only by little children and great sages."[13]

Of particular significance to the overall argument of *How To Tell God From the Devil* is Conrad Hyers's commentary, in "The Celebration of the Commonplace," upon "absurdity" as a term acceptable to Zen. The concept of "absurdity," as representative of "the inadequacy and final frustration of reason," but also of nonsensical methods required in effecting a leap beyond intellection,

> is not a category implying despair or alienation or anxiety as it is in Western existentialism. If anything, it is a perception...[of the kind] that precipitates laughter, not despair, and that moves beyond alienation and anxiety into a joyful wonder. It does not arise out of the loss of a sense of meaning in life. No great light has failed; no sacred vision has been lost or become impossible.... It is not the dark abyss of infinite nothingness that has been entered, but that blissful, wondrous emptiness wherein lies all fullness. It is in no way anxious or estranged or condemned to an alienated consciousness; it is free in that freedom where inner harmony and well-being are not fettered to the attempt at coercing and possessing the world, or turning it into a problem, or offering an academic solution.... The moment of insight, which abruptly perceives with unshrouded clarity things-in-themselves, and at the same time with equal clarity the wondrousness of their inscrutable mystery, is marked as appropriately by laughter as by hushed reverence. Indeed such laughter is itself a form of reverence; it is the laughter of acceptance, appreciation, and wonder.[14]

In "The Folly of the Desiring Self" we are admonished:

> If the ego is seen as one of the elements of the human problem then humor corresponds to the realization of the comedy of the substantial ego, the refusal to take the ego seriously or absolutely in its pretension of being the one secure point of reference in consciousness—as in the philosophy of Descartes where, when all else is in doubt, one retreats to the seemingly impregnable refuge of the reflective self: *cogito ergo sum*. There is no small irony in the fact that what is the fundamental illusion for Buddhist experience is taken as the fundamental axiom of Cartesian thought. In Zen, especially, it is through humor that the ego is revealed as only the mask that the actor puts on, or holds in front of his face (as in the *Noh* play, or ancient Greek drama, or the original meaning of the Latin *persona* as "mask"), hiding his true identity, a mask which is both a tragic mask from the standpoint of ignorance and suffering, and a comic mask from the standpoint of enlightenment and liberation.[15]

In the respect last mentioned, the ego is, in a sense, paradoxically reinstated with aid from humor.

Stress is also placed by Hyers—again with much relevance to the present volume—upon Zen iconoclasm as smashing "rational categories and value structures, the moral judgments and mental discriminations...which we interpose between ourselves and the world of our perception.... [The] 'detached involvement' of humor which refuses to absolutize, and thus to endow with absolute seriousness, anyone or anything, is...a corollary of the Zen emphasis upon nonattachment.... Such an achievement makes possible a living in the world without being conformed to it or bound by it. As Yun-men phrased it, 'He speaks of fire without his mouth being burned by it.'"[16]

In "Socrates in China" Professor Hyers concentrates upon the moral responsibility of Zen. If the Zen master

> assimilates himself to the figure of the clown-fool, or introduces certain comic motifs and stratagems, this is not simply an end in itself, or even a personal actualization of freedom alone, but also a means to an end. In full accord with the Mahayanist emphasis upon the compassionate concern (*karuna*) of the Bodhisattva for the enlightenment of all, the enlightened one seeks, through a variety of techniques, including the *upaya* of humor and clownishness, the awakening of the disciple. This approach has similarities to the Holy Fool tradition in the Greek and Russian Orthodox churches in which certain monks assumed the role of the fool, and engaged in odd or impious behavior, in order to reveal the folly of the people and to awaken piety. The Zen master becomes something of a fool and behaves or instructs in unconventional ways in order to reveal the comedy in a false view of self and to awaken a new perspective on existence.... [The] master functions as a midwife of truth in the Socratic sense. One can at most be awakened to the Truth that is already within, and from which one has never been separated; for it is what one really is in oneself.

The iconoclasm of Zen carries no animus and no self-righteous indignation; "it is grounded in the Bodhisattva ideal of enlightened compassion."[17]

Again, we are offered counsel regarding the nature of nonsense. Nonsense does not mean "without sense" but is instead a question mark "placed after the supposedly firm reality of the world of intelligibility, the irrefutable logic of rationality, or the categories and dichotomies of any system." This "maeutic play upon irrationality in order to move beyond rationality" is conveyed in Hakuin's famous koan, "What is the sound of one hand clapping?"[18]

"Getting the Point of the Joke" entails a state "that cannot be reached in either strictly rationalist or empiricist terms." By contrast, smiling and laughing reflect the intuition "that one has moved beyond a mere discursive comprehension to genuine understanding." Finally, "The Child of Tao" distinguishes childlikeness from childishness.

> The achievement in Zen of the comic spirit and perspective at its fullest may be interpreted as a corollary of the recovery on a higher level of that spontaneity, immediacy, and naturalness enjoyed by the child—the freedom that is prior to the emergence of rationality and order, and the hiatus in experience between self and world, mind and body, good and evil, sacred and profane. Humor in Zen, therefore, at its profoundest, is a humor that transcends all those categories with which we would coerce the world and which, in turn, make us captives in our own prison. It has risen above both the ignorance that is innocence and the ignorance that offers a knowledge of good and evil. It is the playfulness and lightheartedness that lies beyond our restless grasping and clinging, beyond the eternal torment of Tantalus, the sense of gaiety and festivity that lies on the further side of fear of death and attachment to the forms of life. One has learned what it means to become a child again, in the wisdom of the sage, the child of Tao.[19]

III

If it is largely for the purposes of orientation that we have turned to Zen, this does not exempt Zen from critical response. Professor Russell's words are as applicable to Zen as to any and all philosophies/theologies/theodicies/antitheodicies: "The story of the Devil is grim, and any world view that ignores or denies the existential horror of evil is an illusion. Ivan's one child crying out alone in the darkness is worth the whole creation, *is* in a sense the whole creation. If any world view, theist or atheist, minimizes her suffering, declares it nonexistent, gives it elaborate philosophical justification, or explains it in terms of a greater good,...that world view renders her life, and yours, empty and vain."[20]

The pity of Zen. The attack of Zen upon the human theoretical (speculative) reason is devastating. In and through its unique rhetoric of play, mirth, and a paucity of carefully chosen words, the Zen-thing brings the rhetoric of speculation, of reason, of logic to its knees. Put as simply as possible, Zen helps clear the mind and freshen the soul. Yet are we driven, and not without pain and regret, to the side known as "this side": Zen childlikeness is not in fact freed from childishness. For deprived of the stern, apodictic norm of Ivan's single child, childlikeness is made into the real illusion.

The issue is not theological. If Zen transcends/ignores God, its self-lessness and compassion yet mirror things divine. Instead, the issue is diabological. The Zen-thing is strong on works of scorn, of gaiety, and of selflessness. But do not the works of the Devil infect these works with futility?

Tao-hsin (580–651) taught: "Whether you are walking, standing, sitting, or lying down, all that your eyes fall upon and all that you come across is [none] other than the activity of the Buddha. Then you are happy, free from anxiety, and your name is Buddha."[21] In behalf of Frederick Sontag, Jon Levenson, and many others, and never forgetting Ivan's child, we may alter this to read: "Much that your eyes fall upon and much that you come across are none other than the activity of the Devil. Then are you filled with anxiety, even with rage, and your name is changed to Reality."

Prerequisite to authentic comedy are the grace of good *and* the peril of evil. Upon this dual ground, Zen is not authentic comedy. For all its powerful psychological, moral, even theological contribution, there obtrudes a peculiar nemesis. A paradoxical, unhappy irony of Zen is that its abiding inability to vanquish the Devil (an inability the rest of us fully share) is compounded by a studied disallowance or blissful (invincible) ignorance of the radicalness of evil, the Devil's own presence. Thereby is its world of sublime humor made to collapse inward upon itself. The utterly delightful joke upon all things is imploded—what could be more sad?—into a terrible joke upon that very joke.

Notes

1. According to one description of Zen Buddhism, it is primarily an effort "to experience ('actualize') the unitary character of reality. 'I' and 'not-I' are one ('not-two'); both are aspects of Buddha-reality. This becomes clear when one 'sees into one's own nature' in a moment of 'awakening.'" For "deep within everyone there is a Buddha-nature (a nature capable of *bodhi* [enlightenment]), by actualizing which one ceases to reason ignorantly and acquires *prajnaparamita,* the wisdom that has gone beyond—to the beyond that is also within." All dualisms "must be transcended by the realization (through *satori* [Japanese equivalent of *bodhi,* enlightenment]) that the Buddha-reality is not outside Me but is I-Myself and that I-Myself do not stand in contrast to Not-I-Myself, because the Buddha reality includes both a nondualism that is at once, at least to the finite mind, all and yet nothing, full of life and yet void, mind-itself and yet mind-like-empty-space, I-Myself and yet free from self-limitation, formless and unconditioned." (John B. Noss, *Man's Religions,* 5th ed. [New York: Macmillan, 1974], pp. 167–68; in general, pp. 165–70). To "reason ignorantly" is not unrelated to the Western-Kantian theoretical or speculative reason. Consult also D. T. Suzuki, *Zen Buddhism,* ed. William Barrett (Garden

City, N.Y.: Doubleday, 1956); Heinrich Dumoulin, *A History of Zen Buddhism* (New York: Pantheon, 1963).

2. Conrad Hyers, *The Laughing Buddha,* rev. and exp. ed. (Wakefield, N.H.: Longwood Academic, 1991), pp. 57, 124–25.
3. "God" in a Western monotheist sense.
4. Hyers, *Laughing Buddha,* p. 18.
5. As cited in Noss, *Man's Religions,* p. 169. Here is a hint, or more than a hint, of the undercurrent of intellectuality in Zen to which I have alluded.
6. Hyers, *Laughing Buddha,* pp. 14, 18, 19, and 125.
7. Ibid., pp. 13, 18, 24, 29, 32, and 121–22; conversation with my colleague Norman Girardot.
8. Hyers, *Laughing Buddha,* pp. 16, 17, 20.
9. Ibid., pp. 14–15, 21.
10. Ibid., p. 25.
11. Ibid., p. 35.
12. Ibid., pp. 41–2, 45.
13. Ibid., pp. 55–6, 80–1; see also Chap. 6—"The Celebration of the Commonplace."
14. Ibid., pp. 95, 104.
15. Ibid., pp. 111–12.
16. Ibid., pp. 115–16, 118.
17. Ibid., pp. 127–29, 155.
18. Ibid., p. 140.
19. Ibid., pp. 147–48, 166.
20. Jeffrey Burton Russell, *The Devil* (Ithaca, N.Y. and London: Cornell University Press, 1987), p. 260.
21. *The Transmission of the Lamp,* trans. Sohaku Ogata, as cited in Hyers, *Laughing Buddha,* p. 132.

6

The Long and Rocky Road to an Authentic Comic Vision
I

With Moby Dick, *Melville joins the great writers of the middle and last half of the nineteenth century— Kierkegaard, Schopenhauer, Nietzsche, and several decades later, Freud and Spengler.* All of them saw that the error of the Enlightenment was that it lacked a devil.

—*Rollo May[1]*

The specter of radical evil continues to stand erect and powerful, to go out stalking, as the Spoiler not alone of human life and of the world as such but as the very frustration of God. How unrealistic, even irresponsible, it is to deny the Devil as contemporaneously real. By killing off one of the two parties, that denial blurs the entire distinction between God and Devil and thereby aborts the moral task.

Is there a childlikeness abroad that works to rid itself of childishness? Is there a nonutopian comedy? And how can such a comedy help us to tell God from the Devil?—not a final remedy for evil but a Samaritan who will aid us in coming to grips with evil. These questions confront us through the remaining chapters.

I

In a fashion not incoherent with natural theology/natural diabology, but yet in a way unsatisfied by purely theoretical analysis, we may reflect a little further upon pertinent disparities between the Devil and

God. We have already repeated, in Chapter 1 and thereafter, the elementary, established differences: essential evil/essential good; origin of evil/origin of good; destructiveness/constructiveness; archbeing of hatred and abuse/archbeing of love and blessing. But now, there begin to enter in rudiments of a comic vision. A discernible, though not total, shift develops from the more theoretical to the more practical reason. In Chapter 1, we recognized comedy as a certain way or ways of celebrating or coping with the incongruous, the contradictory, the absurd. This understanding is reminiscent of George Santayana's finding that the heart of comedy involves a confusion of categories that are ordinarily kept distinct, such as applying the criteria of theology to cooking, or of cooking to theology (although Santayana was himself dissatisfied with the incongruity theory of humor).[2]

The following fivefold listing will supplement distinctions we have already suggested or implied along the way. It looks back as it also looks ahead.

1. The Devil is very good at theodicy; at this task, God is a failure.

    Jeffrey Burton Russell places several theodicean "answers" under the category of pseudoanswers or evasions, "because none of them faces the existential reality of a universe in which...a little girl is disfigured for life by napalm dropped on her from an anonymous airplane. Once the suffering of that little girl is immediately felt and intellectually grasped as real, *once her suffering becomes our suffering,* once we really face up to the monstrousness of this world in which we exist, we are bound to dismiss these answers as intellectual games" (italics added).[3]

    How could human beings ever resolve the question of evil? (They can and must *fight against* evil; this is a different though of course not unrelated challenge.) For that matter, how could evil ever be justified by anyone, including God?—except the Devil.

    The Devil is the one really successful practitioner of theodicy; indeed, he has made a career of it. The Devil unqualifiedly justifies evil. What makes this effort a case of theodicy is that he dares to carry it out despite and in the very presence of God. Evil is the Devil's business, whereas God ought to know better and do better. Here is one incipient way to differentiate Devil and God—if only between the Devil that already is and the God that God is becoming/may become.

    At its best, human theodicy of any sort is a means to the clarification of existential anguish and forboding, a way of living with evil that may, upon occasion, do a little something to keep at bay the terror that life holds in store. In this major respect, theodicy is not wholly unrelated to comedy, as to various other instrumentalities for confronting despair. Nevertheless, in commenting upon an ancient Greek father's inscription on his son's tomb, "Here Philip buried his son of twelve years, his Nikoteles, his great hope," Professor Russell is right in saying, "To the burial of his father's hope, or of ours, no theodicy has ever spoken convincingly."[4] But the real tragedy of life is that, had the son lived to a hundred and twenty,[5] the comment would carry no less force. Death continues on as the final enemy. I repeat Paul Ramsey's attestation: There is no such thing as dying with dignity.

The comic vision does not seek to justify God before the fact of evil— or at least some of its deputies have grown terribly tired and even discouraged with the spate of efforts to do that. By contrast, the comic vision is not unwilling (though never without a laugh) to speak of God as sonofabitch—in these latter days, daughterofabitch. The elegant comic Carl Reiner teaches us that "the funniest joke of all is the absolute truth stated simply and gracefully." The comic vision dedicates itself to telling the truth about God instead of laboring—futilely—at the defense of God. (Authentic comedy refuses to absolutize.) To behave "simply and gracefully" is, paradoxically, to give the divine simplicity and the divine grace a chance: God is large enough to withstand human rancor (immeasurably justified as that rancor is: no one ever asked to be born). God is a big girl/ a big boy now. A sense of immaturity surrounds theodicy. Alternatively, cannot humankind, in Bonhoeffer's phrase, "come of age"?

2.   There is no way to laugh the Devil to shame. (We can only scorn him.) He laughs right back, and he only revels in the shame. There is a way to laugh God to shame: by calling God to task under the authority of God's own (revealed?) criteria of righteousness and justice.

The prophet Isaiah has the nerve to make righteousness the entire test of holiness, of Godness (Isa. 5:16). But the other incredible thing is that they never brought him up on charges. The implication is: no righteousness, no holiness. Hundreds of years earlier, the patriarch Abraham already confronted God with the identical moral logic: "Far be it from you to...slay the righteous with the wicked, so that the righteous fare as the wicked! Far be that from you! Shall not the judge of all the earth do what is just?" The consequence was a certain measured, divine repentance: For the sake of only ten righteous persons, God promised not to destroy the city (Gen. 18:25–32). (Query: Why not only one righteous person? Maybe they needed a *minyan*.)

That God should repent is biblically crucial (along with the demand that human beings do the same). God's comedic stature is here under formation—what we call today "character development." Because of the interposition of Moses, "the Lord changed his mind about the disaster that he planned to bring on his people" (Exod. 32:11–14). Again:

"O Lord God, forgive, I beg you!
    How can Jacob stand?
    He is so small!"

> The Lord relented concerning this;
> "It shall not be," said the Lord
>
> (Amos 7:2).

The divine repentance falls within the divine compassion:

> For their sake he remembered
> his covenant,
> and showed compassion
> according to the abundance
> of his steadfast love
>
> (Ps. 106:45; see also
> I Sam. 15:35; Jer. 18:8;
> Jonah 3).

A link between the divine humor and the question of miracle—a perennial issue in any Devil/God dialectic—is illustrated in a Talmudic tale. Rabbi Eleazer said, "If the law is as I teach it, let this carob tree give a sign." The carob tree moved two hundred cubits. But the other sages responded, "A carob tree proves nothing." So Eleazer said, "If the law is as I teach it, let the water in this channel give a sign." The water flowed upward, but the sages responded, "the waters prove nothing." Then Eleazer said, "If the law is as I teach it, let the walls of this school decide." So the walls leaned over as if to fall. Whereupon Rabbi Joshua rebuked the walls: "When the pupils of the sages dispute a point of law, what business is that of yours?" Accordingly, through respect for Rabbi Joshua, the walls did not fall, but through respect for Rabbi Eleazer they continued to lean. A divine voice was then heard: "What is the matter with you? Why do you importune Rabbi Eleazer? The law has always been as he teaches it to be." But Rabbi Joshua protested: "The commandment is not in heaven" (Deut. 30:12). Thus may the sages no longer pay attention to a divine voice. For according to Torah, given at Mount Sinai, "the opinion of the majority shall prevail." The tale reaches its climax when the prophet Elijah appears to Rabbi Nathan, who asked him: "What was God doing at the moment when Rabbi Joshua denied the value of miracles?" The prophet replied: "God was laughing and saying, 'My children have triumphed over me.'"[6]

What does it mean to be made in the image of God? (Gen. 1:26) It may mean, among many other things, that to stand up to God and to demand a moral accounting from God is a perfectly justified, even required, reflection of God's own life and will, and hence not inconsistent with God's own wishes. In a sense, God is addressing God: The truth must be told. God has dignity; human beings have dignity (the Devil has no dignity). God's dignity carries the right to stand up to human beings; humankind's dignity implies the right to stand up to God. Human beings say no to God, human beings say yes to God, God says no to human beings, God says yes to human beings. In all such cases the image of God is variously in operation. (The atheist Jean-Paul Sartre speaks for the image of God when he says that God ought to ask forgiveness for the unfairness in human existence.[7] This declaration places Sartre among God's prophets, perhaps among God's saints.)

That God should repent and confess, in effect, "I stand corrected," shows God's sense of humor concerning God's own self. (God is a good comedian.) The Devil never repents; he cannot repent.[8] For C. S. Lewis, evil as such is characterized by the absence of any sense of humor.[9] The Devil has no sense of humor. This is due, I should imagine, to his insecurity. The Devil plays tricks all right, but they are always for his sake. God's jokes redound to the benefit of others: God is not insecure. The senior devil Screwtape has to concede that "the Enemy" (God) is even "cynically indifferent to the dignity of His position." Furthermore, joyous laughter is "disgusting," a "direct insult to the realism, dignity, and austerity of Hell." And fun "has wholly undesirable tendencies; it promotes charity, courage, contentment, and many other evils."[10]

Harry Levin has written an important study, *Playboys and Killjoys: An Essay on the Theory and Practice of Comedy.*[11] Of the two possibilities, the Devil is certainly a killjoy. If it appears frivolous to assign the remaining category to God, calling God a playboy (or playgirl), it is yet hard to separate the divine laughter from a certain playfulness and good cheer. God is a kind of livejoy. Psalm 2:4 and parallels (37:13; 59:8) may seem problematic: "He who sits in the heavens laughs; the Lord has them [the nations] in derision." The laughter of God as derisive might seem to reflect not so much God "proper" but the Shadow of God. Yet in the context of these biblical passages the divine derisiveness is strictly a correlate and consequence of sin and idolatry. The Devil would laugh at goodness; in the Kingdom of God it is those who, having wept, will eventually laugh (Luke 6:20–21).[12]

3. The Devil is a consummate liar, while God and the image of God demand that the truth be told.

Carl Reiner is cited above as marrying authentic laughter to truth. For C. S. Lewis, by attacking the very structure of meaning and rendering reality unintelligible and unlovable, lying reveals itself as the worst of sins.

In Martin Buber's wording, it is in a lie that "the spirit practices treason against itself." In the Persian (Iranian) tradition, the primeval king Yima, born immortal, becomes mortal through his offence, the offence of "taking the lie into his mind." This meant introducing death into the cosmos, for it is "only after him that the rest die." By falsely seeing himself as a self-creator, he commits an inner untruth against both God (Ahura Mazda) and himself; more precisely, "he commits with his existence the lie against being." Buber continues that "truth and lie are the two basic qualities, in whose opposition the opposition of the principles, good and evil, is represented." (As H. Richard Niebuhr would have it, to be immoral is to break one's word.) Buber concludes that to "be true" is ultimately to strengthen, cover, and confirm being at the point of one's own existence; to "be false" is ultimately to weaken, desecrate, and dispossess being at that very same place.

He who prefers the lie to the truth and chooses it instead of truth, intervenes directly with his decision into the decisions of the world-conflict. But this takes effect in the very first instance at just his point of being: since he gave himself over to the being-lie, that is to nonbeing, which passes itself off as being, he falls a victim to it. Thus Yima, the lord of the demons, falls into their power, since he crosses over from being-true to being-false; he becomes first their companion, then their victim. He effects factually a downfall of being—at precisely that point which is called Yima.[13]

A great contribution of Zoroastrianism to the history of morality and of religions has been its identification of Angra Mainyu, the Evil Spirit or Satan, with the Lie (Druj), in total enmity to Ahura Mazda as Truth and Right. The Devil is a liar. Hell is "the House of the Lie."

The question that may be posed is whether God needs the Devil in the way that the Devil needs God. The phenomenon of the lie may throw light upon this question. As H. Richard Niebuhr writes, "lies are an impossibility where there is no truth, whereas the opposite is not true."[14] The truth is not subject to the lie's parasitic condition; the truth does not need the lie in order to prosper and redeem.

An affirmation of the fact that the lie needs truth, but that truth does not need the lie, parallels the way in which evil needs good but good does not need evil. The group of diseases called cancer is paradigmatic of the need of evil for good: A good reality (nature) is turned against itself via an uncontrollable multiplication of cells, occasioned either by internal (genetic?) conditions or by external (environmental? nutritive?) ones. But a good nature does not require evil in order to function. In this respect, a good nature can laugh at evil, whereas nature gone evil can hardly laugh at good. For evil's laughter requires goodness, yet it itself means destruction. (The remission of such a disease as cancer in no way says that good nature needs evil.)

To put in slightly different form the point I have been making: God as Truth is faithful to history. The Devil as Lie specializes in antihistory; for example, there was no Holocaust. Preveniently, Martin Luther put the two things together: The Devil is "not only a liar, he is also a killer."[15]

Authentic comedy collars lying and sends it packing into outer darkness. Let the Lie (Druj) be anathema! Authentic comedy comes to rest upon the bed of truth. This, after all, is how and why human beings are made to laugh: They become at peace with truth, with Being itself. The

Liar has no peace; he can't even trust himself. This forces him into unending, vigilant wakefulness, lest the Shadow of the Shadow plot and deceive himself. To lie upon a bed of lies is to toss and turn forever, never getting any rest. The Devil is the world's leading insomniac.

4. The Devil is pawn of his own necessity; God is free.

By promising Godself to goodness, God is offered self-fulfillment (Comedy); the Devil's promise to evil chains him to destruction, to eventual self-destruction (Tragedy). The responsibility of God for evil is yoked to, even redeemed by, goodness of being, goodness of intent; the responsibility of the Devil for evil (but did the Devil ask to be born?)[16] is yoked to nothing but the being of radical evil, the intent of evil.

Thus is the freedom of God not so much a freedom to think (on days off, if only when playing Scrabble, God may think a little bit) as it is a freedom to act. God's reasoning is not theoretical or speculative, but practical. Accordingly, to speak sensibly of God demands a language of events. God is doer; the Devil is undoer (also of himself). (Jon D. Levenson maintains that the God of the Hebrew Bible is most of the time doing nothing.[17] All right, so God has a little tendency to loaf. Who hasn't? The Devil never loafs, so perhaps a bit of loafing is not all that bad.)

For R. H. Blyth, laughter is "a breaking through the intellectual barrier; at the moment of laughing something is understood; it needs no proof of itself."[18] God laughs, thus breaking the intellectual barrier, even the barrier of some of God's own erstwhile words and deeds. God as Comedian works to remove the barrier between Godself and the Shadow. Stated more simply, when God laughs God is telling the Devil to go to Hell, and God backs up the message with praxis:

Israel is elected; the prophets are taught to elevate justice and righteousness to supremacy; death is fought and a start is made in vanquishing it. These are not words but deeds. Laughter doesn't write a book; laughter laughs. (There are no comic books, only books about comedy.) Is it so that the divine laughter "needs no proof of itself"? Well, that depends. What proof could there be for the laughter of God as such? Yet how could the phenomenon of the divine laughter be written about without that laughter being caught up in a demand for proof? However, there is consolation—of a literary kind but more than that—in the great meaning of "proof": a testing.

Goodness climaxes in love;[19] evil climaxes in cruelty. The enjoyment of love is joy; the enjoyment of cruelty is wanton cruelty, cruelty in the final degree.

5. I put last a point that in a way carries forward point two but also works to encompass all of the other points. The Devil is insolent, God is humble. That the Devil lacks any sense of humor respecting himself is due to his arrogance in contrast to the God of Israel and of Jesus Christ, who is able to repent. We are encountered by the paradox that because God is humble, God can rightly claim divinity, whereas because he is insolent, the Devil

can rightly claim only deviltry. (Cf. Matt. 11:29: "I am gentle and humble in heart." An accompanying paradox is that these words have to be from Matthew rather than Jesus. Were they from Jesus, he would merely be taking on the insolence of the Devil.)

II

We have inspected a few primordial grounds out of which a comic vision might spring, but only within the frame of reference of a Devil/God dichotomy. From the rudiments of such a vision we move on, in the remainder of this chapter and in the next chapter, to a few figures whose persuasions bear in one way or another upon that same dichotomy, but who also stand in some kind of implicit, positive, or creative relation to the comic vision. Despite certain differences in presupposition and affirmation, the interpreters I will refer to and comment upon stand for a priority of deed over idea, existence over essence, life over abstraction, event over theory. But I have particularly in mind the question: How is it that, in opposition to the diabolic Enemy, the divine Enemy may emerge as Friend? Overall, the analyses to follow are highly necessary and/or useful in establishing my own version of a comic vision.

We begin with Martin Luther. This may seem odd, for Luther was hardly a devotee or purveyor of any comic vision and was indeed the sternest of men. He was also, as was noted in chapter 3, something of an antisemite. His inclusion here rests upon two items of pertinence: first, Luther's persuasion that it is the Devil who transmogrifies God into the philosophic concept of an "Omnipotent Being"—as Heiko A. Oberman says in speaking for Luther, "Satan may be no doctor of theology but he is very well trained in philosophy and has had nearly six thousand years to practice his craft"—and, second and more important, Luther's affirmation that the way God is justified is not through the device of arguing over the question of evil but rather through humility. Oberman epitomizes the matter: "Exercising humility means justifying God—that is Luther's unprecedently [sic] bold claim." True, to justify God is, for Luther, to concede the truth of the divine verdict that all human beings are sinners. Luther says that God is always *right* in this verdict,[20] whereas my own theodicean predisposition—indeed, my overall philosophic and theologic stance—rests upon the moral principle or assumption that, since noone ever asked to be born (not even Dr. Martin Luther), God is seen as subject to being wrong almost (though not quite, thank goodness) as readily as to being right. In either case, anyone who exalts humility as a highest virtue cannot be far away from humility's blood sister, humor, and it is this, together with his recognition of the Devil, that qualifies Luther for reference at this juncture.

The subtitle of Professor Oberman's study, *Luther: Man between God and the Devil* together with such chapter titles as "Life between God and the Devil" and "Christianity between God and the Devil," join Oberman's exposition as a whole in mirroring the actual dialectical position of the Protestant reformer.[21] For, at the heart of Luther's point of view is a "coincidence of opposites" all his own, though one that has its grounding and finds its authorization in the New Testament: The "ultimate, bitterest enemy" is none other than Satan;[22] the ultimate, joyous friend is Jesus Christ.

The proclamation of the Christian gospel only intensifies satanic attacks upon the faithful. Luther's world of thought is thus "wholly distorted and apologetically misconstrued if his conception of the Devil is dismissed as a medieval phenomenon and only his faith in Christ retained as relevant or as the only decisive factor. Christ and the Devil were equally real to him: one was the perpetual intercessor for Christianity, the other a menace to mankind till the end. To argue that Luther never overcame the medieval belief in the Devil says far too little"; he actually intensified it and gave it added urgency. "Christ and Satan wage a cosmic war for mastery over Church and world." To be sure, God is possessed of omnipotent power. But this power ever remains hidden. "Faith reaches not for God hidden but for God revealed, who, incarnate in Christ, laid himself open to the Devil's fury." Luther's "*new* belief in the Devil is such an integral part of the Reformation discovery that if the reality of the powers inimical to God is not grasped, the incarnation of Christ as well as the justification and temptation of the sinner are reduced to ideas of the mind rather than experiences of faith. To make light of the Devil is to distort faith." Accordingly, "it is not as a poltergeist that the Devil discloses his true nature, but as the adversary who thwarts the Word of God; only then is he really to be feared. He seeks to capture the conscience, can quote the Scriptures without fault, and is more pious than God—that is satanical."[23]

Spokespersons for the Christian Social Gospel and various protagonists of Christian social responsibility, not excluding Roman Catholics, can be grateful at a very crucial place for Luther's concentration upon the Devil. For the reformer's "own theological and personal turning point" was to become

> a momentous breakthrough for church and society, with his public call to resist the Devil in the spiritual and temporal realms, to unmask him as a liar and brand him a killer. It was typically medieval that Luther had to abandon the world. The end of the Middle Ages drew near when he would not let the world go to the Devil, instead sounding the battle cry for its preservation and improvement. The world, which had previously been the wide gate and the broad way to Hell, and partner to a pact with the Devil, now disclosed itself in the Reformation view to be the world God had ordained and preserved, an environment in which plants, animals, and man could flourish. Where good works had once been done for God's sake, to comply with His high righteousness, they were now redirected to earth for the sake of man, in the service of life and survival until doomsday. Reformation of the Church will be God's work—at the end. Improvement of the world is the reformation's work now.... [The] Reformation turning point can only be fully gauged as an event and a revolution when it is understood that Luther's discovery [rediscovery—A.R.E.] of the righteousness of God also revealed the Devil to be the enemy of woman, world, and well-being.[24]

We are presented with the well-nigh incredible case history that Martin Luther could serve in this way to advance the *Weltanschauung* and cause of biblical-prophetic faith as at the same time he could come to disclose himself as no mean antisemite.[25] That Luther should do all this with solid help from (his certainty of) the Devil, Chief Antisemite, constitutes a mind-blowing laugh at the Devil himself, as to a lesser degree at Luther. A little German sometime-monk afflicted with chronic illness succeeds in working the Devil *against* the Devil, and for all his own representation (as antisemite) *of* the Devil. Now *that* is something worth thinking about.

One cheer for the Devil, two for Luther.

Yet, as Oberman points out, when the vision of a world pervaded by the Devil ends in repudiation of one or another group identity, the results can only be an appalling betrayal of individual dignity. "Where the battle against Satan's forces leads to collective judgments in the face of a rapidly approaching doomsday, the voice of the prophet becomes a shrilly fanatical battle cry. That, too, is Luther."[26] Perhaps the worst moral danger for all who affirm the Devil—*caveat scriba!*—is fanaticism toward opponents.

Luther's viewpoint comprises, in any case, "a radical deviation from the medieval concept of the Devil, according to which the evil one is drawn by the smell of sin, the sin of worldly concern. In Luther's view, it is not a life dedicated to secular tasks and worldly business that attracts and is targeted by the Devil." On the contrary, wherever Christ is present, the Adversary is nearby as well. "[The] closer the Righteous One comes to us on earth through our belief in Christ, the closer the Devil draws, feeling challenged to take historically effective countermeasures." All in all, "the Reformation symbol of Christ's presence is not the halo of the saint, but the hatred of the Devil." As Oberman comments, "the issue is not morality or immorality, it is God and the Devil. This patent encroachment on conscience desecrates the very thing that elevates man above the beasts—his knowledge of the difference between good and evil. The two great turning points of the Reformation age, the Lutheran and the Copernican, seem to have brought mankind nothing but humiliation. First man is robbed of his power over himself, and then he is pushed to the periphery of creation."[27]

It is my wish, not to contradict Luther, but to go at least a short way beyond him, to accept and live with our humiliation as a necessity, yet to chasten it a bit in and through the grace of comedy. The paradox is that in comedy our rightful humiliation is itself humiliated a little. We are even made to stand straighter and taller. For the meanwhile, the final paragraph of the Oberman study is apropos:

> Luther must have had a very strong constitution, or he would never have been able to bear strain, overwork, and constant physical ailments for so long. But there is a deeper source for his exceptional vitality. Health is God's domain; death the Devil's intent. Luther learned to draw life from the struggle against the Devil. For the just shall *live* by faith, and "life" does not begin in Heaven. According to the medieval *memento mori*, in the midst of life we are surrounded by death. Luther's faith enabled him vigorously to turn this on its head: "In the midst of death we are surrounded by life."[28]

This, in the end, is what would make it wrong, I should say, wholly to dissociate the reformer from Christian comedy. Comedy is life; tragedy is death. I mentioned above that Luther is hardly representative of any kind of comic vision. Yet it would be unjust to ignore, not only that his sternness was matched by personal cheerfulness and jocularity, but that he could write of how he knew the tricks that the Devil liked to play on him: Satan "is a sad, sour spirit, who does not like the heart to be glad." From Luther's perspective, any comic vision will naturally, i.e., diabolically, end up truncated, yet even the reformer was thankful for small blessings. As Oberman interprets, "God is the God of joy. Dark thoughts cannot be avoided, yet Luther comforts a depressed friend; it is the same as in nature; you cannot stop birds from flying over your head, but you can stop them from nesting in your hair. So seek company, play cards, or do something else you enjoy—and do it with a good conscience, for depressions come not from God but the Devil."[29]

How naïve the last eight words of the previous sentence sound in our time (the "God" side in depression has been largely replaced by "physiological imbalance"). Professor Oberman speculates that were Luther somehow around today, psychiatric analysis would come up with a "persuasive" diagnosis: *Paranoia reformatorica*—though only upon irritatingly uncertain grounds, "ranging from neurosis to psychosis, from Oedipus complex to mother fixation. Fear of the Lord and abhorrence of the Devil" are held to be "indicators of disturbed childhood development." Notwithstanding all this, Martin Luther could well accept such a diagnosis because "Reformation madness" encompasses "the foolishness that is an intrinsic part of faith." (I might interject that such madness may also be able to reckon with the foolishness that is entirely outside faith.) Furthermore, and most relevant of all, Luther's persuasion that God is at work and hence can be trusted furnishes "the other side of the 'phobia'; courage and contempt for the Devil issue from faith."[30] Finally, we may find seeds of comedy within the reformer's "unprecedently [sic] bold claim" for humility.

To epitomize Martin Luther's vision in language consonant with this book—a vision that, once we manage to escape one or another form of genetic fallacy, is no longer seen as subject to psychological reductionism—the Christian gospel together with Christian theology are constituted of a twinning process: Christology demands diabology; diabology cries out for Christology. To deny the Devil is to deny God. It is the Devil himself who proves (tests) God's reliability. The other side of the coin is that only God can fight the Devil. The Shadow of God here takes on a distinctly Lutheran visage.[31]

III

Reinhold Niebuhr, brother of H. Richard, conserves much of Luther in his theology and particularly in his anthropology, as at the same time he, on the one hand, tones down the intensities of Reformation diabology (any explicit twinning of Christ and Devil is absent) and, on the other hand, explicitly ties religious faith to comedy and humor in ways that Luther could never have developed. Niebuhr is, at once, son of the Reformation and son of the Renaissance. Let us see how this is so.

Although Reinhold Niebuhr does not "preach" the Devil after the fashion of Martin Luther, certain of his historical allusions and theological commentaries give due notice that he is not prepared to negate devilish reality (for all his softening of the word Devil to devil). However, it is on the basis of assertions (needs?) within his anthropology that his somewhat fragmentary diabology comes to expression—this in contrast to Luther, who, as we noted, goes so far as to correlate all Christology with diabology.

While, as we shall emphasize, Niebuhr concentrates upon human sin[32] and its all-decisive place in the moral evil of our world, he yet affirms as a "mystery" the truth that sinfulness appears to "posit itself."

[There] is always a devil in classical religious mythology, and the devil is a symbol of the belief that evil is regarded as an actual rebellion against God. Of course this realism is always balanced by an ultimate optimism, because it is never believed that the devil can seriously threaten the rule of God.[33] [Niebuhr here passes over certain expressions of radical dualism, as for example the view of Mani and Manicheism—A.R.E.]

There is...great profundity in the biblical myth of the serpent who "tempted" Eve by suggesting that God was jealous of man's strength and sought to limit it.... It is man's unbelief and pride that tempt to sin. And every such temptation presupposes a previous "tempter".... Thus, before man fell into sin there was, according to biblical myth, a fall of the devil in heaven. The devil is a fallen angel who refused to accept his rightful place in the scheme of things and sought a position equal to God.

This then is the real mystery of evil, that it presupposes itself. No matter how far back it is traced in the individual or the race, or even preceding the history of the race, a profound scrutiny of the nature of evil reveals that there is an element of sin in the temptation that leads to sin; and that, without this presupposed evil, the consequent sin would not necessarily arise.... This is what Kierkegaard means by saying that "sin posits itself."

Purely sociological and historical explanations of the rise of evil do not touch the depth of the mystery at all.... In dealing with the problem of sin the sense of meaning is inextricably interwoven with the sense of mystery.[34]

To believe that there is a devil is to believe that there is a principle or force of evil antecedent to any evil human action. Before man fell the devil fell.... [The devil's] sin and fall consists in his effort to transcend his proper state and to become like God.... The importance of biblical satanology lies in the two facts that: (1) The devil is not thought of as having been created evil. Rather his evil arises from his effort to transgress the bounds set for his life, an effort that places him in rebellion against God. (2) The devil fell before man fell, which is to say that man's rebellion against God is not an act of sheer perversity, nor does it follow inevitably from the situation in which he stands. The situation of finiteness and freedom in which man stands becomes a source of temptation only when it is falsely interpreted. This false interpretation is not purely the product of the human imagination. *It is suggested to man by a force of evil that precedes his own sin.* Perhaps the best description or definition of this mystery is the statement that sin posits itself, that there is no situation in which it is possible to say that sin is either an inevitable consequence of the situation nor yet that it is an act of sheer and perverse individual defiance of God" (italics added).

Sin can never be traced merely to the temptation arising from a particular situation or condition in which man as man finds himself or in which particular men find themselves. Nor can the temptation which is compounded of a situation of finiteness and freedom, plus the fact of sin, be regarded as leading necessarily to sin in the life of each individual, if again sin is not first presupposed in that life. For this reason even the knowledge of inevitability does not extinguish the sense of responsibility.[35]

These passages suggest three essential considerations, one negative, the other two positive. First, no orthodox Reformation thinker would agree or would be able to speak of the Devil as a "symbol" or to conceptualize the biblical account of the Fall as a "myth"; Renaissance and Enlightenment influences upon Niebuhr shine through. Second, Niebuhr's resort to "mystery" respecting the origin and causation of evil is consonant with traditional attestations to the Devil, with particular reference to the phenomenon of temptation. Third, and most significant for the argument of this book, an insistence upon the evil of the Devil as preceding the evil of humankind helps to counteract the dastardly assumption that humanity is unqualifiedly or solely culpable for the terrible evils of the world. I have already stated my conviction regarding how morally crucial the stubborn fact is that no human being ever asked to be born, with the grave import that this has respecting the blameworthiness of God (or at least of someone or something other than humankind). I have cited the dictum of Albert Camus, which I find unanswerable, "Man is not entirely to blame; it was not he who started history." As Emil Brunner has said, humankind is not great enough to introduce evil and sin into the cosmos. And as Reinhold Niebuhr puts it, the human rebellion against God "is not an act of sheer perversity." W. Burnet Easton, Jr., used to picture the Fall as "up" as much as "down." Thereby humanity actualizes a God-given dignity. Paradoxically enough, it is the phenomenon of a Devil given over to radical evil that helps to offset the immorality of placing humanity, rather than God, at the center of blame for the horrors of this world. The Devil carries blame, and the

Devil is the Shadow of God (a "fallen angel"). Nevertheless, we are cautioned again and again that the human being is not exempted from moral liability (*Verantwortlichkeit*)—any more than, I would add, is God: The "knowledge of the inevitability" of human sin and evil "does not extinguish the sense of responsibility." On the contrary, such responsibility is at the center of the teaching of *imago dei*. The biblical myth of the Fall "seeks to do justice to both the universality of sin and self-regard and to the element of personal responsibility in each sinful act."[36] In a word, humankind remains proximately blameworthy for evil but not ultimately blameworthy.

Human sin, or what I should prefer to call humankind's proximate blameworthiness, comes to evil blossom in and through the willful corruption of freedom. Reinhold Niebuhr's anthropology of humankind's anxiety, idolatry, and guilt, his sociology and politics of the power of tragedy and the wrongness of utopianism, and his morality of concentrating upon the pain of a fallen world, all play a part within his theory of evil. True to the Reformation, Niebuhr finds evil rampant in the world, although his insistence upon humankind as culprit does not seem to rule out transhuman factors, as when, in a prayer, he speaks of "the tumults, pains, and afflictions of life."[37] True to Enlightenment and Renaissance affirmations, Niebuhr rejects total human depravity and insists upon humanity's freedom for good. An intimate and intricate relation obtains between "the creative and the disruptive tendencies of human freedom."[38]

With Søren Kierkegaard, Niebuhr concentrates upon the ontologic-psychic condition of anxiety. Anxiety is both "the condition of human achievement and the precondition...of sin—the former because anxiety is at once the prerequisite and the inspiration of creative acts, the latter because of the accompanying temptation to make idols out of the very same attainments and to gather the universe into ourselves instead of trusting in God as redeemer. Idolatry is the primal sin."[39] Humankind "stands at the juncture of nature and spirit"; accordingly, human beings are equally "involved in both freedom and necessity. The strange residency upon the very border between the world of nature and the world of spirit is what ensures the essential incongruity of human existence [the primordial ground of comedy—A.R.E.]. Evil is to be apprehended "as not simply the consequence of temporality or the fruit of nature's necessities. Sin can be understood neither in terms of the freedom of human reason alone, nor yet in terms of the circumscribed harmonies in which the human body is bound." With humankind as such, sin "lies at the juncture of spirit and nature, in the sense that the peculiar and unique characteristics of human spirituality, in both its good and evil tendencies, can be understood only by analyzing the paradoxical relation of freedom and necessity...."[40]

Here we observe the marriage in Reinhold Niebuhr of Reformation and Renaissance: In opposition to anthropological naturalism on the one hand and anthropological idealism on the other, Niebuhr is a Christian anthropological (and political) realist. Christian realism means a double recognition: of the reality of persistent evil and of the reality of persistent goodness. The amphibious status of humanity as a creature of nature and a being of spirit, "but yet an unqualified unity of these two aspects, means that the conflicting [doctrines]...of naturalism and idealism are equally judged and found wanting."[41] The biblical-Jewish-Christian conception of human being avoids "pretension, complacency and naïveté on the one hand, and despair and flight from the human struggle on the other."[42]

The radical freedom of humankind is indeterminate. The essence of the human being is "free self-determination."[43] Humanity can rise to untold heights of goodness and it can fall to untold depths of evil.[44] In the collective life of humankind "most evil arises because finite men involved in the flux of time pretend that they are not so involved. Biblical faith has always insisted upon the embarrassing truth that the corruption of evil is at the heart of the human personality.... Thus the same freedom which gives human life a creative power, not possessed by other creatures, also endows it with destructive possibilities not known in nature."[45]

This dialectical interpretation by Niebuhr suggests an anthropological counterpart to a cosmic condition: the sublime goodness and empowering grace of God versus the base evil and destructiveness of Satan; the image of God and the rebellion against God; God Godself and what we are calling the Shadow of God. The tale of humankind recapitulates the war in heaven. Of great significance here is Niebuhr's welcome rejection of the Augustinian notion we earlier encountered, according to which evil is subsumed under non-Being. On the contrary, "the devil is possible only in a world controlled by God and can be effective only if some of the potencies of the divine are in him. *Evil, in other words, is not the absence but the corruption of good;* yet it is parasitic on the good. In such a mythical conception evil is more positive than in monistic philosophies, and more dependent upon the good than in religious and philosophical dualisms" (italics added). Niebuhr cites approvingly Luther's assertion that the Devil is "God's Devil," used by God to divine ends. "Devil," declares God in the reformer's words, "thou art a murderer and a criminal, but I will use thee for whatsoever I will. Thou shalt be the dung with which I will fertilize my lovely vineyard. I will and can use thee in my work on my vines.... Therefore thou mayst hack, cut, and destroy, but no further than I permit."[46]

For Reinhold Niebuhr, the human story is "too grand and too awful to be told without reverence for the mystery and the majesty" of the God who transcends all human knowledge. Only humble persons "who recognize this mystery and majesty are able to face both the beauty and the terror of life without exulting over its beauty or becoming crushed by its terror." Accordingly, Niebuhr has much to say of relevance to the question of the divine Enemy become Friend. In one of his prayers he conveys the paradox of divine wrath and judgment vis-à-vis divine compassion and grace: "We are consumed by your anger and sustained by your mercy." He refers with sympathy to the theme of the Reformation, "God's grace is nothing but the forgiveness of sinners," and to Luther's avowal that "the final sin" of humankind is its effort to prove itself sinless.[47] Even God's judgment can be a source of hope, since it tells us that human sin is no more than penultimate and that its defeat, quoting Robert McAfee Brown, "provides the seedbed in which mercy and grace can be sown and take root in human life."[48]

In *The Nature and Destiny of Man,* Niebuhr poses the question of a divine resource capable of overcoming the tragic character of human history and of curing as well as (rightfully) punishing the "sinful pride" in which humankind "inevitably involves" itself.

> From the standpoint of Christian faith the life and death of Christ becomes the revelation of God's character with particular reference to the unsolved problem of the relation of His judgment to His mercy, of His wrath to His forgiveness. Christian faith sees in the Cross of Christ the assurance that judgment is not the final word of God to man; but it does not regard the mercy of God as a forgiveness which wipes out the distinctions of good and evil in history and makes judgment meaningless.... The good news of the gospel is that God takes the sinfulness of man into Himself; and overcomes in His own heart what cannot be overcome in human life, since human life remains within the vicious circle of sinful self-glorification.... [Without] this divine initiative and this divine sacrifice there could be no reconciliation....

So the all-legitimate judgment of God upon human sinners is not abrogated, for that would mean an impugning of justice—yet "the final word is not one of judgment but of mercy and forgiveness."[49]

In keeping with the incompleteness of his diabology, Reinhold Niebuhr here overlooks his own admission, referred to above, that humanity is not the solitary culprit for sin. This means that we are required to qualify Niebuhr's stress upon the legitimacy of the divine judgment, lest we turn God into the Devil whose specialty is unrighteousness. I propose that the divine acceptance and forgiveness of (admittedly sinful) humankind is a moral necessity to be applied to God, if God is to be received as a truly moral being. For, as we have repeated, humankind has no say in its creation and "is not entirely to blame" (Camus). The evil Shadow ever seeks to overtake and vanquish the divine goodness. Without requisite acts of acceptance and forgiveness, God remains a reprehensible tyrant. So God had better forgive human beings if God knows what is good, not alone for humankind, but for God Godself. Furthermore, there is a sense in which God Godself must seek to be forgiven, not only for the creating of humankind (a humankind that, admittedly, involves itself in sin), but for the element of responsibility that God ultimately bears for evil (unless we are to fall into the unfortunate habits of the unqualified dualists).

Upon this foundation of Reinhold Niebuhr's thought, we can turn at last to his view of humor. In ways not unreminiscent of the "Zen-thing," Niebuhr analyzes the perils of making coherence into the fundamental test of truth: The phenomena of life are often too unique to satisfy any simple system of meaning; areas of coherence and meaning may be seen rationally to contradict each other; various configurations and structures stand athwart any rationally conceived system of meaning; and human freedom in its indeterminacy cannot be encompassed by any natural or rational notion of coherence.[50]

The suggestion is made in Chapter 1 of this book that comedy and humor may be received as a certain way or ways of celebrating the incongruous, the contradictory, the absurd. Incongruity is the precondition and ground of humor.

In two essays of Reinhold Niebuhr, "Christianity and Tragedy" and "Humour and Faith," the traditionally contrasting categories of the tragic and the comic are examined. "Tragedy" is often used in a loose way that unfortunately confuses it with "the pitiful." In authentic tragedy "the hero defies malignant power to assert the integrity of his soul. He suffers because he is strong and not because he is weak," as against pathos. And "he involves himself in guilt not by his vice but by his virtue." However, in ordinary life the tragic and the pitiful are mixed, as when people become enmeshed in suffering, not only because of weakness but because of strength, not only through blindness but due to some noble purpose. Yet in true tragedy—the purest conception of tragedy is found in Greek drama—the suffering of the hero is self-inflicted. The tragic motif in Greek drama is of two sorts, Promethean and Dionysian. In Promethean tragedy "the perennial self-destruction of man by his willfully overreaching himself," and with no solution to the problem, is accentuated, whereas the closer Greek tragedy stays to the Dionysian myth, the more a "titanic defiance" of rational and traditional morality is present—a "conscious affirmation of unconscious human impulses in defiance of society's conventions," all this in the name of a seemingly higher duty.[51]

In contrast to the Christian teaching that sin emerges out of freedom, the myth of tragedy insists upon the inevitability of guilt-ridden consequences and maintains that the hero is caught within a web of circumstance from which he cannot escape. I suggest that the outcome of authentic tragedy is the closure of life, life closing in upon us, whereas in comedy, life remains open. Tragedy means fate (*moira*); comedy comes out upon the side of freedom and hope.

In the influential essay "Humour and Faith" Reinhold Niebuhr conceives of humor as a prelude to faith and of laughter as the beginning of prayer.

> The intimate relation between humour and faith is derived from the fact that both deal with the incongruities of our existence. Humour is concerned with the immediate incongruities of life and faith with the ultimate ones. Both humour and faith are expressions of the freedom of the human spirit, of its capacity to stand outside of life, and itself, and view the whole scene. But any view of the whole immediately creates the problem of how the incongruities of life are to be dealt with; for the effort to understand life, and our place in it, confronts us with inconsistencies and incongruities which do not fit into any neat picture of the whole. Laughter is our reaction to immediate incongruities and those which do not affect us essentially. Faith is the only possible response to the ultimate incongruities of existence which threaten the very meaning of our life.
>
> ...If laughter seeks to deal with the ultimate issues of life, it turns into a bitter humour. This means that it has been overwhelmed by the incongruity. Laughter is thus not merely a vestibule to faith but also a "no-man's land" between faith and

despair. We laugh cheerfully at the incongruities on the surface of life; but if we have no other resource but humour to deal with those that reach below the surface, our laughter becomes an expression of our sense of the meaninglessness of life.... That is why laughter, when pressed to solve the ultimate issue, turns into a vehicle of bitterness rather than of joy. To laugh at life in the ultimate sense means to scorn it. There is a note of derision in that laughter and an element of despair in that derision.

Again, once we recognize the real power of sin, we know that laughter is not able to deal with that problem. As Niebuhr points out, "if we continue to laugh after having recognized the depth of [human] evil, our laughter becomes the instrument of irresponsibility. Laughter is thus not only the vestibule of the temple of confession but the no-man's land between cynicism and contrition." And when our own sin is at the fore, we see that the joy of reconciliation with God, "the fruit of genuine repentance, is a joy which stands beyond laughter though it need not completely exclude laughter."

Niebuhr concludes his essay with these words:

Our provisional amusement with the irrational and unpredictable fortunes which invade the order and purpose of our life must move either toward bitterness or faith, when we consider not this or that frustration and this or that contingent event, but when we are forced to face the basic incongruity of death.

Faith is...the final triumph over incongruity, the final assertion of the meaningfulness of existence. There is no other triumph and will be none, no matter how much human knowledge is enlarged. Faith is the final assertion of the freedom of the human spirit, but also the final acceptance of the weakness of man and the final solution for the problem of life through the disavowal of any final solution in the power of man.

Insofar as the sense of humour is a recognition of incongruity, it is more profound than any philosophy which seeks to devour incongruity in reason. But the sense of humour remains healthy only when it deals with immediate issues and faces the obvious and surface irrationalities. It must move toward faith or sink into despair when the ultimate issues are raised.

That is why there is laughter in the vestibule of the temple, the echo of laughter in the temple itself, but only faith and prayer, and no laughter, in the holy of holies.[52]

Is this last negation to be accepted? It is related to Niebuhr's earlier restriction of humor and laughter to the immediate incongruities of life. For him, humankind's incongruous position in the universe—the human being is so great, yet so small—is the problem of faith and not of humor.[53] I should respond that the ultimate incongruities of life may eventuate not alone in faith but also in humor. Unfortunately, once the objective comic dimension is limited in the way Niebuhr proposes, there is very great difficulty in speaking of truly divine comedy. Accordingly, I do not accept the Niebuhrian delimitation. I suggest that Conrad Hyers is right when he says that the faculty of humor knows no limits; human beings are capable of laughter respecting the ultimate incongruities as well as the immediate ones.[54] Again, Niebuhr's judgment that faith is "the only possible response to the ultimate incongruities of existence" is questionable, not only for, in effect, excluding God as comic but also for underestimating such widespread alternatives to faith as stoicism, fatalism, and hedonism. However, it is certainly so that grandiose claims for the efficacy of humor are forbidden. As Niebuhr rightly puts it, laughter alone never destroys the tyrannies of power.[55]

Notes

1. Rollo May, *The Cry for Myth* (New York: W. W. Norton, 1991), p. 283.
2. George Santayana, *The Sense of Beauty*, as cited in Conrad Hyers, *The Laughing Buddha* (Wakefield N.H.: Longwood Academic, 1991), p. 69; John Morreall, ed., *The Philosophy of Laughter and Humor* (Albany, N.Y.: State University of New York Press, 1987), p. 90. Santayana went so far as to hold that existence is inherently comic: "This world is contingency and absurdity incarnate, the oddest of possibilities masquerading momentarily as fact." (*Soliloquies in England and Later Soliloquies* [New York: Scribner, 1922], pp. 141-42).
3. Jeffrey Burton Russell, *The Devil* (Ithaca, N.Y. and London: Cornell University Press, 1987), p. 225.
4. Ibid., pp. 167-68.
5. We remember the wish that Jewish people often express, "May you live to a hundred and twenty."
6. William B. Silverman, *Rabbinic Stories for Christian Ministers and Teachers* (Nashville, Tenn.: Abingdon Press, 1958), pp. 65-6.
7. As cited by Frederick Sontag, *The God of Evil* (New York: Harper & Row, 1970), p. 87.
8. Consult Jeffrey Burton Russell, *Satan* (Ithaca, N.Y. and London: Cornell University Press, 1987), p. 69.
9. On the seemingly contrary eventuality of a comic Devil, consult Jeffrey Burton Russell, *The Prince of Darkness* (Ithaca, N.Y. and London: Cornell University Press, 1992), pp. 150-56, 161-62, 173, 233-34.
10. C. S. Lewis, *The Screwtape Letters* (London: Collins Fount, 1977), pp. 26, 58. For word on the historical/biographical background of this work of Lewis's, consult A. N. Wilson, *C. S. Lewis* (New York and London: W. W. Norton, 1990), Chap. 13—"Screwtape 1939-1942," particularly pp. 176-79.
11. Harry Levin, *Playboys and Killjoys* (New York: Oxford University Press, 1988), pp. 5, 10. Levin's analysis is oriented to the stage, but this has good foundational authorization: Was not the theater comedy's initial "social matrix"?
12. For Luke, in contrast, the rich, who laugh now, will one day "mourn and weep." (Luke 6:24-25).

13. Russell, *Devil,* p. 102; Martin Buber, *Good and Evil* (New York: Scribner, 1953), pp. 7, 107, 109, 110–12.

14. H. Richard Niebuhr, *Faith on Earth,* ed. Richard R. Niebuhr (New Haven, Conn.: Yale University Press, 1989), p. 78.

15. As cited in Heiko A. Oberman, *Luther* (New York: Doubleday Image Books, 1992), p. 179.

16. Consider in this regard the conversation between Satan and the Lord in Job 1:6–12.

17. Jon D. Levenson, *Creation and the Persistence of Evil* (San Francisco: Harper & Row, 1988), p. 163.

18. R. H. Blyth, *Oriental Humour* (Tokyo: Hokuseida Press, 1959), p. 91.

19. If love is divine, is hatred necessarily devilish? God Godself is said to hate evil. For example, God hates lying and other evils (Zech. 9:3). Yet the God/Devil dichotomy is retained: God hates and loves; the Devil hates but does not love.

20. Oberman, *Luther,* pp. 156, 162.

21. It is surely a sign of today's changed times that I was able to purchase my copy of Oberman's study of Luther in a book shop attached to the Roman Catholic Chapel of the Holy Cross in Sedona, Arizona (Sept. 1992).

22. Oberman, *Luther,* p. 3.

23. Ibid., pp. 72, 104–05.

24. Ibid., pp. 179, 283. "Luther's own behavior contradicts the caricature of servility to princes." Yet it remains so that "the only progress he expected from the reformation was the Devil's rage, provoked by the rediscovery of the Gospel." And it must be acknowledged that, for Luther, "violent resistance against the authorities, particularly in the name of the Gospel, was the work of the Devil—and only possible in the chaos of the Last Days." (ibid., pp. 256, 267, 278).

25. With respect to Luther's antisemitism, consult the lengthy citation from the reformer in Ibid., p. 290; in general, pp. 290–97. Of course, parties other than Jews lay victim to Luther's vituperations: Romanists, the pope himself (special ally of the Devil), nationalists, church reformers, princes, witches, and others.

26. Ibid., pp. 229, 291; see also pp. 300–04.

27. Ibid., pp. 106, 155. Oberman rather effectively disposes of attempts to psychologize Luther in the latter's dealing with such realities as the Devil. See, e.g., ibid., pp. 106ff., "God's Word in Filthy Language"; also pp. 154–56.

28. Ibid., p. 330.

29. Ibid., pp. 309–10. Luther looked upon music as a great gift of God: "without music man is a stone, but with music he can drive away the Devil." Ibid., p. 310. Fittingly, the senior devil Screwtape dubs music a "detestable art." (Lewis, *Screwtape Letters,* p. 57).

30. Ibid., pp. 314–15.

31. The world of C. S. Lewis appears to be far removed from that of the warring prophet Martin Luther. Yet in *The Screwtape Letters,* as elsewhere, the two are shown to have much in common. The paradox is at once delightful and sobering: The urbane, intellectualist, Oxford don, and the rough, obsessed German ex-monk hardly appear companionable; yet the Devil's courtesy brings them together.

32. For a feminist critique of Reinhold Niebuhr's teaching on sin, also of Paul Tillich's, consult Judith Plaskow, *Sex, Sin and Grace* (Washington, D.C.: University Press of America, 1980). A full review of Plaskow's critique is found in my *Black-Woman-Jew* (Bloomington, Ind.: Indiana University Press, 1989), Chap. 10. Consult also Mary McClintock Fulkerson, "Sexism as Original Sin: Developing a

Thea-centric Discourse," *Journal of the American Academy of Religion* 59 (1991): 653-75.

33. Reinhold Niebuhr, *Christianity and Power Politics* (New York: Scribner, 1940), p. 199.
34. Reinhold Niebuhr, *Discerning the Signs of the Times* (New York: Scribner, 1946), pp. 166-67. In an early work Niebuhr writes that "according to the myth of the Fall, evil came into the world through human responsibility." But he tempers this claim by observing that the serpent, "symbol of the principle of evil, does justice to the idea that human rebellion is not the first cause and source of evil in the world." (*An Interpretation of Christian Ethics* [New York: Harper & Bros., 1935], pp. 72-3).
35. Reinhold Niebuhr, *The Nature and Destiny of Man*, Vol. I (New York: Scribner, 1941), pp. 180-81, 254.
36. Reinhold Niebuhr, *The Self and the Dramas of History* (New York: Scribner, 1955), p. 99. Cf. Henry A. Murray: According to one tenable position, "the Satanic sin" is to shatter "man's faith in the existence of…necessary potentialities within himself and to reduce him to cynicism and and despair until the demoralization and abasement of his personality has reached a state beyond recovery and in one disgraceful debacle of genocidal fury he terminates the long, long history of his species." (*Endeavors in Psychology*, ed. Edwin S. Shneidman [New York: Harper & Row, 1981], p. 534).
37. From a prayer by Reinhold Niebuhr, *Justice and Mercy*, ed. Ursula M. Niebuhr (New York: Harper & Row, 1974), p. 22.
38. Reinhold Niebuhr, *Man's Nature and His Communities* (New York: Scribner, 1965), p. 31.
39. A. Roy Eckardt, *For Righteousness' Sake* (Bloomington, Ind.: Indiana University Press, 1989), p. 169. Reinhold Niebuhr applies this reasoning to the issue of *fanaticism*. Specific causes of fanaticism, "such as the claim of ultimate truth on religious, philosophical, and scientific grounds" cannot be allowed to "obscure the more general cause, namely the tendency of men, who are both *creators* and *creatures* in the historical process, to seek to obscure their creaturely finiteness and pretend to possess more transcendence over the historical process than is within the competence of creatures." (Niebuhr, "The Present Heritage of the Long Encounter Between Christian Faith and Western Civilization," *Harvard Divinity Bulletin* 26 [Oct. 1961]: 4-5).
40. Niebuhr, *Nature and Destiny of Man*, I, p. 181; in general, chaps. 1-4; *Interpretation of Christian Ethics*, p. 76.
41. Eckardt, *For Righteousness' Sake*, pp. 166, 168.
42. Gabriel Fackre, *The Promise of Reinhold Niebuhr* (Philadelphia: Lippincott, 1970), pp. 34-5.
43. Niebuhr, *Nature of Man*, I, p. 16.
44. Correspondingly, political life entails the "perennial predicament" of seeking "proximate solutions of insoluble problems." (Niebuhr, *Justice and Mercy*, p. 82). The Devil is, so to speak, to be used against the Devil. St. Augustine was right: Such peace as the world may achieve is only gained by strife. But Niebuhr finds Luther's approach to political problems far too pessimistic. (*Christian Realism and Political Problems* [New York: Scribner, 1953], pp. 145-46).
45. Reinhold Niebuhr, *The Structure of Nations and Empires* (New York: Scribner, 1959), p. 298; Reinhold Niebuhr, *Faith and History* (New York: Scribner, 1949), pp. 122-23.

46. Niebuhr, *Interpretation of Christian Ethics*, pp. 73, 75. The words of Luther are taken from Herman Obendiek, *Der Teufel bei Martin Luther.*
47. Niebuhr, *Justice and Mercy*, pp. 9, 75, 92. Consult Niebuhr's essay "Mystery and Meaning" in *Discerning the Signs of the Times*, pp. 152-73.
48. Robert McAfee Brown, ed., *The Essential Reinhold Niebuhr* (New Haven, Conn. and London: Yale University Press, 1986), pp. xii-xiii.
49. Niebuhr, *Nature of Man and Destiny*, I, pp. 141-43, 147-48.
50. Reinhold Niebuhr, "Coherence, Incoherence, and Christian Faith," in *Christian Realism*, pp. 176-79.
51. Reinhold Niebuhr, "Christianity and Tragedy, " in *Beyond Tragedy* (New York: Scribner, 1937), pp. 156, 159, 160-63.
52. Niebuhr, "Humour and Faith, " in *Discerning the Signs of the Times*, pp. 111-12, 114-15, 121-22, 127-28, 130-31.
53. Ibid., p. 113.
54. A. Roy Eckardt, *Sitting in the Earth and Laughing* (New Brunswick, N.J. and London: Transaction Publishers, 1992), p. 176; Conrad Hyers, *The Comic Vision and the Christian Faith* (New York: Pilgrim Press, 1981), p. 31.
55. Niebuhr, "Humour and Faith," p. 116.

7

The Long and Rocky Road to an Authentic Comic Vision
II

> *Experience has taught me to believe in no fixation*
> *of beliefs, but in the exciting process of perpetually*
> *reconstructing them in order to encompass new*
> *facts, experiences, and conditions. This, as I see it,*
> *is the essence and the responsibility of freedom.*
> *—Henry A. Murray[1]*

The part of our exposition that is begun in Chapter 6 is concluded in this chapter.

I

What do the Eisleben/Wittenberg of Martin Luther, the Union Theological Seminary of Reinhold Niebuhr, and Harvard University have to do with one another?

As faithful servants of the Enlightenment, Harvard and like places of today do not suffer gladly any propagation/superstition of the Devil[2]— though, to be sure, certain forms of devilishness are allowed to enter for purposes of study and research, not to mention, in the eyes of some skeptics, for purposes of adoration. On the other hand, in such a personage as Harvey Cox, Harvard makes wide room for the comic vision. Further, as we shall see, there is a sense in which Professor Cox does not wholly abandon the Devil, at least retaining him in demythologized form.

If Reinhold Niebuhr's thinking moves between Reformation and Renaissance impulses, Harvey Cox is closer to the second of these

Weltanschauungen, though not without strains of ambivalence. Cox has acknowledged Niebuhr's substantial influence upon him, particularly at the point of the latter's biblical-Christian realism, leading to Cox's own decision to become a theologian.[3] Again, Cox keeps alight the torch of the Christian Social Gospel, a position we were able to associate, if in a somewhat revisionist sounding way, with the name of Martin Luther.

Withal, in theology as broadly construed by him, Cox opts, not for modernism, but for postmodernism. As he asserts in *Religion in the Secular City,* "modernity" is "the world view of the entrepreneurial class which seized the tiller of history from the weakened grip of its feudal forerunner." Concretely, modernity boasts five pillars: the legal and moral sovereignty of the nation-state; science-based technology as authoritative for life and its possibilities; bureaucratic rationalism as the decisive method for organizing thought and praxis; profit maximization as the way to motivate human labor and distribute goods and services; and the secularization and trivialization of religion, with "the spiritual dimension harnessed to profane purposes."[4]

While for Cox "the moral and legal gains of modernity are genuine and must not be lost," he still hears the preacher of his boyhood declaim that "the devil is a modernist"[5]—although he also remembers having been "strangely drawn," like Rousseau and Saint-Preux, toward *le tourbillon social,* the social whirlwind, adding that "the devil can be terribly intriguing." With Reinhold Niebuhr, Cox clothes the evil one in lower-case dress, and nowhere can he bring himself to say that the Devil is the Devil.[6] (In *The Secular City* Cox makes Eve's serpent into something "quaint,"[7] while for Niebuhr the serpent remains at least mythologically viable.) Yet Cox does go on to show that all the pillars of modernity "are being eaten from the inside," and to proclaim that the modern world "has cracked" and is decomposing, although he does not link the present and coming debacle to any Devil *as such.* On the other hand, we note the tantalizing ending to his description of today's giant airport as "modernity incarnate": "Maybe Our Lady of the Airport can help us in our quest for a Christianity that deals with the devil of modernism by constructing a world in which that Old Tempter may still cause trouble but *in some other guise*" (my emphasis). We note as well Cox's judgment that to apprehend what responsibility for exorcism is to mean in the "secular city," we will have to "get behind the prescientific images of spirits and demons to the reality they expressed. Men of New Testament times used this language to designate the subpersonal forces and suprapersonal influences which warped and twisted human life. They represented the 'principalities and powers' as they functioned in a particular personality, something that is still very much with us."[8]

The subtitle of Harvey Cox's more recent study *Religion in the Secular City* is *Toward a Postmodern Theology.* Here is his summation of the latter outlook:

> A viable postmodern theology will be created neither by those who have completely withdrawn from the modern world nor by those who have affirmed it unconditionally. It will come from those who have lived within it but have never been fully part of it, like the women in Adrienne Rich's poem who, though they dived into the wreck, have not found their names inscribed within it. It will be created by those who, like black American Christians, have refused to accept the slave-master's gospel.... but have also refused to jettison the Gospel altogether. What is needed... is not some measured middle ground, some mellowed balance of what has been good and what bad in modern liberal theology, but a theology forged by those who have been both inspired and abused, both touched and trampled on by the religion of the modern age.[9]

The task of a postmodern theology is to recover the essential purpose of Christianity, "a conscious means of personal self-discipline and of social control. It is to begin exploring the full implications of Pablo Richard's statement that 'for those who suffer its injustice, the reconciliation between religion and the modern world is a sacralization of oppression.'"[10] It is in the human oppression of yesterday, today, and tomorrow that the demons live. Harvey Cox's "some other guise" on the part of the Devil—perhaps Cox will pardon my capitalization (isn't "new guise" methodology one of the Devil's oldest tricks?)—is social and political injustice. Reinhold Niebuhr's influence probably enters here, but Cox is taken with and concentrates upon the post-Niebuhrian "radical critique of modern theology" on the part of a variety of Christian liberation thinkers and also, no less significantly, on the part of Christian *campesinos,* who live and meet today in the many scattered *comunidades de base* (grass-roots communities).[11] For example, in a *pueblito* called La Chispa a certain lady named Ana speaks of human sin in this way: "Sin is seeing what's wrong in the world, how the supervisors treat the field workers, how the children are ignored when they are sick—and then not doing anything about it." Liberation thinking is biblical but also experiential; its representatives know well that sin "expresses itself in institutional injustice more than in individual failings."[12] (Cf. Reinhold Niebuhr's *Moral Man and Immoral Society.*)

Particularly in its Latin American version, liberation theology teaches that "the special locus of God's presence is the poor." Over many pages Cox speaks on behalf of the "carnival faith" associated with Our Lady of Guadalupe. "A dark-skinned *mestiza* [halfcaste], she personifies the anger and persistent dignity of people of color everywhere. A woman, she embodies the never-completely-dominated *jouissance* of the second sex. A poor person, she inspires the hope of all those who believe that God is preferentially present in the lives of the disinherited." The poor have a singular role to play "in the divine intention for human history. The poor are those through whom God chooses to mediate the coming of the divine reign." This compelling idea of the *dios pobre,* central to the Bible, "was lost sight of and denied during much of modern history and in nearly all modern theology. But, like the *sola fide* of the sixteenth century, the idea of *dios pobre* has always been there. Smoldering, it has now been fanned into flames and become the central idea of the new reformation."[13]

Gustavo Gutiérrez is cited by Cox in a passage that links the devil in "some other guise" to a major thrust of the present book: "The poor know that history is theirs and that if today they must cry, tomorrow they will laugh. That laughter turns out to be an expression of profound confidence in the Lord—a confidence which the poor live in the midst of a history they seek to transform. It is a joy which is subversive of the world of oppression, and therefore it disturbs the dominator; it denounces the fear of those who tremble and reveals the love of the God of hope."[14]

From Cox's perspective, to free human beings from oppression is the one available and sure way to put the demons to flight. True, justice is not equatable with comedy, as comedy is not equatable with justice. However: Justice decrees that the poor, who weep now, are going to laugh, rejoice, and leap for joy, whereas the rich are fated to mourn and weep. So justice is a crucial ingredient in any recipe for authentic comedy. I think here of Elayne Boosler's declaration—the culminating epigraph of *How To Tell God From the Devil*—that "real comedy can't be learned; it comes from a need for justice."

Religion in the Secular City provides a helpful apperceptive mass for approaching and understanding Cox's *Feast of Fools,* his major contribution to the theory and practice of Christian comedy. This is one reason

I have reviewed the former work first, despite the fact that *Religion* appeared fifteen years after the other volume. One further passage from *Religion* provides a good transition to *The Feast of Fools*: "Cultural elites, including religious elites, almost always view festivals as dangerous. Carnivals generate an energy that cannot be turned off. They loose passions that cannot easily be called back. Consequently the history of festivals in the modern world is the history of attempts to ban and control them, and of ordinary people fighting to keep their festivals from being abolished, altered, or turned into tourist attractions."[15]

In a frame of reference of postmodern theology, the implication of *The Feast of Fools* is that any such theology misses something essential if it fails to preserve and advance "festivity and fancy." We are told that if Cox's previous work and companion piece, *The Secular City,* was "Apollonian," *The Feast* is "more Dionysian, more playful, more generous to 'religion'" than is *The Secular City.*[16] *The Feast* strongly emphasizes "the noninstrumental significance of celebration and liturgy," and wants to help close the "unnecessary gap" between "the world-changers" and "the life-celebrators." The title is drawn from the medieval "Feast of Fools," an annual occasion for merrymaking and for satire directed, interestingly enough, against both church and court. One part of the study deals with festivity, the peculiarly human "capacity for genuine revelry and joyous celebration," and involving socially sanctioned occasions for expressing feelings ordinarily repressed or neglected; another part is concerned with fantasy, the distinctively human "faculty for envisioning radically alternative life situations." If festivity is closely akin to human *memory,* fantasy is closely tied to human *hope.*[17]

It is Cox's purpose "to examine both the loss and the reemergence of festivity and fantasy in our civilization, and to evaluate both processes from a theological perspective." He is insistent that real celebration is not a retreat from injustice and evil but takes place with greatest authenticity when these realities are identified and fought. Genuine celebration is "a way to cool history without fleeing from it." Celebration provides a perspective upon history without removing us from "the terror and responsibility" we bear as the makers of history. Celebration reminds us that "history is not the exclusive or final horizon of life" and recalls for us "the link between the two levels of our being—the instrumental, calculating side, and the expressive, playful side." As for fantasy, this faculty exceeds festivity. In fantasy, called by Cox "advanced imagining," "man not only relives and anticipates, he remakes the past and creates wholly new futures. Fantasy is a humus. Out of it man's ability to invent and innovate grows. Fantasy is the richest source of human creativity. Theologically speaking, it is the image of the creator God in man. Like God, man in fantasy creates whole worlds *ex nihilo,* out of nothing."[18]

In the discrete area of theological responsibility Professor Cox advocates "a theology of juxtaposition" (cf. the exposition above of postmodern thinking): The theological method we require "cannot be content to explain and interpret the past. Nor can it focus entirely on present experience or bind itself wholly to future hope. Most importantly, it cannot try to smooth over the obvious contradictions in these dimensions of faith and experience nor attempt to reduce or reconcile them to each other. Rather it will exemplify the difference among these dimensions by juxtaposing them to each other. Recalling one of the principal ingredients of festivity, let us call this theological method the 'method of juxtaposition.'"[19]

Cox is here referring to something closely related to "the element of excess." Juxtaposition refers to the fact that "festivity must display contrast. It must be noticeably different from 'everyday life.'"[20]

> Traditional theologies emphasize faith's dependence on the past; they are historical. [Today's] radical theology, the "theology of creative negation," focuses on the present crisis of faith; it is incarnational. Theology of hope is oriented toward the future; it is eschatological. A theology of juxtaposition plays off the tensions among these three not by neatly balancing them but by maximizing the creative friction among all three. So it focuses precisely on those discomforting points where memory, hope, and experience contradict and challenge each other. It recognizes our estrangement from much of the tradition, but it is somewhat estranged from the ethos of today. It is unwilling to reconcile itself to either. It delights in the disrelation.[21]

To run ahead for a moment, via a comment elicited by Harvey Cox's image of "juxtaposition": In the next chapter, I seek to address the question of a comprehensive Christian comedy (theology) for today with aid from a concept of "Realized Incongruity." That concept, as we shall see, is able to embrace traditional theology (the past), radical theology, not excluding the recent "death of God" (the present), theology of hope (the future), and, indeed, the very theology that juxtaposes these opposites. Disrelated, yet to be related, are history, incarnation, and eschatology. A viable postmodern theology will entail a revolutionary theology of comedy.

This brings us to Cox's climactic essay "Christ the Harlequin," which serves to apply his theology of juxtaposition and that is of special relevance to our present work.

St. Paul's determination, "the foolishness of God is wiser than men, and the weakness of God is stronger than men," is the epigraph of Cox's chapter. God is a fool. As far as Christ goes,

> he has come to previous generations in various guises, as teacher, as judge, as healer. In today's world these traditional images of Christ have lost much of their power. Now in a new, or really an old but recaptured, guise, Christ has made an unexpected entrance onto the stage of modern secular life. Enter Christ the harlequin: *the personification of festivity and fantasy* in an age that had almost lost both. Coming now in greasepaint and halo, this Christ is able to touch our jaded modern consciousness as other images of Christ cannot.... [Today] clowns and troubadors are back tumbling and frisking through our cultural imagination. They help set the stage for a new iconography of Christ.[22]

Cox tells us that elements of the biblical record "easily suggest clown symbols": "Like a wandering troubador [Christ] has no place to lay his head. Like the clown in the circus parade, he satirizes existing authority by riding into town replete with regal pageantry when he has no earthly power. Like a minstrel he frequents dinners and parties. At the end he is costumed by his enemies in a mocking caricature of royal paraphernalia. He is crucified amidst sniggers and taunts with a sign over his head that lampoons his laughable claim." Today's "weak, even ridiculous church, somehow peculiarly at odds with the ruling assumptions of its day, can once again appreciate the harlequinesque Christ. His pathos, his weakness, his irony—all begin to make a strange kind of sense again." By dressing Christ in a clownsuit, we not alone express such persisting impulses as doubt, disillusionment, fascination, and ironic hope; we also say something "more distinctively contemporary. We say that our whole relation to Christ, to any faith at all, and to the whole of existence for that matter, is one of conscious play and comic equivocation. Only by assuming a playful attitude toward our religious tradition can we possibly make any sense of it. Only by learning to laugh at the hopelessness around us can we touch the hem of hope. Christ the clown signifies our playful appreciation of the past and our comic refusal to accept the spectre of inevitability in the future. *He is the incarnation of festivity and fantasy.*"[23]

"Christ the harlequin, the man of sorrows in the foolscap," represents a combination we of today greatly need but also can understand, "merriment and seriousness." As sophisticated and self-critical moderns, we are at a place where we no longer bother even to *doubt* our traditional religious symbols. "The coming of Christ the harlequin means, however, that symbols, belief, and faith need not simply be jettisoned. That was the simple-minded critical response of an earlier generation, one that had not yet uncovered for itself the playful element even in such a serious thing as faith. Our ability to laugh while praying [contra Reinhold Niebuhr's dichotomization, at the ultimate level, of faith and humor —A.R.E.] is an invaluable gift. It is not understood either by the sober believers or by the even more sober atheists among us."[24] (My experience is that more than a few Jews understand it, and not all of them are Hasidim.)

"Christ the harlequin is the joke in the middle of the prayer. Even better, perhaps, he is the prayer as joke or the joke as prayer. He is the spirit of play in a world of calculated utilitarian seriousness." Cox turns here to Hugo Rahner, the Roman Catholic philosopher, whose description of play, we are told, could almost be used to speak of prayer: "To play is to yield oneself to a kind of magic, to enact to oneself the absolutely other, to preempt the future, to give the lie to the inconvenient world of fact. In play earthly realities become, of a sudden, things of the transient moment, presently left behind, then disposed of and buried in the past; the mind is prepared to accept the unimagined and incredible, to enter a world where different laws apply, to be relieved of all the weights that bear it down, to be free, kingly, unfettered and divine."[25]

Among passages that conclude *The Feast of Fools* the following should be singled out:

> The comic sensibility can laugh at those who ferment wars and perpetuate hunger, at the same time it struggles to dethrone them. It foresees their downfall even when their power seems secure. The comic,...because it ignites hope, leads to more, not less, participation in the struggle for a just world.
>
> This gift of comic hope is not something on which religious people hold a monopoly. But it may be the special responsibility of men of faith to nourish this gift, to celebrate this sense of comic hope, and to demonstrate it.... [Where] laughter and hope have disappeared man has ceased to be man.
>
> ...Christian hope suggests that man is destined for a City. It is not just any city, however. If we take the Gospel images as well as the symbols of the Book of Revelation into consideration, it is not only a City where injustice is abolished and there is no more crying. It is a City in which a delightful wedding feast is in progress, where the laughter rings out, the dance has just begun, and the best wine is still to be served.[26]

The writings of Harvey Cox contribute much to a trialectic of God/ Devil/Comedy. Unfortunately, *The Feast of Fools* leaves him with a problem of his own making: the relation between comedy and history, with special reference to Christology. True, and as we have noted, Cox does not turn his back upon the historical record. In *The Feast* he affirms that even though Christianity, with other religions, utilizes myth, "it is founded on specific historical events." He laments radical theology's "ritual immolation of history." Again, in *Religion in the Secular City,* he rightly rejects, with all liberation thinking, the notion that a "neutral theology or any detached understanding of who Jesus was and is" is possible.[27] The fact remains that Cox's remarkably (and properly) childlike stance sometimes carries him away. (I shouldn't talk; I also go out of control.) Thus, it is really quite ridiculous to turn Christ into "the spirit of play in a world of calculated utilitarian seriousness." Indeed, for all the beauty of the words "harlequin" and "harlequinesque"—I am myself infatuated with these words—it is simply farfetched to personify Christ as a harlequin. The dialectical quality of myth as an uneasy balance of fact and imagination is here lost. Fact is subordinated to fancy. (Notably, it is "Christ" whom Cox identifies as harlequin, never "Jesus Christ.") A harlequin is a designedly comic character or performer dressed in bright colors, as is a clown. The *historical* materials Cox alludes to in *The Feast* suggest not a harlequin but more an earnest prophet of the Reign of God.

Religion in the Secular City is much more sound on the matter of Jesus: "The purpose of Jesus' life was the coming of the kingdom [*sic*] of justice and peace, of which he was himself the chief exemplar. Hence the struggle for the reign of divine justice provides the only appropriate context within which any meaningful discussion about Jesus can go on."[28] We are not to ignore the fact that this latter rendering comes fifteen years after *The Feast of Fools*; it can therefore be received as more definitive for Cox's point of view. But, regrettably, this does not resolve the question of what judgment must still be tendered respecting a harlequin Christ. I doubt that Cox would even today wish to withdraw that symbolization; it is a pillar of his theory of Christian comedy, a vision that, for him, postmodern humankind very much needs. It may be in order to refer to Cox's own agreement that Christological arguments have always been as much political as theological,[29] a view with which I agree as well. Here is precisely the reason a valid Christian *Anschauung* of comedy cannot overlook the Jesus who is *campesino,* embodiment of *el dios pobre,* an identity that is anything but that of harlequin. In this regard it is refreshing to note that even in *The Feast* Cox makes one allusion to Jesus as a "Nazarene peasant."[30]

I suggest that a convincing Christology, not excluding a liberation Christology, is obliged to link the Christ of faith more closely than Cox does in *The Feast* to the Jesus of historical experience, the Jesus who was a Jew utterly loyal to his people and their faith.[31] Yet even when we take into account the exposition in *Religion in the Secular City,* Professor Cox does not provide us with a Christology of comedy. A uniquely Christian comedy must proffer something that God does in Jesus; imaginative representations of Jesus of Nazareth, while relevant, are quite insufficient. We will return to this requirement.

II

We have been impelled more and more to mark and espouse the affinities of the comic and the cause of justice. In the presence of a God who means to be secular, we remember that the divine is justice, justice is the divine. Injustice to females is high, perhaps highest, on the list of the Devil's preferential options. With this state of affairs before us, an appropriate and much needed final source for reference and learning for this and the previous chapter is Nancy A. Walker's *A Very Serious Thing: Women's Humor and American Culture,*[32] already a classic in its field. I particularly have in mind the lessons Professor Walker's study teaches respecting a paradox: the happy opportunities and the sad limitations of humor.

For over 150 years American women have been writing and acting out humor in ways that deliciously violate and destroy something "everybody knows": A sense of humor is simply absent in woman. The American humorous tradition has been thought—even by females—to have been and even to remain the preserve of males (primarily white males, and very often with women as their butt); the half has been taken for the whole. The great tradition of American women's humor "has been effectively submerged or hidden." The only anthologies of that humor have been prepared by women. A dominant theme of women's humor is "how it feels to be a member of a subordinate group" in a culture that boasts of equality but from which one is estranged and "what it is like to try to meet standards for behavior that are based on stereotypes rather than on human beings." But an equally important theme in female humor is woman's unabating claim to autonomy and power. To be a woman and a humorist is not alone serious business; it is also dangerous business. It means confronting and subverting "the very power that keeps women powerless, and at the same time [a risk of] alienating those upon whom women are dependent for economic survival." For, whether it is "viewed from the perspective of psychology, anthropology, sociology, or linguistics [we may add theology and philosophy—A.R.E.], humor is tied to power, autonomy, and aggression in ways that directly affect gender relationships. In general, women's humor "reinforces our emerging realization of the extent of women's essential powerlessness over time and, simultaneously, belies the assumptions of nonintellectuality and essential passivity that have been used to justify women's subordinate status."[33]

In her essay on "Humor, Intellect, and Femininity," Walker shows how the issue of women's sense of humor is "part of a complex web of cultural assumptions about women's intelligence, competence, and 'proper role.' .... The 'lady' and the 'real girl' are not funny; at best, they appreciate the humor of the male.... Whether in the form of overt satire or in more subversive ways, women have laughed at the accusation that they are 'witless,' and through that laughter have spoken to each other about the absurdity of their common dilemma." A further essay on "The Humor of the 'Minority'" dwells upon similarities and differences between women's experience and that of other minorities. Women's humor exhibits a strong sense of shared oppression together with an indictment of "the values of a culture that trivializes her life."[34]

Walker is careful to distinguish *women's humor* from *feminist humor,* though she points out that the latter is highly significant within the former. Feminist humor takes two forms, of subtly challenging stereotypes and other evils and of explicitly challenging sources of discrimination, subordination, and oppression. Lesbian humor is singled out for its power to help women "define themselves *for* themselves rather than being defined by men or their relationships with men." We are offered the impression that lesbian humor is able to break out of subservience to men more effectively than is feminist humor, and even more so with respect to women's humor as such.[35]

I want to give you as many of Professor Walker's own words as I can. She concludes:

> Reformulating the canon of American humorous literature so that it represents both male and female humor would compel us to acknowledge that the American humorous tradition, and therefore some important aspects of American culture itself, arises from at least two central conflicts that have heretofore been considered peripheral: the conflict between genders and the conflict between public and private spheres of experience.... As long as humor was considered a male-defined activity, and male humor identical with American humor, such issues as female economic dependence, child-raising practices, and the effects of technology on housekeeping—all of which are basic to social attitudes and values—were denied their centrality in the American social fabric.

> For Louis D. Rubin, as for many others, the "approved American mode of humor" is "that in which cultural and social pretension are made to appear ridiculous and artificial." The humorist, this suggests, prefers the ordinary to the elaborate, the commonplace to the celebrated. Yet ironically, it is precisely the commonplace, the routine, and the ordinary that women's humor has depicted, at least until recently, rather than the formal, official transaction. But because it has done so, it has been seen as reflecting the experience of a private minority rather than dealing with fundamental conflicts that are reflected in the public sphere: male dominance over women in the domestic setting mirrors the submerging of the individual by bureaucratic hierarchies of all sorts; the struggle to achieve ideal performance in an assigned role characterizes not only women's experience, but also that of every group of immigrants that has sought acceptance and assimilation into the mainstream of American life.

> Perhaps most important, women's humor challenges the basic assumptions about women that have justified their public and private subordination. Instead of passive, emotional beings, women in their humorous writing show themselves to be assertive and insightful, alert to the absurdities that affect not only their lives but the values of American culture in a larger sense. The tradition of women's humor is a record of women's conscious denial of inferiority and subordination and a testament to their spirit of survival in a sexist culture.[36]

How may we respond to such an accounting?

The Devil is very clever. He invades, manipulates, and corrupts the beauties of life as much, or more, than anything else. What more demonic a thrust could there be than the ideology that only males can do humor, that females are without humor! But the Devil does not stop there. A more ultimate level of devilishness is to fabricate as the primary female function the reformation of the male.[37] Here is sexism in most diabolic form, for it very convincingly obscures behind a good cause the treatment of the female as means rather than as end. The Devil always goes to the party dressed in the gorgeous robes of good intentions.

But the Devil is not all that clever. Feminist humor's power to reveal "the fundamental absurdity of one gender oppressing the other"[38] makes the Devil look sick. When put to use by those who are oppressed—not alone women but blacks, Native Americans, et al.—humor is an effective social weapon in exposing the Devil and his praxis, a male-imperialist and male-dominated culture: Men have special ways of being creeps. On the other hand, the sexist story of American humor, together with its historiography, helps teach us that humor as such is no messiah. Paradoxically, the Devil teaches us not to idealize the world of humor. He teaches us to stay on watch for those who fantasize a soteriological role for human comedy/humor/laughter. For any genuine messiah we have to look, in blessed moments, to God, though it appears that we also want to look, in perverse moments, to the Devil. This forces the question: Who will deliver the goods?

It is time to gather together certain things we have learned upon the long and rocky road to an authentic comic vision, also to go beyond that learning, for the sake of a constructively Christian comic vision, a post-theodicy of the practical reason and a contribution to postmodern thinking.

Notes

1. Henry A. Murray, *Explorations in Psychology: Selections from the Personology of Henry A. Murray* (New York: Harper & Row, 1981), p. 613.
2. Any more, perhaps, than Martin Luther himself would have done, had he been born much later—at least on Heiko Oberman's speculation ("Luther Today: A Test," *Luther* [New York: Doubleday Image Books, 1992], pp. 313–14).
3. Consult the Cox review of Richard Wightman Fox's book, *Reinhold Niebuhr: A Biography,* in the *New York Times Book Review,* 5 Jan. 1986, p. 24.
4. Harvey Cox, *Religion in the Secular City* (New York: Simon and Schuster, 1984), pp. 82, 183.
5. Such is, indeed, the title of Chap. 16 of *Religion in the Secular City.*
6. In *The Feast of Fools* Cox affirms the dual Christian teaching of the goodness but fallenness of the world (Cambridge, Mass.: Harvard University Press, 1969, p. 42). Cf. his comments about the "principalities and powers" of the New Testament, also on Jesus as exorcist, in *The Secular City,* rev. ed. (New York: Macmillan, 1966), pp. 110–12, 130.
7. Ibid., p. 20. It is interesting to note the historical fate of such identities as the serpent of the Garden of Eden. For premodern Christianity the serpent is the serpent; for Reinhold Niebuhr the serpent is to be handled as a symbol; for Harvey Cox the serpent is quaint.

8. Cox, *Religion,* pp. 181-89, 219; Cox, *Secular City,* p. 130. Cox places "the demons" under "sociocultural neurosis." Exorcism means scraping "the stubborn deposits of town and tribal pasts" from the social consciousness and freeing people to face the world "matter of factly." (Ibid., pp. 132-36). An implication here seems to be that to make the Devil something supernatural would deflect attention from the very real demons that afflict contemporary social and cultural life— to name two examples, the might of possessors of inordinate power and the antisexual enterprise of *Playboy.* See *The Secular City,* Chap. 8—"Work and Play in the Secular City," and Chap. 9—"Sex and Secularization."

9. Cox, *Religion,* p. 209. "The devil may be a modernist, but the entire modern world is not of the devil" (p. 219).

10. Ibid., p. 204.

11. Ibid., Part Two—"How Shall They Possess the Earth? The Radical Critique of Modern Theology." See also A. Roy Eckardt, *For Righteousness' Sake* (Bloomington, Ind.: Indiana University Press, 1987), pp. 199-223.

12. Cox, *Religion,* pp. 98-101, 138.

13. Ibid., pp. 260, 263. See also pp. 243-61 passim, referring to Our Lady of Guadalupe. Chap. 21 is entitled "Carnival Faith in People's Religion and Postmodern Theology."

14. Gustavo Gutiérrez, "La Fuerza Historica de los Pobres" [The power of the poor in history], cited in Cox, *Religion,* p. 107. See the larger selected writings of Gutiérrez, *The Power of the Poor in History* (Maryknoll, N.Y.: Orbis Books, 1983).

15. Cox, *Religion,* p. 249.

16. For our purposes, a full exposition or appraisal of Harvey Cox's influential work of 1965 and 1966, *The Secular City,* is not needful. Much in that work is preparatory for his later books, while his later books help provide a balance to *The Secular City.* For Cox, secularization—*not* secularism but "the liberation of man from religious and metaphysical tutelage" (*Secular City,* pp. 15, 18)—is a morally right outcome of biblical faith. Secularization entails the disenchantment of nature, the desacralization of politics, and the deconsecration of values (Chap. 1). Cox affirms the biblical understanding of God and of humankind as God's partner (p. 72).

17. Cox, *Feast of Fools,* pp. vii, viii, 3, 7, 8, and 22.

18. Ibid., pp. 17, 25, 46, 59, and 62.

19. Ibid., p. 131.

20. Ibid., p. 23.

21. Ibid., p. 133. Under the heading of radical theology, Cox speaks of Thomas J. J. Altizer and Richard Rubenstein; under the theology of hope he speaks of Jürgen Moltmann and Johannes Baptist Metz. See also the appendix to *The Feast,* "Some Relevant Theological Currents."

22. Ibid., pp. 139, 140 (italics added).

23. Ibid., pp. 140-42 (italics added).

24. Ibid., p. 144.

25. Ibid., p. 145; Hugo Rahner, *Man at Play* (New York: Herder and Herder, 1967), p. 65, as quoted in Cox, *Feast,* pp. 146-47.

26. Ibid., pp. 153, 157, 162.

27. Ibid., pp. 79-80, 124; Cox, *Religion,* p. 234. See the latter source, pp. 234-36— "The Postmodern Christ: A Convergence of Theologies?" In this frame of reference we have to keep before us an essential distinction between *Historie,* centering

in "controlled, objective facts of historiography," and *Geschichte,* "a paradigm, above the historical; attached to history but by no means limited by it." (Zev Garber, review of Sidra DeKoven Ezrahi, *By Words Alone,* in *Religious Education* 76 [1981]: 226).

28. Cox, *Religion,* p. 234.

29. Ibid.

30. Cox, *Feast,* p. 80. In *The Secular City* Cox has Jesus coming to people primarily through social change (p. 128).

31. See A. Roy Eckardt, *Reclaiming the Jesus of History* (Minneapolis: Fortress Press, 1992).

32. Nancy A. Walker, *A Very Serious Thing: Women's Humor and American Culture* (Minneapolis: University of Minnesota Press, 1988).

33. Ibid., pp. ix-x, 4, 8-9, 11, 13-14, 22, 30, 44, 120, and 169-70.

34. Ibid., pp. 98-9, 119, 125.

35. Ibid., pp. 13, 152, 160. For more on lesbian humor, see pp. 160-63, 180.

36. Ibid., pp. 182-83.

37. Such was, I regret to report, the persuasion of Mark Twain. See Mary Ellen Goad,"The Image and the Woman in the Life and Writings of Mark Twain," *Emporia State Research Studies* vol. 19, no. 3 (1971): 5. I am indebted to Nancy A. Walker for this reference.

38. Walker, *Very Serious Thing,* p. 163.

8

A Stop Along the Road to Hear Three Jokes: Comedy and the *Campesino*

> *It happened that a fire broke out in a theater. The clown came out to inform the public. They thought it was a jest and applauded. He repeated his warning, they shouted even louder. So I think the world will come to an end amid general applause from all the wits, who believe that it is a joke.*
> —*Søren Kierkegaard[1]*
>
> *Compassion is that power which survives to resist tragic suffering.*
> —*Wendy Farley[2]*
>
> *Hope has two beautiful daughters. Their names are anger and courage; anger at the way things are, and courage to see that they do not remain the way they are.*
>
> —*Augustine[3]*

In this chapter, I wish to explore (and to bring to conclusion in the next chapter) a vision—remember, we are only doing metaphysical poetry—that has nobody but me to blame.[4] The vision benefits from the virtues and faults of the views we have reported and assessed, but it moves in added directions. I offer the rudiments of a trialectic of God/ Devil/Comedy, employing the third of our three variables as the primary working tool. The practical reason keeps plugging away. It may be useful to recall Henri Bergson's finding that a comic situation arises if it belongs at once to two series of events that are independent of each other, and if it is capable of being assigned two entirely different meanings simultaneously.[5] Yet surely, human reactions to the incongruous, the contradictory, and the absurd vary greatly. As one who stands upon the threshold of being a geriatric case—well, maybe not quite that—I am more and more leaning toward risibility, a comic treatment of the absurd, a celebration of the absurd almost in spite of itself.

I

Blameworthiness for radical evil and radical suffering[6] is carried ultimately, if not proximately, by God. God is the first and final sinner. We are the subjects of *thrownness,* consequent upon God's evident decision to make a world.

Such judgments can be tendered only by the religious believer; humanists and atheists can rest content, if it does manage to content them, with human beings and/or natural forces as exclusive culprits for all the world's ills. The question of evil is thus viewed quite differently within a nontheological frame of reference. The theological view can be said to take evil much more seriously and poignantly than do humanist or atheist representations, since nothing could be more serious or poignant than associating evil with God.

If there is to be any reconciliation between God's culpability and God's goodness, it has to come from beyond theodicy. Only from a dimension beyond argument could the Enemy ever be enabled to emerge as Friend, only under the aegis of the divine praxis, word-become-action. Otherwise we are left in our anguish. Promises are of no avail. The eventuality of divine action enters in whether we speak of Judaism, Christianity, or Islam. Expressions of redemption in such traditions as these are made possible by, and thereby limited by, the language of events, historical events, and the dimension of history.

How do history, faith, and comedy relate to one another? Alternately put: How, if at all, is the Absolute to break through into human life? Put yet a third way: What does God do, if God does anything, before the fact of incongruity in ultimate form? For that matter, what does the Devil do, if anything, before the fact of such incongruity? (Phenomenologically and morally speaking, any question we fabricate respecting God can be duplicated respecting the Devil.)

This chapter centers in my concept of Realized Incongruity, a form of incongruity-in-action that does battle with the absurdities of life, particularly those tied to radical evil and radical suffering.

Reinhold Niebuhr declares that it is impossible to resolve with the aid of humor the contradiction between divine mercy and divine judgment, because "the divine judgment is ultimate judgment."[7] We have cited Niebuhr's avowal that "to laugh at life in the ultimate sense means to scorn it." I should think that everything depends upon the object of the laughter. If "life in the ultimate sense" refers to the divine life, Niebuhr cannot be questioned. Ultimately to laugh at God is sacrilege. But if "life in the ultimate sense" extends to the life of the Devil, father of radical evil, the scorn that is present is suffused with goodness. Here is a further aspect to the quest to tell God from the Devil: There is unrightful scorn and there is rightful scorn.

I suggest that humor and faith contain, along with so many of life's dualities, e.g., freedom and fate, elements of a dialectical relation, with each side driving toward the opposite side. Humor and the comic dimension are incapable in themselves of any final victory over evil, suffering, and the many vicissitudes of life. But such challenges are met or lived with in and through some kind of faith—unless they are reacted to in and through despair. And among the byproducts of faith is a comic vision that can accept even life's incongruities under the rubric of a certain nonchalance, an accompaniment of grace. Within the Christian outlook, the comedy of God is, as we shall emphasize, capable of providing a certain Joy. By virtue of the grace of God, the Devil is laughed to scorn. The comic vision is fulfilled in the divine comedy.

Reinhold Niebuhr's claim has been cited that were we to continue to laugh after recognizing the depth of our evil and sin, our laughter would become an instrument of irresponsibility. Niebuhr is talking about human laughter; he does not sufficiently distinguish between humor as human and humor as divine. Is it or is it not the case that the test of the very legitimacy of God—in God's own eyes, not to mention ours— is righteousness? The ultimate judgment of God has to be tempered by humor; otherwise, it is God who becomes irresponsible. Humankind remains utterly blameless for its creation and as well for the devilishness of temptation. Thus are we entitled to turn to the phenomenon of the laughter of God—not the idea of laughter but laughter as God's act. The question can be posed concerning the moral indispensability of God's mercy—for which Niebuhr himself pleads—not only for our sake but for the sake of God's own integrity. We humans laugh *at* ourselves and *with* God; God is required to laugh *at* Godself and *with* us.

To Niebuhr, God's vicarious suffering, as reconciling mercy and judgment, is "far removed from laughter."[8] Even were we to agree that the same applies respecting the laughter of human beings, it is definitely not the case either with regard to the divine laughter or with regard to the suffering of human beings. Precisely because the divine judgment is ultimate, the divine mercy must be ultimate. For we never asked to be born! It is the norm of the divine righteousness itself that demands the comedy of God.

II

One means for exploring the relationship among history, faith, and comedy is to consider continuities and discontinuities between Jewishness and Christianness. (For parsimony's sake and as a special tribute to me as ignoramus, I omit Muslimness.)

"Tragedy knows of tears and of death alone; comedy knows not only of tears and death, but of song, dance, and resurrection. The Comic Vision is Sarah's; it ends in birth and it ends in laughter. 'And Sarah laughed' (Gen. 18:12)."[9]

We consider first whether there is a peculiarly Jewish comedy. Four interpreters are called upon.

1. In Lionel Blue's study, *To Heaven With Scribes and Pharisees,* we read that "the most typical weapon of Jewish spirituality is humor."[10] This is a piquant line, although later I assay to emend it. The rabbi's aphorism opens up intriguing, even delectable, questions, such as: Where does this leave *other* weapons of Jewish spirituality? Where does Blue's finding leave *Christian* spirituality? At a minimum the rabbi is reminding us that comedy is a uniquely and terribly serious business—much more vital (life-affirming, life-sustaining) than its twin, tragedy.
2. In *The Jewish Way,* his study of the Holidays, Irving Greenberg attests that "ultimately, laughter is a unique reflection of Judaism's conception of life and reality. One of the Torah's central, positive teachings is that there is no other God.[11] If one believes in the infinite One God, then everything else is relative. No other value source, no other power has the right to claim absolute status.... The presumptuousness of the demand for absolute loyalty on the part of human systems is best undermined by mockery and laughter, which puncture pretensions without giving weight to the pretender."[12] The parents of comedy are nonabsoluteness and the struggle against idolatry.

    Greenberg's rendering of Jewish humor centers upon the "quintessential Jewish holiday" of Purim, with its unmatched "fun and games, masquerade and mummers, drinking, partying, and gift-giving." The rabbis speak of Esther as "the book of the hiding God. God's name is not mentioned; the redemption is brought about by flawed human effort. As one scholar [Elliot Yagod] put it, 'Wear masks, get drunk, for meaning is hidden beneath the visible.'"[13]

> The celebration of Purim grows out of a wise acceptance of vulnerability.... Health, success, children can be snatched away overnight. The sweetness of life should be savored today, for that is all one really has for sure.... [Purim's] dialectical resolution of the tension between dream and reality is to celebrate the victory while poking fun at it.... The way to deal with reversals is to *play* with them; humor can be the key to sanity. It is the only healthy way to combine affirmation with ongoing doubt....

> ...[The] tradition satirizes its own pretensions, affirming yet recognizing the contradictions to its own fundamentals....

> ...If people insist on having extraterrestrial redeemers, they will perceive themselves as living in a world abandoned by God, when in fact God is the Divine Redeeming Presence encountered in the partial, flawed actions of humans. The truth of this salvation eludes both those who explain everything away as coincidence or random occurrence and those who insist on 'out of this world' revelation....

> ...Humor expresses transcendence of unredeemed reality, and it takes sanctity itself with a sense of limits.... The unchecked tendency to respect religion all too often leads to deifying the ritual and the outward form of God.

> ...One can only respond with laughter and mockery and put-on, satirizing God and the bitter joke this world threatens to become.... But as the hilarity reaches its climax, Jews move beyond bitterness to humor.... Through the humor, Jews project themselves into future redeemed reality that transcends the moment. Thus, hope is kept alive and the Messiah remains possible....

> Purim is the balance to Passover; it is the humor that admits that the Shabbat is still a dream. To act as if Shabbat and the final redemption are fact would be insane; but not to affirm the totality of hope would be a sellout. Purim offers an alternative humorous affirmation. Thus, Purim's laughter preserves integrity and sanity together. This is Purim's remarkable role in Jewish history.[14]

One Talmudic midrash "tells us that in Messianic times, all the holidays will pass. Purim alone will endure and be celebrated (Talmud Yerushalmi Megillah 1:5)." We may comment that there could never be a Purim celebration of the Devil, because the Devil takes life too seriously and is thereby prohibited from joining in the fun.

There follows, in summary form, Irving Greenberg's viewpoint upon the foundation of Jewish humor. "In poking fun, we affirm the presence of contradiction. We speak with ultimate seriousness, but with a tentativeness that admits the alternatives. It is the way we testify in a world that appears to contradict our hope."[15]

3. I turn to two elements within the thinking of Emil L. Fackenheim that are pertinent to the comic vision. (1) The initial entry in Michael Morgan's collection of Fackenheim's writings is the older but prevenient essay,"Our Position Toward Halacha" (1938). Once Halacha, Commandment, is accepted as representative of the Absolute, the truth is equally clear that "Halacha confronts the [Jew] of today as a system with fixed content, with commandments that contain small, infinitely detailed minutiae that, vis-à-vis no less than Divinity, must necessarily appear as a totally incongruous *Kleinigkeitskrämerei* (pettifoggery)."[16]

Apart from the clear connection between humor and lengthy German words, we note *incongruous* as the most jussive term here, for does not the soul of comedy live (at least when theologically construed) amidst a dialectical incongruity between the Absolute (Nonpettifoggeriness, as we may put it with a little smile) and the "minutiae" of our very small planet? Thus is the (unbelievable?) point to be made that, in principle, the Absolute will "break through" into human life under the aegis of "totally incongruous" triflings—or *seeming* triflings.

From this perspective, we may be impressed anew with the force of Rabbi Blue's aphorism: "the most typical weapon of Jewish spirituality is humor."

(2) In his much more recent study *What Is Judaism?* (1987), Professor Fackenheim alludes to a Talmudic ambiguity upon the hiding of God. "Does [God] hide in wrath against or punishment of, His people? God forbid that He should do so at such a time [as ours]! Does He hide for reasons unknown? God forbid that He should, in this of all times, be a *deus absconditus*! Then why does He hide?" It is his weeping that he hides. "He hides His weeping in the inner chamber, for just as God is infinite so *His pain is infinite, and this, were it to touch the world would destroy it.... God so loved the world that He hid the infinity of His pain from it lest it be destroyed...*"[17]

If, as we note in Chapter 6, the laughter of God in the Psalms is a laughter of derision, it makes moral sense to indicate weeping as the fitting human response. But insofar as God Godself engages in the act of weeping, insofar as the pettifoggery of tears becomes the Way of the Absolute, in embodiment of the divine love, then is the human response reversed. Laughter bursts into laughter.

4. Mark Shechner addresses directly the question of the nature of Jewish humor, but strictly within the American milieu. (I submit that reflection upon Jewish humor in its relation to American culture ought to begin with a singular datum: While Jews constitute only 2.7% of the population

of the United States, yet no less than 80% of all people at work in various aspects of the comic enterprise are Jewish. [Comment by the Devil, Chief Antisemite: "Everybody knows, stupid, that the Jews control all our entertainment."])

Professor Shechner proposes the paradoxical phrase "ghetto cosmopolitanism," which describes a condition that "arose out of the striking conjunctions of oppression and spirituality in the ghettos and *shtetls* of Ashkenazic Jewry." The ghetto cosmopolitan "combines a parochialism bred of poverty and confinement with a universal consciousness bred of study and intellectual ambition. In him, vulgarity and sensibility go hand in hand; his coarseness of manner is not inconsistent with a high degree of intellectual and aesthetic discrimination."

In and through the concept of ghetto cosmopolitanism we are aided in apprehending the two worlds that combine to educe Jewish comedy: an exalted (transcending), spiritual world, blessed as it is with its very own language of Hebrew, and a lowly (immanent) world of ordinariness, also blessed with a language of its own: Yiddish. Professor Shechner observes that "a mind nurtured upon a higher and a lower language" is "accustomed to shuffling between the transcendent and the worldly and defining its relationship to reality in terms of the ironies generated by such travel."[18]

As I have written elsewhere:

Instances of humor that live upon the unique incongruities generated by the two worlds of Jewry are legion. Mrs. Fishbein answers the telephone to hear a cultured voice, "Can you and your husband come to a tea for Lady Windemere?" Mrs. Fishbein breaks in, "Oy, have *you* got a wrong number!" Dahn Ben-Amotz asks, "What if the people of Israel hadn't been elected the Chosen People?," and replies, "Some other people would have got it in the neck." An elderly Jewish lady art collector is apprised of a chance to secure another Picasso. She responds, "With Picassos I'm up to my ass already." And Woody Allen can agree that there is an intelligence to the universe all right—save for "certain parts of New Jersey." As Shechner points out, it was the "juxtaposition of higher and lower worlds within the mental economy of the Jewish people that established the terms for a *comedy of deflation,* whose basic trope was a sudden thrusting downward from the exalted to the workaday. From Sholom Aleichem to Woody Allen, this comedy of internal juxtaposition has been fundamental."[19]

In another source Mark Shechner verifies the relation between Jewish comedy and the religion of Judaism: Comedy is Judaism's "inversion, its negative, its shadow. The reversal of figure and ground. Where both comedy and religion acknowledge the interdependence of two worlds, a higher and a lower, each gives primacy to a different world. Religion...translates upwards, while comedy undercuts the transcendent, criticizes it, subordinates it to the common. The one, in effect, Hebraizes, the other Yiddishizes."[20]

To review the identity of the two Jewish worlds: We have respectively, via Irving Greenberg's conceptualization, the infinite One God vis-à-vis the realm of relativity and vulnerability, and under Emil Fackenheim's conceptualization and respectively, the Absolute vis-à-vis minutiae. Jewish comedy/humor is actualized in and through the tension between God/Absoluteness and relativity/pettifoggery.

Wherein lies the integrity of the bond between the Absolute and comedy as such? What is it that enables the comic vision to sustain itself—or, better, to be sustained by resources beyond itself, contra, say, a tragic vision?

I cite Emil L. Fackenheim's application of the "commanding Presence"—his morphology of human freedom—in *God's Presence in History*: "As *sole* Power, the divine commanding Presence *destroys* human freedom; as *gracious* Power, it *restores* that freedom, and indeed *exalts* it, for human freedom is made part of a covenant with Divinity itself. And the human astonishment, which is *terror* at a Presence at once divine and commanding, turns into a *second* astonishment, which is *joy*, at a Grace which restores and exalts human freedom by its commanding Presence."[21]

Human freedom is here apprehended as neither autonomous (master of its fate, captain of its soul) nor heteronomous (subject to dictates alien to itself),[22] but as, ideally, theonomous (consonant with the proper thrust of the *imago dei*). And we can then be grasped by the "second astonishment": Joy, *verbum ipsissimum* for, the *essentia* of, comedy/humor/laughter.

Jewish thinking and experience have, of course, always been cognizant of tragic elements within the human world. We are reminded, for instance, that the very ground of Sholom Aleichem's humor was the persuasion that "the prevailing social conditions oppressed and crippled...[the Jew] until he became not only miserable but ridiculous."[23] Nevertheless, Jewry never allows ultimacy to tragedy. For within the *Weltanschauung* of tragedy, human structures (also divine structures) must fall prey to an impersonal, remorseless Fate (*moira*), which boasts as well the power of inexorable suffering and the power of Nemesis, retribution. It is no accident that Judaism and the Jewish heritage forever refuse to exalt the "tragic hero." Again, Sigmund Freud was being a good Jew in testifying that in view of its repudiation of suffering, humor must be numbered among the great and historic foes of the human compulsion to suffer. In humor is found a nonvindictive liberation from the wounds of life.[24] The eventuality of Jewishness ever remains the eventuality of comedy, never of tragedy. Against the entire dimension of Fate, the Jewish ethos is affirming an open present and an open future. It is often said that Jews are a most historical people. To turn Jewish life into tears alone would be to subject that life to Fate. (It is possible to argue, although I do not pursue the matter here, that a central reason for the gradual eclipse of the Devil in the development of Judaism and Jewish life is the triumph of freedom over Fate.) Even the fatefulness of German Nazi demonry was to be overpowered. And since that evil time, the act of perpetual remembering (*zachor*) carries forward the struggle. In tragedy, things must be what they have been, are, and will be; in comedy, the future explodes into openness, into the spontaneity of play and dance. In Frederick Buechner's aphorism (from the Christian side), the tragic is the inevitable, the comic is the unforseeable. But Buechner goes even farther and suspects that from the divine perspective, "it is the tragic that is seen as not inevitable whereas it is the comic that is bound to happen."[25] (I may insert that the "freedom" of the Devil and his minions is held prisoner to tragedy or necessity, the fate of having to do radical evil.) Where there is hope there is comedy; where there is comedy there is hope. As Peter Berger writes, while tragedy may imbue a sense of human courage, only comedy can foster a sense of hope.[26]

The opportunity ever remains of choice, of decision. Humanness is freedom; freedom is humanness. Freedom means: responsibility (obligation *and* culpability), creativity, a transcending response to incongruity, life as in the end eligible for redemption, for final wholeness. Correspondingly, as Sharon Weinstein observes, Jewish humor embodies "a prevailing optimism that this too, no matter how horrible, shall pass, and that Jews as a people will endure."[27]

III

We come to the eventuality of peculiarly Christian comedy/humor/laughter.

The Jewish teaching upon the *Anknüpfungspunkt* (meetingplace, point of confrontation) of history and the transhistorical, of immanence and transcendence, is embodied in the "giving of the Torah," the major Jewish event of Realized Incongruity, the divine implementation of, or action upon, incongruity as such, a cosmic, deliberate juxtaposing of categories.[28] The Torah makes for joy: "The law [teaching] of the Lord" is Israel's delight (Ps. 1:2).

Christian comedy, never in violation of the Jewish envisionment, keeps that affirmation going under the aegis of additional, crucial, and unique historical events. Continuity is thereby shown, yet also discontinuity, between Jewish comedy and Christian comedy. In and through divine acts of Realized Incongruity, the dimension of incongruity is fully recognized but is then pitted against itself, thus making possible the way to laughter and joy.

Christian humor is grounded, of course, in the two-world symbiosis of Jewishness. This is exemplified in the church's appropriation of Torah as "Word of God." However, while in the Christian comedy the transcendent is subordinated to the common all right, nevertheless and by way of contrast, it is faith itself that "translates" downwards. This difference obtains because of the essential fact that while Jewishness is comprised of the dual elements of religion and people (*laos*),[29] Christianness is limited to a faith. Out of its *continuity* with Jewishness, the church has kept viable the higher and lower worlds that compound into the distinctiveness of Jewish comedy. But out of its *discontinuity* with Jewishness, and while attesting to *some* kind of comedy of deflation, the church has yet seen fit to alter the juxtaposition into a translation downwards that, although it does not undercut the transcendent, does radically transform it. In the Christian schema, the ordinary is peculiarly assimilated to sacredness, to the story of salvation (*Heilsgeschichte*)—or, more carefully, certain selected elements of the ordinary are thus assimilated (since Judaism too assimilates the ordinary to sacredness). In a word, Christian comedy could never be embodied in the Marx brothers, whereas Jewish humor could.

Quite expectably, therefore, Jewish comedy can be primarily and properly directed toward secularity while Christian comedy is perforce thrust toward religious faith. (That the Feast of Purim is not free of religious elements, or at least of religious application, reminds us that the differentiation here is relative in character, a matter of emphasis, though of a distinctive and noteworthy sort.) More precisely, the Christian community has taken onto itself, or has been assigned, the propagating of no less than three Basic Incongruities. That is to say, in and through three claimed events—Incarnation, Crucifixion, Resurrection—the transcendent is linked redemptively to the immanent.

Professor Shechner points out that within the Jewish outlook, "religion translates upwards," whereas comedy subordinates the transcendent "to the common." Christians are enabled to lift out this latter subordination and utilize it to confess, in some contrast to Judaism, that *in essence* the Christian faith is in and of itself, *kiveyachol,* a uniquely unique (=transcendingly unique) Joke.

The sentence just above requires at least two midrashim before we proceed further. (1) I call attention to Heinz Moshe Graupe's identification of the Hebrew term *kiveyachol,* as just used. The concept is an appropriate one in Hebrew literature to convey religious content "that almost seems blasphemous." It is variously translated as "so to speak," "as if it were possible," and "as one might be allowed to say."[30] I should want to tie this conceptualization substantively and decisively to my relating of *myth* and *the comic* near the beginning of this book, both of which are, as was said, alternate ways of reckoning with the dialectic of transcendence/immanence, ways that try to mediate between the mystery of fact and the mystery of interpretation. The concept *kiveyachol* serves to do the same thing, if in modest and simple syntactical fashion.

(2) The word "Joke," used to signify one or another basic Christian event, may sound offensive or demeaning to some readers, whereas the phrases "Christian comedy" and "divine comedy" probably do not. There is etymological support for such a negative reaction. *The Oxford Universal Dictionary* defines "joke" as "something said or done to excite laughter or amusement," and then adds: "a ridiculous circumstance." "Ridiculous" is defined as "exciting ridicule or derisive laughter; absurd, preposterous, comical, laughable"; also, a second meaning is "outrageous." I certainly do not mean "Joke" in such superficial or even trivial ways. Christian sacred acts or events are far from being amusing. The constructive purpose of the expression "Christian Jokes"—"Joke" and "Jokes" must always be capitalized, otherwise the point is lost before we have started—is threefold: (a) The usage points up the objectively incongruous character of the events involved (as Christian doctrine has always acknowledged and insisted upon). (b) More crucially, the usage accentuates the *active* quality of the Christian mysteries. To joke is to *do* something, whereas "to be comical" is to remain in a state or condition. According to the Christian *Anschauung,* God *acts* to be incarnate, God *acts* in the death of the Crucifixion, God *acts* in the Resurrection of Jesus Christ—just as God *acts* in the giving of Torah. The Christian comedy is a set of *doings* (in direct opposition to such philosophical

speculation as tries to "think God's thoughts after" God). (c) All in all, a Christian Joke, an act of Realized Incongruity, is a most serious business. The Joke is not simply a joke. Yet the pure comedy of "jokes" is itself far removed from triviality. Our stand-up and sit-down performers are telling the truth about themselves, and us, and life. Humor worth its salt is always a moral creation, with moral lessons to teach. To repeat a marvelous line from Carl Reiner, a most elegant comic, "The funniest joke of all is the absolute truth stated simply and gracefully." The world of "jokes" and the world of "Joke" are bound together. The world of "jokes" is the world of God's creation; the world of "Jokes" is a pointer toward redemption. In a word: "Christian Joke" is a means of communicating with a secularized culture that is considerably devoted to comedy.

We must, accordingly, keep in mind the essential dichotomy, referred to above, of Jewishness as entailing a *laos* (people) and Christianness as delimiting itself to a faith. As we have noted, Jewish comedy arises out of the juxtaposing of spirituality and ordinariness, God and relativity, the Absolute and pettifoggery. This is where the Jewish view locates the incongruity that is the ground of its humor. Thus is there a formidable difficulty in identifying Judaism (as a faith) under the rubric of Joke (Essential Incongruity). In the general frame of reference of Jewishness (a context broader than Judaism as such), we have a comedy of deflation: the humor is directed downward, "a sudden thrusting downward from the exalted to the workaday." All this suggests that Rabbi Blue's aphorism, "the most typical weapon of Jewish spirituality is humor," might better read, "the most typical weapon of the Jewish *double world* is humor"—whereas, in contrast, the most typical weapon of *Christian spirituality* is seen to be, *kiveyachol*: a Joke. For, on the Christian side, it is the faith itself that is so much more the Joke, because now the juxtaposition of spirituality and ordinariness is channeled and remains wholly inside that faith. Now, as previously indicated, it is the faith itself that "translates" downwards. In consequence, the faith itself remains at the center of the comedy. Christian comedy is, in essence, religious comedy. Nothing less than the domain of the transcendent is transformed in the process.

We are a little more prepared now to epitomize the Christology of comedy, deriving as that Christology does from three Jokes:

1.   *The Birth.* God hides Godself and lives singularly in *this* baby (John 1:14; 3:16).

This affirmation is not incongruent with the persuasion that God hides Godself in Torah, the holy in the profane, a *kenosis* (emptying) of Eternity into Time (cf. the Zen Buddhist teaching of *Sunyata*, emptiness).[31] While it is often insisted upon that Judaism and Christianity are wholly disparate when it comes to the teaching of incarnation, the truth is that the disjunction is not total and may not even be essential. Here are three citations from Jewish scholars. Lional Blue declares: "God has no human form in Jewish theology but He reveals a very human psyche in Jewish jokes. There He enters into the suffering and paradoxes of the world, and experiences the human condition. There He is immanent, if not incarnate, and a gossamer bridge of laughter stretches over the void, linking creatures of flesh and blood to the endlessness of the *Ein Sof*, and the paralysing power of the Lord of hosts."[32] Norman Lamm writes: "God is especially immanent in Torah, and the study of Torah is therefore a means of achieving an encounter with the divine presence.... Torah, as such, is far more than a document of the divine legislation; it is in itself, mystically, an aspect of God."[33] And Michael Wyschogrod states: If man "is to have a relation to Hashem [The Name]...then Hashem must be near man wherever he is. And not only near man but in man, or more specifically, in the people of Israel."[34]

Judaism does not, of course, accept *this* Incarnation, the Christian one.

2.   *The Life and the Death.* In the clown, everything seems a jest.[35] But in the *campesino* Jesus, there can be authentic Christian comedy. For it is *el dios pobre* who, in and through the *campesino*, goes to every length to embody the divine compassion and the divine forgiveness. Here is found the Joy of the Incarnation. The *campesino* is one with *el dios pobre* (John 10:30). And the *campesino* will lay down his life for the sheep, including the many sheep that "do not belong to this fold" (John 10:15–16). Christian comedy is triadic. It is the comedy of *el campesino nazareno*, of *el dios pobre*, but also of *Nuestra Señora de Guadalupe*, of these who suffer yet laugh, laugh yet suffer. *"The Christian God had hands laid upon him."*[36]

A final laugh (judgment) upon the antisemite, Christian and other, is that the incarnational Joke, the Joke of the Cross, should consist of the minutia of a poor Jewish woodworker from the lowly town of Nazareth.[37]

Christianity is able to manifest a certain foolishness that does not obtain on the Jewish side. True, the discontinuity is not total. For when Paul declares that the message of the cross is foolishness, he can readily cite the prophet Isaiah, "I will destroy the wisdom of the wise" (Isa. 29:14; I Cor. 1:18–19). Yet the cross remains not only "foolishness to Gentiles" but "a stumbling block to Jews"—the latter with very good justification: Jesus as alleged Messiah failed to realize the hope that links Messiah to objective peaceableness and justice in the world. By contrast, it was the cross that led Paul to discern, with joyousness, that his God of Israel is at once a fool and a weakling: "God's foolishness is wiser than human wisdom, and God's weakness is stronger than human strength" (I Cor. 1:25).

However, we must go back for a moment to the concept of *kenosis*. In *Religion in the Secular City* Harvey Cox agrees that Christ "gives up the power and privilege associated with deity and becomes poor in order to reveal the love of God." But Cox alerts us to a danger in that teaching as stressed among today's liberation thinkers, especially by women theologians "aware of the subtle forms of domination that persist in many time-honored ideas." The danger is the perpetuating of "a concept of condescension in which all the inherent dignity is on the divine side and none on the human side. God stoops to the essentially worthless human condition to bring salvation; but the idea of an inherent human powerlessness and dependency remains." Women theologians are rightly insisting "that what they and other dominated peoples need to hear are not further assurances that deliverance will come from an outside source; rather, they need to hear that God can strengthen and undergird their own struggle, that they are not devoid of power or potential—as the sexist culture tells them they are—but are capable of standing up. God is not the St. George who saves the hapless maiden by slaying the dragon, but the One who supports and inspires her to slay it herself." Further, as far as Jesus is concerned, his choice "was not to lower himself to an inferior station but to become a defender and representative of people with whom he already had close ties."[38]

The powerful and the powerful interests are ever and again on the lookout to utilize ideological fabrications to keep the powerless and downtrodden "in their place." Divine *kenosis* is an earnest sign of redemption all right, but human *kenosis* can easily compound and prolong oppression. To bring together theological affirmation and moral insistence: Forgiveness never forgets that wrongness is not good. On the contrary, acts of forgiveness only point up sin in the starkness of its evil. But then these acts go beyond and against evil by judging judgment through the power of mercy. Thus is evil put to shame, and the door is opened to freedom and comedy.

3. *The Resurrection.*[39] In the presence of death, human comedy is powerless. It dies, along with everything else.[40] But what of the Comedy of God?

Is God Enemy or is God Friend? It is told that once upon a time, the *campesino* was taken out of death, *este campesino, this* peasant. Some of us still believe that, somehow, *el dios pobre* was there, and indeed brought the whole thing off. (It seems, *kiveyachol,* that God couldn't stop laughing, and this turned out to be something of a drag. This explains why things were delayed for nigh on to three whole days. But we humans can sympathize here; once in a while we too have a spell where we just can't stop laughing, try as we might.)

To return to a statement I have submitted more than once: We never did ask to be born. Neither do we now ask to be subjected to Death, the final insult and final evil vis-à-vis Life. William Hazlitt calls it, fittingly, the "ugly Customer." The responsibility, at both places, our birth and our death, has, ultimately speaking, nothing to do with us. It lies wholly elsewhere. To many persons, here is grievous cause for pessimism, for emptiness, for despair, indeed for the hatred of God, even for a kind of avenging flirtation with the Devil. Yet to others, the door stays open, if only barely ajar, to a salvation wrought by God, perhaps as recompense, in a dominant respect, for our travail in the life we did not seek and for the specter of death we find so difficult to endure.

One means that righteousness utilizes in order to vindicate God (Isa. 5:16) is the resurrection. Here is "theodicy" wholly beyond theodicy. In this Friend, friendship comes to completion and to rest. And here is how, at an ultimate level of reckoning, we tell God from the Devil. In other language, a provisional dualism of Enemy versus Friend is replaced by a modified monism that is finally able to assimilate Enemy to Friend.

The triumph of God over the Devil, the Shadow of God, and the triumph over God as Enemy is the Christian parallel to the Persian victory of Ahura Mazda over Angra Mainyu. Yet the promise of the resurrection also remains eschatological (as does the Zoroastrian hope). In the Final Joke the evil of death is itself subjected to death, but only in principle and proleptically. In the words of Harvey Cox, "merely to reconcile theology to existing reality is to forget the crucial eschatological factor, the one that reminds us that existing reality is provisional, is part of 'this passing age,' and therefore cannot be taken with ultimate seriousness."[41] And Wendy Farley declares, "It is in history that we live, struggle, think, act, and suffer. Without denying the legitimacy of eschatological hopes, theology must seek a historical response to evil. Otherwise, consolation and hope may degenerate into excuses for remaining passive or indifferent in the face of radical suffering and injustice."[42]

The all-decisive reason we are made to insist that redemption is "not yet" lies in the fact that radical evil continues to afflict the life of God as well as the lives of human beings. We are not out on some utopia trip. For the saving incongruities/congruities of God can themselves be subjected to incongruities that are nothing less than diabolic. I adduce one example from a domain earlier referred to, today's feminist revolution.

Divine incarnation tied to a male human could turn into a Bigger Joke than God Godself, and certainly we, may comprehend or master. Many women rightly want to know how "redemption" could ever be possible in the form of a male. At least two related questions are involved here: (1) Is God's Joke of Realized Incongruity itself subject to a comic, cosmic veto?: "You thought you were redeeming us, and all you sent was a *son*! What a joke!" (2) How is it possible to perform an act of authentic Realized Incongruity when the prejudices and sins of human beings infect the subject matter of the act with their own incongruity of immorality?

About the best I can say is that a Bigger Joke does not actually drive us out of the comic realm, although it does remind us that comedy is never exempt from tragedy, and it does tell us that the comic act is a most difficult thing to pull off, even for God. Put differently but pertinently: The Devil is the expert *par excellence* in fouling things up—so expert that he may even be tempting us (God too?) to downplay our own blameworthiness and responsibility. All in all, the three Jokes that comprise the Christian faith are not immune to contamination by radical evil.

I repeat from chapter 1: The "how to" of this book does not pretend to do something substantive to vanquish the Devil. It tries only to distinguish Devil and God, and thereby, perhaps, to help us a little in our own battles against evil, particularly the evils of repression.

Withal, the resurrection does abide as a present reality. This is seen in at least three ways. First, the resurrection-event remains as a norm respecting various kinds of Christian affirmation—for example, the authority of the New Testament. As Clark M. Williamson writes, "It is the living Christ who explains the New Testament, not the New Testament that explains the living Christ."[43] Second, to bring H. Richard Niebuhr back into our company, "a universal teleology of resurrection," contra "a universal teleology of entombment," means that an ethic of death is countered by an ethic of life, and an ethic of life bespeaks an open future, an open society. We may add to this that an open future at once points up and reinforces the solidarity of faith and comedy. Third, and still with H. Richard Niebuhr, if the resurrection reconciles us to God the erstwhile Enemy, after "enemies are reconciled, they no longer [have to] ask why it was that the animosity had developed in the past."[44]

"A curious custom in the Greek Orthodox tradition gathers believers on Easter Monday for the purpose of trading jokes. Since the most extravagant 'joke' of all took place on Easter Sunday—the victory, against all odds, of Jesus over death—the community of the faithful enters into the spirit of the season by sharing stories with unexpected endings, surprise flourishes, and a sense of humor. A similar practice occurs among the Slavs, who recognize in the resurrection of Jesus of Nazareth a joy that it is Jesus who has the last laugh"—thus does Doris Donnelly begin her essay on "Divine Folly."[45] William H. Willimon provides a counterpart of the same point: At Duke University Chapel "we do it [Easter] for no better purpose than the sheer fun of it."[46] Yet the Christian as Christian is not engaged—to borrow phrasing from today's academic humor studies—in "funny ha-ha" jokes but rather in "funny strange" or "funny peculiar" Jokes. They are in no way conducive to light laughter; their closest relatives are awe and penitence (cf. Rudolf Otto's concept of "the numinous"[47]).

And the Devil? Where does he come in? Well, some hope is being sounded here that he may be on the way out. Here is the way my mentor, Jeffrey Burton Russell, closes his study *Mephistopheles*:

> I look tonight from my winter window and name the stars, Procyon, Sirius and Mirzam, Aldebaran, and here in the warm south Canopus in

Carina, low on the rim of the sea. I name them, but I know them not by naming but only by loving, for love is the stuff of their being and mine. O blue blazing Rigel, O long twins with burning heads, O stars grape-clustered in the vineyards of the night. For knowledge pauses when the blood stops beating to the brain, but love never ceases, because it is the true stuff of reality that moves the sun and the other stars. *Che move il sole e l'altre stelle*. And that is why the Devil in whatever way he exists, is negation negated, denial denied, meaninglessness exploded into galaxies of meaning blooming bright in the darkness with the light of love.[48]

The Devil is ugly, and will not endure. Beauty must win, and, laughing, She will win.

IV

In summary: To respond to the divine action, which liberates people from their "theoretical reason," is to move over to the domain of the "practical reason," which entails fresh forms of behavior: freedom to contend for justice, a life in which meaningfulness fights off despair, a kind of nonchalance and playfulness, and the whole undergirded by hope. "Blessed are you who are poor, for yours is the kingdom of God.... Blessed are you who weep now, for you will laugh" (Luke 6:20, 21). If good is nothing more than an aspect of evil, the fate of hopefulness is bleak. But if evil somehow falls under the authority of good, hope can persist.[49]

To attest to Incarnation-Crucifixion-Resurrection is to remain at home, but also to be transfixed, wholly within the Hebraic province. Thus does the *restaurazione*, the *rinnovamento* of *this* Jewish person embody and vindicate afresh the life-struggle against Necessity. The revolution contra Fate moves forward and outward. The struggle is successively—not supersessionistically—joined by the Christian community of faith. The reason our matriarch Sarah laughed was the birth of her son Yitzhak, the one who also laughs, the one who will laugh (Gen. 18:12; 21:1-7). *El campesino* Yeshua ("God saves") revitalizes the memory of Yitzhak, when he says to the few persons before him, "You have pain now," but one day "your hearts will rejoice, and no one will take your joy from you" (John 16:22).

We have listened to Emil Fackenheim's words, "God so loved the world that He hid the infinity of His pain from it lest it be destroyed."

The dialectic of Continuity/Discontinuity fairly shouts at us: "God so loved the world that he gave his only Son..." (John 3:16). Yet it is continuity that must win the day. For it is the love of God that is heard from the opposable sides of the Grand Canyon: In the giving of God, God's love is hidden (the witness of the church). In the hiding of God, God's love is given (the witness of Israel). A bridge is built. In love is found a strange symbiosis of righteousness and forgiveness. Tragedy is counterveiled by Comedy—by what Frederick Buechner calls "confession and tears and great laughter":

> [George Buttrick was preaching] that unlike Elizabeth's coronation in the Abbey, this coronation of Jesus in the believer's heart took place among confession—and I thought, yes, yes, confession—and tears, he said—and I thought tears, yes, perfectly plausible that the coronation of Jesus in the believing heart should take place among confession and tears. And then with his head bobbing up and down so that his glasses glittered, he said in his odd, sandy voice, the voice of an old nurse, that the coronation of Jesus took place among confession and tears and then, as God was and is my witness, *great laughter*, he said. Jesus is crowned among confession and tears and great laughter, and at the phrase *great laughter*, for reasons that I have never satisfactorily understood, the great wall of China crumbled and Atlantis rose up out of the sea, and on Madison Avenue, at 73rd Street, tears leapt from my eyes as though I had been struck across the face.[50]

The laughters that burst forth from the two opposable sides of the canyon are not triumphalist or arrogant. Together they spread upon their winds the blossoms of grace, the "amazing grace" that brings into being the "second astonishment": Joy.

Notes

1. Søren Kierkegaard, *Parables of Kierkegaard*, ed. Thomas C. Oden (Princeton: Princeton University Press), p. 3 (taken from *Either/Or*, II).
2. Wendy Farley, *Tragic Vision and Divine Compassion* (Louisville, Ky.: Westminster/John Knox Press, 1990), p. 29.
3. Augustine, as quoted by Robert McAfee Brown in "What Keeps You Going?," *Christianity and Crisis* 51 (1991): 381.
4. This chapter is in substance found under the title "Comic Visions, Comic Truths," in A. Roy Eckardt, *Collecting Myself: A Writer's Retrospective*, ed. Alice L. Eckardt (Atlanta: Scholars Press, 1993).
5. Henri Bergson, "Laughter," as referred to in Harvey Cox, *The Feast of Fools* (Cambridge, Mass.: Harvard University Press, 1969), p. 144.
6. Wendy Farley uses the phrase "radical suffering" for "suffering that has the power to dehumanize and degrade human beings and that cannot be traced to punishment or desert." (Farley, *Tragic Vision*, p. 12).
7. Reinhold Niebuhr, "Humour and Faith," in *Discerning the Signs of the Times* (New York: Scribner, 1946), p. 118.

8. Ibid., p. 119.

9. Maria Harris, "Religious Educators and the Comic Vision," *Religious Education* 75 (1980): 431.

10. Lionel Blue, *To Heaven With Scribes and Pharisees* (New York: Oxford University Press, 1976), p. 75.

11. "In order to protect the oneness of God from every multiplication, watering down, or amalgamation with the rites of the surrounding world, the people of Israel chose for itself that verse of the Bible to be its credo which to this very day not only belongs to the daily liturgy of the synagogue but also is impressed as the first sentence of instruction upon the five-year-old schoolchild. This is the confession which Jesus acknowledged as the 'most important of all the commandments,' and which is spoken by every child of Israel as a final word in the hour of death: 'Hear, O Israel! The Lord our God is One' (Deut 6:4)." (Pinchas Lapide, in Lapide and Jürgen Moltmann, *Jewish Monotheism and Christian Trinitarian Doctrine*, trans. Leonard Swidler [Philadelphia: Fortress Press, 1981], p. 27).

12. Irving Greenberg, *The Jewish Way* (New York: Summit Books, 1988), pp. 254–55.

13. Ibid., pp. 224, 227, 235. There is a kind of overwhelmingness in the fact that Elie Wiesel's play, *The Trial of God*, should be set upon the Feast of Purim. (New York: Random House, 1979).

14. Greenberg, *Jewish Way*, pp. 236, 237, 246, 251, 254, and 257.

15. Irving Greenberg, *Guide to Purim* (New York: CLAL, National Jewish Conference Center, 1979), pp. 17, 20.

16. Emil L. Fackenheim, "Our Position Toward Halacha," in *The Jewish Thought of Emil Fackenheim: A Reader*, ed. Michael L. Morgan (Detroit: Wayne State University Press, 1987), p. 22.

17. Emil L. Fackenheim, *What Is Judaism?* (New York: Summit Books, 1987), p. 291.

18. Mark Shechner, "Dear Mr. Einstein: Jewish Comedy and the Contradictions of Culture," in Sarah Blacher Cohen, ed., *Jewish Wry* (Bloomington, Ind.: Indiana University Press, 1989), pp. 142–46.

19. A. Roy Eckardt, "Is There a Christian Laughter?," *Encounter* (Indianapolis) 53 (1992): 111. The quotation here included from Mark Shechner is from Shechner, "Comedy, Jewish," in Glenda Abramson, ed., *The Blackwell Companion to Jewish Culture* (Oxford: Basil Blackwell, 1989), italics added.

20. Shechner, "Dear Mr. Einstein," pp. 154–55.

21. Emil L. Fackenheim, *God's Presence in History* (New York: New York University Press, 1970), pp. 15–16.

22. Emil L. Fackenheim, *Quest for Past and Future* (Boston: Beacon Press, 1970), pp. 219–20.

23. Meyer Wiener, "On Sholom Aleichem's Humor," in Cohen, ed., *Jewish Wry*, p. 50.

24. Sigmund Freud, "Humor," in John Morreall, ed., *The Philosophy of Laughter and Humor* (Albany, N.Y.: State University of New York Press, 1987), p. 113.

25. Frederick Buechner, *Telling the Truth* (San Francisco: Harper & Row, 1977), pp. 57, 72.

26. Peter L. Berger, *The Precarious Vision* (Garden City, N.Y.: Doubleday, 1961), p. 273. Cf. Harvey Cox: "When tragedy fails you still have pathos. When comedy fails it becomes ridiculous. When tragedy succeeds it reveals to us a vision of the relentless wholeness of life. When comedy succeeds it shakes us into a new stance, it prepares us for new experiences." (Cox, *Feast of Fools*, p. 137).

27. Sharon Weinstein, "Jewish Humor: Comedy and Continuity," *American Humor: An Interdisciplinary Newsletter* 3 (Fall 1976): 1. On the question of Jewish humor in the context of other kinds of humor, consult Christie Davies, *Ethnic Humor Around the World* (Bloomington, Ind.: Indiana University Press, 1990).

28. In Islam we have the Realized Incongruity of the Qur'ān as Word of Allah.

29. Insofar as the event of the restoration of the State of Israel in 1948 (after some nineteen hundred years) is to be looked at within the purview, not only of Jewish faith but also of Jewish peopleness (*laos*), it is possible to argue that the conceptualization being applied here to the understanding of Jewish humor can be applied to Israel. The reasoning might begin something like this: With Eretz Israel, we witness a unique case of the transcendent being translated downward into the immanent. Israel is the contemporary Jewish community's special joke—a joke upon all antisemites and Nazis, upon the rest of humankind, perhaps also upon itself, perhaps even upon God Godself (whose own holy language has now been pettifogged into a worldly *lingua franca*). Thus, in the measure that the event of the new Israel goes beyond the reality of Judaism as such (while of course sustaining Judaism) and falls within Jewish two-world incongruity, it becomes eligible as a joke. But, further, since Israel may also be regarded as an earnest of redemption—sometimes Israel receives a place in Jewish life comparable to the one Jesus Christ occupies in Christian life—we may be driven beyond "joke" to "Joke." But cf. Arthur Waskow's alternative rendering of the divine comedy, "God's Joke: The Land Twice Promised." To Waskow, God promised the land twice: to Isaac and his children (Israel and Jews) and to Ishmael and his children (the Palestinians). This, Waskow argues, is God's real joke. (See Otto Maduro, ed., *Judaism, Christianity and Liberation* [Maryknoll, N.Y.: Orbis Books, 1991], pp. 73-80). We may, in addition, take note of an interesting literary sequence of events in Luke 2. Herod's slaughter of the infants is said to fulfill Jeremiah's word that tells of Rachel weeping for her children. But then, once Herod is dead, Joseph in Egypt is told in a dream to take the infant Jesus and go up to Eretz Israel (vss. 16-21). The eventuality of a convergence of Jewish comedy and Christian comedy can here be glimpsed.

30. Heinz Moshe Graupe, *The Rise of Modern Judaism: An Intellectual History of German Jewry 1650–1942*, trans. John Robinson (Huntington, N.Y.: Robert E. Krieger, 1978), p. 249.

31. Consult John B. Cobb, Jr. and Christopher Ives, eds., *The Emptying God: A Buddhist-Jewish-Christian Conversation* (Maryknoll, N.Y.: Orbis Books, 1990).

32. Blue, *To Heaven*, p. 78.

33. Norman Lamm, as cited in David Birnbaum, *God and Evil* (Hoboken, N.J.: Ktav Publishing House, 1989), p. 243.

34. Michael Wyschogrod, *The Body of Faith* (San Francisco: Harper & Row, 1989), p. 101.

35. I should be the last to denigrate the jester's role, for it is irreplaceable. Leszek Kolakowski writes: "Although an habitué of good society, [the jester] does not belong to it and makes it the object of his inquisitive impertinence; he...questions what appears to be self-evident. The jester could not do this if he himself were part of the good society, for then he would be, at the most a drawing room wit. A jester must remain an outsider; he must observe 'good society' from the sidelines, for only then can he detect the non-obvious behind the obvious and the non-final behind what appears to be final. At the same time he must frequent

good society so as to know what it deems holy, and to be able to indulge in his impertinence." ("The Priest and the Jester," *Dissent* 9 [1962]: 233). I am indebted to Harvey Cox for this reference. Were Kolakowski willing or able to substitute "she" and "her" for "he" and "him," he would have it made.

36. Frederick Sontag, *The God of Evil* (New York: Harper & Row, 1970), p. 96, italics added.

37. For a treatment of the life and death of Jesus as a parable and analogy for interpreting the present, see H. Richard Niebuhr, *The Meaning of Revelation* (New York: Macmillan, 1941), pp. 124–25.

38. Harvey Cox, *Religion in the Secular City* (New York: Simon & Schuster, 1984), pp. 141–43.

39. It is essential to their professional health and professional ethics that scholars keep up to date upon the work of other scholars in their fields and do not misrepresent them by reproducing earlier viewpoints rather than later, and perhaps changed ones, as definitive. Darrell J. Fasching refers to my 1978 and 1982 position upon Jesus' resurrection as though it comprises my final say on the matter, all the while ignoring the diametrically opposite position I came to and published repeatedly in more than adequate time for him to use in his book, *Narrative Theology After Auschwitz* (Minneapolis, Minn.: Fortress, 1992), pp. 26–7. Consult the following: A. Roy Eckardt, *Jews and Christians* (Bloomington, Ind.: Indiana University Press, 1986), pp. 85–7; *For Righteousness' Sake* (Bloomington, Ind.: Indiana University Press, 1989), pp. 310–12; and, a most explicit attestation to Jesus' resurrection, "Why Do You Search Among the Dead?", *Encounter* (Indianapolis) 51 (1990): 1–17.

40. Cf. Ernest Becker, *The Denial of Death* (New York: Free Press, 1973).

41. Cox, *Feast of Fools,* p. 135.

42. Farley, *Tragic Vision,* p. 22.

43. Clark M. Williamson, *A Guest in the House of Israel* (Louisville, Ky.: Westminster/ John Knox Press, 1993), p. 195.

44. H. Richard Niebuhr, *The Responsible Self* (San Francisco: Harper & Row, 1978), p. 143. See also H. Richard Niebuhr, *Faith on Earth,* ed. Richard R. Niebuhr (New Haven, Conn. and London: Yale University Press, 1989), especially Chap. 6—"The Reconstruction of Faith" and Chap. 7—"The Community of Faith."

45. Doris Donnelly, "Divine Folly: Being Religious and the Exercise of Humor," *Theology Today* 48 (1992): 385–98.

46. William H. Willimon, comp., *Last Laugh* (Nashville, Tenn.: Abingdon Press, 1991), p. 16.

47. Rudolf Otto, *The Idea of the Holy* (New York: Oxford University Press, 1958).

48. Jeffrey Burton Russell, *Metphistopheles* (Ithaca, N.Y.: Cornell University Press, 1990), p. 301.

49. According to the theory of panentheism (not to be confused with pantheism), all things exist somehow "inside" the being of God, although God continues to transcend them. From this perspective, suffering and evil are not beyond the reality of God, and hence are not entirely meaningless or dispurposive. I remand this comment to an endnote because panentheist reflection falls primarily under the theoretical reason as against the practical reason, although it certainly has practical, existential import.

50. Frederick Buechner, *The Alphabet of Grace* (San Francisco: HarperSanFrancisco, 1989), p. 44.

9

End of a Road: God/Devil/Comedy

*The Devil is a necessary component in male
religion because a God without an adversary is
inconceivable to the masculine mind.*
                    —Charlotte Perkins Gilman[1]

*What is truth? said jesting Pilate; and would not
stay for an answer.*
                              —Francis Bacon[2]
*The highest values of the true comedian are
freedom and honor.... False comedians have no
concern for freedom...[and] are devoid of any
sense of honor.*
                        —Edward L. Galligan[3]

*The more one suffers, the more, I believe, has one a
sense for the comic.*
                      —Søren Kierkegaard[4]

This chapter brings to a culmination the constructive venture initi-
ated in chapter 8.

I

Some readers may feel that this book fails to avoid the very intellectualism it claims we ought to question. Any such inheritance would probably not occur to me did I not sense an element of truth in it. I take a
little comfort in the rule that commissions writers to accumulate words
in campaigning against other words. Even the Zen-thing subjects itself
to that hazardous but inevitable procedure. Further, the comic cause may,
paradoxically, gain a little boost right here: The incongruity of setting
the dogs of reason upon reason is anything but unfunny.

Christian comedy, together with other comedies, has more than one job to do. (People other than Christians have their own precious laughters, their own inimitable comedies; nothing triumphalist or supersessionist is allowed the Christian. *The most Christians can do is to engage in jokes and laughter as pale though hopeful reflections of the Joke they have envisioned.*) Christian comedy proclaims the futility, even evil, of traditional theodicy. It is a sharp knife in the great arsenal that fights human oppression. It joins its sister Love in celebrating the Jokes of God. It finally runs beyond all human, perhaps all divine, functionalisms; it laughs that it might laugh that it might laugh. But Christian comedy also has as a prime task to discern ways that help us tell God from the Devil.

To pave the way for my offering of a comparative table upon God vis-à-vis Devil, I might, for reminder's sake, return us to our first chapter and Jeffrey Burton Russell's sevenfold expression of "what he knows about the Devil." Once again I resort to paraphrase: Direct experience of a force perceived as evil, possessing unity and purpose, and coming from outside the human subject; such experience as common to sane people in a variety of cultures; an admission that the experience, arising as it does out of one's unconscious, may not in fact be beyond the self; yet a necessity to take the experience seriously, because the element of beyondness is constituent to the perception itself, and is widespread within the perceptions of other people; the experience as interpreted by individuals through their personal and cultural preconceptions; the need to correct one's preconceptions to accord with the methodology one has chosen; and an emphasis upon the fact that the methodology selected manifests a definable development of historical tradition, asserting as the tradition does the reality of a principle. In that same chapter, I apply Professor Russell's formulation to God, substituting "good" for "evil" at requisite places. Russell had declared, you will recall, that it is fallacious to identify belief in the Devil as outdated and superstitious, and that the proper question to ask of any idea "is not whether it is outdated but whether it is true." No idea "that fits into a coherent world view can properly be called superstitious." The same criteria apply, I need hardly add, to belief in God.

Perhaps we are ready for the listing that follows, a concoction that reflects nuances and emphases appropriate to a comic-poetic orientation. I might call it: A New Septuagint: Seventy Ways TTGFTD—or *Coincidentia Oppositorum,* Texas-Style.[5]

I gave up trying to make the two columns come out all nouns, or all adjectives, or all whatever. In the end, I decided to sacrifice tidiness and syntactical propriety to vitality. I have left out some of the more truistic candidates. To offset a bit any prejudicial influence on me, I list marks of the Devil alphabetically. The result is that on God's side, first letters fall where they may. But that's okay; God's creation itself is still unfinished. (Incidentally, I demand to know why "Devil" and "God" are both missing from *The Devil's Dictionary* of Ambrose Bierce.)

DEVIL	**GOD**
Adversary	Mediator
Always right	Sometimes wrong
Amalekite	Irish*
Answerer	Questioner
Antisemite	Israelite
(Not to mention	(Wrestler with
racist, etc., etc.)	Godself)
Anxious	Nonchalant
Arrogant	Penitent
Believer	Skeptic
Boring**	Youthful
(Minimum of 7	(Probably not
gezillion years old)	over 17)
Bureaucrat	Daydreamer
Careful dresser	Rather disheveled
Childish	Childlike

---

* I can't resist inserting a little poesy at this juncture. (I swear I have not had the benefit of any Irish whisky—not for the last twelve hours. Involved here is a strictly fasting text.)

HAIKU UPON EMPLANING AT SHANNON

To move
From Earth to Heaven
You will pass through Eire.
Eire is the turnkey.

Please see Michael Downey, ed., *In Praise of the Irish.*

** Popular gossip has it that the Devil makes his home in Boring, Maryland, having moved there from Nazareth, Pennsylvania. While the accusation is completely false, the Devil does have a few relatives in Boring. Come to think of it, he has relatives just about everywhere. Even in Rome. Even in Brooklyn.

Clever	Sometimes a little slow
Coercive	Nurturing
Comforter	Nuisance
Compulsive dieter	Tendency to overeat
Compulsive hand-washer (Cf. Matt. 27:24)	Blameworthy
Constipated	Regular
Dedicated	A little unsure sometimes; maybe even ambivalent
Dignified	Baseball fan
Dinosaur	Piglet*
Empty of humor (and Full of Baloney, not to mention Dissimulation)	Full of nonsense (and Empty of Guile)
Expert at good intentions	Good intentions get you nowhere.
Fanatic	Live-and-let-liver
Fascist	Democrat
Father of depression	Mother of joy
Full of knowledge	Full of wonder
Idealist (Boycotts the polls on Election Day.)	Politician (Always gets out to vote.)
Idol worshiper	Not very religious
Immutable	Changeable
Insolent	Low-handed
Insomniac	Sound sleeper**

---

* In *Winnie-the-Pooh* Piglet laments, "It is hard to be brave when you're only a Very Small Animal." Consult Benjamin Hoff's *The Tao of Piglet* and *The Te of Piglet.*

** At least ten hours a night, and never forced to get up to do you-know-what. But how am I ever going to deal with Ps. 121:4: "He who keeps Israel will neither slumber nor sleep"? The actor here is hardly the Devil, not even the divine Shadow. I suppose that one exegesis could be simply that whenever God is watching after Israel, God naturally stays alert (perhaps with a bit of help from pep-up pills). Beyond this, a little gender-eisegesis could note that in the translation the verse definitely refers only to the male side of God. The female side is then left occasionally to drop off. The trouble with this reading is that it goes against everything we know of Dagwood Bumstead and his unnumbered male cronies. I leave to the gentle reader to take things from there.

Intellectual	Electrician
Irresponsible	Responsible
(The Devil made me do it; I myself am not really the Devil.)	(Yes, I did it.)
Killjoy	Livejoy
Learned in Scripture	Out on the streets
Liar	Comedian
Loved but hated	Hated but loved
(First laugh)	(Last laugh)
Made in his own image	Made in the image of humankind (but without forgetting animals, plants, and very small things)
Matter-hater	Materialist
Modernist	Postmodernist
Moral absolutist	Moral relativist
Orthodox	Heretical
Party-pooper	Life of the party
Patrón rico	*Campesina pobre*
Philosopher	Grocery store clerk
Pious	Pipe smoker (of decarcinogenic tobacco*)
Preferential option for lackeys	Preferential option for critics and people who talk back
Presentist	Eschatologist
(Do everything now.)	(Wait and you'll see.)
Pristine	Eclectic
Prude	Given to festival and fantasy
Reactionary	Radical
Religious	Secular
Resident of Third Reich	Resident of Guadalupe
(1933–1945)	(no special dates)
Sage	Fool

---

* Why does not God provide us with the same? Seems a bit discriminatory.

Sexist	Sexual
Shortsufferer	Longsufferer
Slaveholder	Emancipator
Snob	Trombone player
Sorcerer	Clown
Specialist in antihistory	Historian
Spectator	Actor (i.e., Activist)
Teetotaler	Winebibber
Trickster	Jokester
Tyrant	Pluralist
Undoer	Doer
Very capable	Certain tendency to klutzhood
White and macho	Dark and gentle
Workaholic	Sometimes given to loafing
Worldclass blackbelt in theodicy	Dropout from theodicy school

II

In struggling against God and people, the Devil seeks to make life inhuman, i.e., antipolitical. When and if we are able to venture into the full sunlight of God, the Shadow of God is no longer seen. (Within the night of the Devil, the figure of God is very hard to make out.) The Shadow needs God, whereas, freed of the Shadow, God can laugh. And give birth. Repentance (divine and human) carries the seeds of humor, while, once it is born, humor enables repentance to keep going, even to thrive.

Harvey Cox's Christology is low. Can anything be said for a higher one? Cox translates "Christ" into a "joke in the middle of a prayer," a "spirit of play." Alternatively, we may discern, not a joke, but a Joke within a divine story of incongruity: the Word made flesh in a Jewish human being, the death of God, the resurrection of one who had been crucified. This is where the humor is found, in all its unbelievableness, not just because humor as such is the offspring of incongruity, but because peculiarly Christian humor is the outcome of an impossibly possible Incongruity: the objective clash between Eternity and Time. The clash occurs between things incommensurate yet never unrelated; therefore, it at once explodes/implodes. On the scene—upon the very "place of the skull" (Mark 15:22)—the Devil knows humiliation, gets what is coming. Then is the Other One seen to emerge from the Shadow.

I am, nonetheless, wholly in accord with Harvey Cox in his determination that the jester's function be to mock and ridicule "the very things we are most reticent to reexamine."[6] Severely, this word applies to our repression of the Devil as it does to all the perils that stem from such repression. For one (mostly unspoken) major threat or challenge throughout our story is that very element of *repression,* which, psychoanalytically interpreted, entails a burying or driving out of impulses, fears, unbearable memories, ideas, and ideologies from consciousness into the unconscious, the latter apprehendable as at once individual and collective.

In and through a full acknowledgment of the phenomenon of the Devil, the way is opened to a beginning trialectic of God/Devil/Comedy. Without God, radical evil is left to prosper. But without the Devil as Shadow of God, the unqualified burdening of humankind as culprit for radical evil continues its unspeakable course, perpetuating the terror and the anxiety. Accordingly, an overall way to tell God from the Devil is through the comedy, i.e., the joy, that may be eventuated once the two previous sentences are placed side-by-side and given equal voice. Comedy is freedom—from guilt, from anxiety, from lostness, from loneliness—yet the created freedom of the human being does not come to full dignity apart from the evil/good interposition of the Shadow. The Devil here emerges as defeating his own ends; his destructiveness becomes self-destruction. Such are among the mysteries of the grace of God.

III

Our little posttheodicean venture in metaphysical poesy (poetic metaphysics) draws to an end. It has intended a convergence of philosophy/theology/psychology/morality/politics. Perhaps we have reflected sufficiently together to be able now to say "God as myth"—"Devil as myth"—"Comedy as myth," yet all the while sternly reminding ourselves, not only that each of the three kinds of myth is very different from the other two,[7] but that God as truth, Devil as truth (thereness), and Comedy as truth are not to be lost. Literalism may be anachronistic all right, but truth is not. The three concepts/realities abide somewhere within the enchanting, sometimes frightening, universe between hard data and subjectiveness.

In radical monism Devil and Comedy are, in effect, ousted (repressed, sent into exile). In absolutist diabolism, or what might be called the Devil's private religion, God and Comedy are, in effect, ousted (repressed, sent into exile). In the Zen-thing, God and Devil are, in effect, ousted (repressed, sent into exile).[8] The beginning of an end to such pervasive repression, an end to powers that are able to terrorize, each in a distinctive way, is found via provisional, partial alliances—in Jungian language, via moves toward integration.[9]

Integration may be given its start via deciduous, if ultimately abortive, partnerships between any two contestants. Whenever God is dead or remanded to exile, Comedy and Devil are encouraged to negotiate a liaison—yet only to be assailed by despair. Whenever Devil is eclipsed for a time, God and Comedy are inspired to venture upon a marriage of convenience—yet only to find that the castle they have erected is hanging in the air of Polyanna-town, utopia, noplace. And whenever Comedy flags or is sent away, God and Devil are licensed to slug it out as twins—but without surcease and with Tragedy left to leer at them, and at us, from ringside.

How is full integration, or reintegration, possible? How is a needfully complete trialectic of God/Devil/Comedy to come to birth, or to gain rebirth?[10] An authentic postmodern theology will nourish that trialectic. At a minimum, one cheer can be heard, perhaps even two, for a Western ethos—yes, I am mouthing the forbidden W-word—that has never quite lost, or forsworn, or succeeded in getting rid of any one of our three protagonists. None of them has wholly stopped breathing, and, with help from a few desperate but openminded survivors, they just may revive themselves. Beyond this, yet in a certain continuity with it, there is always the eventuality of intervention from "beyond." (One cheer for a transcending mysticism.[11])

Should God return here/there, the despair that afflicts Devil and Comedy just might be inoculated with Joy. Should the Devil return here/there, God and Comedy just might be saved from sentimentality, being forced to own up to the horrible way things are. And should Comedy return here/there, the war of God and Devil just might ease a bit, if only in and through the frail grace of a smile. For Jews and Christians, at any rate, the smile widens perceptibly whenever they truly remember the beginnings and the story of Israel: "Once upon a time...." Nevertheless: Already in the primordial, universal rainbow (Gen. 9:13) every Jew and every Christian and every Muslim can freely find the smile's own curve—well before Jews and Christians and Muslims were ever heard of. (Except that to know that the rainbow really is a smile, you have to be and do as a child, bending way over and looking at it upside-down through your legs; otherwise it's only a piece of very beautiful but dubious news.) The divine war against the Devil goes way, way back. But yet, in the tale of Israel, in the tale of the church, in the tale of the people of Islam, the laughter of God comes down/up/over to meet the laughter of humans, working together to entice God, perhaps even deci-sively so, out from the Shadow.[12] Comedy steps to center stage as one viable partner in the most vital task of juxtaposing God and Devil. But then, carrying the shield of Hope, it goes on to act out, in anticipation, the victory of God over all devilishness. The compassionate deed is laugh-ter; laughter is the compassionate deed. Forgiveness is the comic; the comic is forgiveness. Land o'Goshen, two partners in the trialectic are starting to gang up on the Old Tempter! The last laugh is not funny, and it is not a joke. It is a Joke.

Notes

1. Charlotte Perkins Gilman, as cited in Gloria Kaufman, ed., *In Stitches* (Bloomington, Ind.: Indiana University Press, 1991), p. 171.
2. Francis Bacon, *Of Truth.*
3. Edward L. Galligan, *The Comic Vision in Literature* (Athens, Ga.: University of Georgia Press, 1984), p. 52.
4. Søren Kierkegaard, *Parables of Kierkegaard,* ed. Thomas C. Oden (Princeton, N.J.: Princeton University Press, 1978), p. 30 (taken from *Stages on Life's Way*).
5. Should you prefer primary sources here and wish to read what God and the Devil have themselves had to say, see *God: The Ultimate Autobiography* (London: Pan Books, 1989) and *Satan: The Hiss and Tell Memoirs* (London: Pan Books, 1989). Symptomatic of the intense rivalry of the two parties today is that they should together utilize the one publisher and write in exactly the same year. (Some of you may think I am making up these books, but I am not.)
6. Harvey Cox, *The Feast of Fools* (Cambridge, Mass.: Harvard University Press, 1969), p. 136.
7. See below, n. 10 to this chapter.
8. Yet, by virtue of its norm of compassion, Zen shows itself open to "amazing grace." This opportunity applies to any and every human gestalt of compassion.
9. Jeffrey Burton Russell, *Mephistopheles* (Ithaca, N.Y. and London: Cornell University Press, 1990), p. 231.
10. This wording may imply the personifying of Comedy, along with God and Devil. I don't quite know how to handle the implication, and I am tempted to concede it. Some people have spoken of this or that incarnation as God, others of Hitler as the Devil, others of their favorite stand-up as Ms. or Mr. Comedy. Comedy cer-tainly *lives* in human beings. But that such Comedy is *more than* a "phenom-enon" (as we have indeed postulated of both God and Devil), I have not quite claimed, although I also do not think that Comedy, as an independent entity, is

necessary to my case. We speak of the laughter *of* God and of the laughter *of* the Devil, but I have never heard anyone say that Comedy-as-such laughs.

11. My old teacher Reinhold Niebuhr might be disappointed with me here. He used to say that mysticism is "mist" at the beginning, "I " in the middle, and "schism" at the end. I would be glad to settle for a substitute concept, but I just can't think of one. The word "transcendent" by itself tries to do the two jobs that the phrase "transcending mysticism" does. As a believer in the God of history, Niebuhr was in fact saying what I am here trying to say. On Harvey Cox's sympathy for recent and contemporary "neomysticism," consult his *Feast of Fools,* Chap. 7—"Mystics and Militants."

12. The laughter of the Devil only intensifies the Shadow.

10

Epilogue: Parting Sense and Nonsense

Unattributed pieces to follow are, I fear, by me. Most titles assigned to other pieces are mine. Readers will know which items are "sense," which are "nonsense," and which are both of these.[1] Excepting the first item and the last, I resort to the alphabetizing device I stumbled upon at the start of Chapter 9. This makes for the vice, familiar to habitués of dictionaries, of constantly changing the subject. On the other hand: Here's to Chaos! (For William F. Fry, humor may be construed as a chaotic phenomenon to be played with and to serve as entertainment, in contrast to the frustrations that stem from contemplating natural chaos, which is in any case beyond our control.[2])

TRIADIC INTRODUCTION

An old pond.
A frog jumps in.
Plop!
                    —Bashō (1643–1694)

Wise men hear and see
As little children do.
            —Lao Tzu (b. 604 B.C.E.)

If you wish to write haiku
Find a three-foot child.
                    —Bashō

ABSURDITY AND THE WORD

There is an element of absurdity in even the most accepted truths and established facts and conventions, as in the experience of using a familiar word that suddenly looks or sounds funny, that suddenly is absurd, like all words.

—Conrad Hyers[3]

1. *Gone, On Sabbatical.* Under the aegis of Lady Constantina Scraftsbite—not to mention her effgis, geegis, hgis, igis, and jgis—I have been enabled to engage in a year's research upon the origin and history of the gis.

2. *The Guaranteed Annual Diet.*

> Do we pchew?
> No.
> Do we qchew?
> No.
> Do we rchew?
> No.
> Do we eschew?
> Yes.

3. *News Conference.*
Ambassador: The Banian representative will be joining us.
Correspondent: Excuse me, Sir, do you mean the representative of Albania?
Ambassador: Of course. How could it be otherwise?
Correspondent: But you said, "the Banian representative."
Ambassador: Well, yes, the Banian representative represents all Bania.
Correspondent: In other words, Excellency, you might better have said, "The Albanian representative will be on hand."
Ambassador: Stupid! I am referring to the sovereign principality of Bania—*all* Bania.

4. *Our shrinking Vocabulary.* The word "circumcision" is in fact a contraction that somewhere lost its apostrophe. The full spelling is "circumnavigatethecision."

A similar fate applies to the very word "contraction." The full word is "contractoffortyeightacrestion."

In truth, there has never been a word that is not a contraction of something else—not excluding even ostensibly single-letter words such as "a." The complete word in this case is "ashtoodle."

5. *Transliteration and its Problems.* There is a Chinese lady named Ha.
The difficulty is that when put into English, her name comes out Malicadooslaw.

6. *Witwrit for Nitwrits.*

Your wit is writ too small:

You want to write wit but all you've done is write writ.

Should you ever come to write wit when intending to write wit,

Your wit will be writ large—every bwit, fwit, hwit, jwit, kwit, lwit, nwit, pwit, swit, twit, writ;

Or better, every bit, fit, hit, jit, kit, lit, nit, pit, sit, tit (well, maybe twit here), and wit.

THE ACCOLADE

Whenever I think of Carl Reiner, two words come to mind: Carl, and Reiner.

—Steve Martin

ALIEN STATUS IN ABERDEEN

I have not quite come to identify myself as an old man. I like to think of me as an older man.

The definition of this older man is a man for whom different brands of Scotch whisky—*not* whiskey—have come to taste more or less the same.

Since, by definition, such a plight could never beset a Scotsman, no matter how antique his taste buds, we have proof that I, as an older man, am nothing but a foreigner.

ASTROMATH

Men reach their sexual peak at eighteen. Women reach theirs at thirty-five.

Do you get the feeling that God is playing a practical joke?

—Rita Rudner

BARBRA STREISAND'S JEANS

I keep wondering if Barbra Streisand is happy.

Ever since I read in *Star* magazine that she will only wear a pair of jeans one time because she likes them stiff, and hence, took sixty pairs of new jeans with her on location—I just keep wondering if she's happy.

—Nancy Jo Batman[4]

BEST SELLERS

The list to come is taken from the North Umbria *Post-Times-Dispatch-News-Chronicle-Press-Express-Eagle.* (There have been buy-outs.) The first column on each side gives the book's standing this week relative to the others; the second column on each side shows the number of weeks the book has been a best seller.

Editor's note: The increasing popularity of "how to" books of nonfiction is evident, welcome, and not surprising.

	Mystery-Crime-Adventure			Nonfiction-Science	
1	*Whatever Happened To The Yellow Stream?* James Daily	70	1	*How To Bake Thousand-Grain Bread* Lemuel Kitsch	27
2	*Lovers Who Cannot Stand To Love* Linda Belinda	83	2	*How To Master Sanskrit In Forty Years* Nelly Stall	23
3	*If Nostrils Could Testify* Antonia Disraeli	9	3	*The Construction Of The Sydney-Cairo Bridge: An Engineer Remembers* Elizabeth Duckling	8
4	*The Night The Devil Sang Falsetto* Sarah Tipperary	1	4	*How To Turn The Other Buttock, Vol I—Move To The Left* Desmond Quaking	24
5	*The Nine Loves Of Aloysius Woodworth* Sally Grindge	17	5	*How Old Is Water?* Geraldine Thimble	13
6	*From Pimp To University President* Algernon Drenchmouth	6	6	*From The Eschatological To The Scatological, And Back* Pamela Gracenote	25
7	*The Dagger That Was All Blade* Harry Szabo	3	7	*How To Separate Being From Nonbeing* Omar Hadash	40
8	*Hit-And-Run Drivers I Have Loved* Lisa Bee	18	8	*How To Hold Kidnappers For Ransom* Engelbert Tinn	16
9	*Seven Brides For Sidney Erskine* Penelope Watt	7	9	*A Stiffnecked People And The Origins Of Chiropractic* Barbara Gloon	2
10	*The Strange Case Of The Single Eyebrow* Moses Brinkley	41	10	*Rope And Its Proper Length* Helena Montana	10
11	*Escape From An Anteater* Sidewinder Watkins	28	11	*The Fascination Of Dust* Donald Daygan	27
12	*Holding One's Water In Ancient Macedon* J.C.K. Bryce-Jones	63	12	*The Decline Of The Long Fingernail In North Chinese Culture* Miles Standoff	35
13	*Playing Potsy With God: A Mystic's Dream* Tera Blend	4	13	*Bypass Surgery And The Right Of Privacy* Robert Jones, M.D.	80
14	*The Corpse That Retched* Sir Alastair Fleck	4	14	*The Place Of The Barrel Stave In Paris Fashion* Helene Patois	5

CENTURY MARKS

The last time Oral Roberts needed a few million to sustain his ministry he announced that God would "call him home" unless he was able to raise the necessary cash. This time Satan is after him. In order to fight off a "satanic conspiracy," Roberts, along with his son Richard, has appealed for more money. In a letter mailed to more than a million of his contributors, Roberts pleads that "we've got to have a financial breakthrough or all hell is going to break loose against this ministry. Please understand we've got to have the finances. There is no other way! Hear me, there is no other way!"

—*The Christian Century*[5]

CHAIN OF COMMAND

Field Marshal to Beauregard:
    "General Beauregard, seize them!"
Beauregard to Field Marshal:
    "It is done, Excellency."
Field Marshal to guard:
    "Guard, seize Beauregard!"

THE CLOWN IN THE BELFRY

In the year 1831, this church [in Rupert, Vermont] was repaired and several new additions were made. One of them was a new steeple with a bell in it, and once it was set in place and painted, apparently, an extraordinary event took place. "When the steeple was added," Howard Mudgett writes in his history, "one agile Lyman Woodard stood on his head in the belfry with his feet toward heaven."

—Frederick Buechner[6]

COINCIDENTIA OPPOSITORUM

Ought there not be provision for a clown's clown?
At the circus the clown's clown would be an ordinary looking person walking around dressed in a dark business suit, to whom no one pays any attention.

ETYMOLOGY AT WORK

The term "satellite phallus" was first coined by a man who, coincidentally enough, was named Satellite Phallus, even though there was no relation. Phallus was a Welshman long known for an ability to walk on a middle finger.

FOR THE SAKE OF NO SAKE

What in limbo do they mean when they speak of God's sake? Over and over again I hear them: *"For God's sake!"* What sake? I have no sake. Yet they invoke it so often I sometimes think they revere my sake more than me myself. I have had my entire estate inventoried item by item and have found no sake and nothing even resembling one.

—God[7]

FROM LOYOLA TO PARIS

How many angels can
Dance on the head of
A pin? None, not
Even one.
Only in
France do angels
Dance, along the Champs
Élysées. Don't crowd, please.

FROM PAULA

(My arithmetically-alert daughter, talking to her father)
In 1974 you had a heart attack. In 1983 you were struck by a car. In 1992 you had kidney cancer.
If I were you, I'd watch out for 2001!

FUNNIEST EXPRESSION IN ENGLISH

The giggles.

GOD, ON THE INCARNATION

What did you expect? I *am* only human!

GOD'S PERSONAL CONCEPTION OF THE DEVIL

I have always wondered whether any documentary proof is available that God has something to say about the Devil, and if so, what God has said. I finally found the answer in Robert Graves:

IN BROKEN IMAGES

He is quick, thinking in clear images;
I am slow, thinking in broken images.
He becomes dull, trusting to his clear images;
I become sharp, mistrusting my broken images.
He continues quick and dull in his clear images;

I continue slow and sharp in my broken images.
He in a new confusion of his understanding;
I in a new understanding of my confusion.[8]

THE GOOD SAHARATAN

Clarence Flipover is out there in the desert separating out and confiscating the many defective grains of sand.
His project can be calculated to revolutionize desert warfare.

HALF A WHEEL IS BETTER THAN ONE

Conrad Hyers and others teach us that authentic comedy cannot be pushy or arrogant. To the end of the modesty that is demanded, I have invented the half-wheel.
The purpose of this note is not to extol the half-wheel's virtues, of which there are many, but merely to show that I am not unaware of certain problems. The main difficulty is that every time the half-wheel goes half way around, you have to jack up the vehicle and give the half-wheel a half spin so that it can get back to work. This state of affairs is complicated by the fact that on a four-half-wheel vehicle, you have to follow the same procedure on all four half-wheels.
Problems such as this are more than offset by the half-wheel's innumerable advantages, such as enabling you to make quick stops. A complete listing of these advantages must await another exposition. In the meantime, I recommend that you purchase one of my half-wheelbarrows.

HEALTH WORKERS AND H.I.V.

Judy Wesley said she was having a particularly hard time because an 8-year-old was very near death.
"I can't cry," she said. "I don't sleep. If I don't sleep I won't have the strength to deal with it and everyone else who is counting on me. I feel angry. Angry at the illness, angry at my helplessness, angry at God. I have a problem with anger and if you feel anger at God then you're in trouble."
A colleague, Sharon Billig, said: "It's O.K. to be angry with God. I figure He can handle it."
Ms. Wesley disagreed, saying: "But I need Him. I need to be able to say, 'Please help me!'"
The room fell silent. Mr. Doka asked if they were familiar with the story of Job.
"Job doesn't take it quietly," Mr. Doka said, giving his interpretation. "He rails against God. He's angry. He finally has a meeting with God, and God commends him for his anger, for not suffering in silence."

—J. Peter Zane[9]

(For any who react to Mr. Zane's accounting by asking how I could ever be so graceless as to fling this story into the midst of laughs and nonsense, I suggest a look, indeed more than a look, at Steve Lipman's study, *Laughter in Hell: The Use of Humor During the Holocaust.* Again, my own book is about God and Comedy but it is also about the

Devil. I believe that the sudden intervention of radical evil into human joy is at once a special act, and an ever-needful reminder, of the Devil.)

THE HIGHER EDUCATION

I teach at a place where they've asked me the difference between a Jew and a genital.
—Mary Boys

HOW I CAME TO CALM DOWN

I was never able to contain my excitement until one morning I stumbled upon an excitement container someone had put out for the rubbish.

HOW TO ANSWER A QUESTION WITH A QUESTION

Question: Who invented the martini?
Question: Does disaster befall a city,
    unless the Lord has done it?
(Amos 3:6)

HOW TO BEAT THE WIDE TIE/NARROW TIE CYCLE

Wear a vest.

HOW TO OUTWIT ANOTHER SYSTEM

Dear Diary:
The scene is a card store in Bronxville, N.Y. The time, a week or so before Valentine's Day. The cast, a couple, apparently married; they are examining valentine cards in the husband and wife sections. After making selections, they exchange and read the cards.
He: It's really beautiful. Thanks.
She: How very thoughtful. Thank you, dear.
They wish each other Happy Valentine's Day and kiss. Then they return the cards to the rack and walk out.
—Joseph A. Coyle[10]

HOW THE PATRIARCH WAS ENCOURAGED TO
TAKE UP THE SAXOPHONE

Abraham
Took it on the lam
From Ur
Which persecuted.
Abraham
Went off the lam
Once God
Had rooted-tooted.

If Men Could Menstruate

Men would brag about how long and how much.
Boys would mark the onset of menses, that longed-for proof of manhood, with religious ritual and stag parties.
Congress would fund a National Institute of Dysmanorrhea to help stamp out monthly discomfits.
Sanitary supplies would be federally funded and free.

—Gloria Steinem[11]

The Imperial Animal

It did the tyrannosaurs no good to blame one another for their failure. They could not adapt to reality, and they became extinct. If and when we are gone, our quarrels about which of us was to blame will merely seem funny—except that there will be nobody there to laugh.

—Lionel Tiger and Robin Fox[12]

Inkstands and Casters

Where is the Devil?
The Devil lives in the northeast caster of my inclined writing desk—or did until last week.
For what has seemed like ages (it is only fifty-three years) I have tolerated the Devil. Whenever the offending caster would fall off—it did so three of every eight rolls of the desk—I would suffer the vertigo of trying to write with a three-caster desk. Eventually, I would be forced to stoop down to put the caster back, but in the process at least one other caster and usually two would fall off. I came to formulate my Writer's Law: There is no way to put back a caster of your writing desk without losing another one.
By last week I had finally had it. It is said that Martin Luther fought the Devil by heaving an inkstand at him. The story is apocryphal. Mine is not. I fought the Devil by removing all four casters from my writing desk, getting rid of my vertigo in the bargain. But to slide a heavy writing desk towards you that lacks casters is not good for either the rug or your back—two reminders that the Devil is quite peripatetic.

Late Bloomer

After thirty-seven years as a leading theologian, Fabius Maximus concluded it might be a good idea to learn how to read.

Minimal Rights

Do we really *need* white chocolate? I mean, we blacks don't have very much. Can't we at least have *chocolate?*

—Arsenio Hall

The Mystery Of The Disappearance Of Being

If you put flour and water together, you have glue.
If you add butter and eggs, you have the makings of a cake.
Where did the glue go?

—Rita Rudner

North American Lovecall

Tom was arrested for peeping.
He was booked as a Peeping Tom Tom.

One Cheer For The Welsh

The Welsh seem to have a strong belief in the power of language. It is sometimes more important that an argument should be passionately put than that it should be right. They seem to believe that passion convinces. They are wrong, but what a splendid illusion.

—Ivor Richard[13]

Out To Lunch

Dear Miss Manners:
As a businessman, how do I allow a businesswoman to pay for my lunch?
Gentle Reader:
With credit card or cash, as she prefers.

—Judith Martin[14]

A Proboscidean Note, Complete With Two Morals

Across the entire, prodigious history of humankind upon Planet Earth, Milky Way, no small child has ever picked its nose.
A small child picks its nostril.
Things are different on Planet Simpleface, also Milky Way. People there have one nostril. But isn't this to say that they have no nostrils? They only have a nose.
On Simpleface a small child picks its nose.
Moral No. 1: Not even God can pick a nostril and a nose simultaneously.
Moral No. 2: What's all this about the cruciality of left brain/right brain research? Quite old hat! The future of physiological investigation on Planet Earth belongs to Left Nostril/Right Nostril Studies, together with everything in between. With reference to the region last-mentioned, the next generation of criminologists will experience a real breakthrough. For they will have benefited from my doctoral dissertation, to be published with 20/20 vision, "The Relation Between the Deviated Septum and Social Deviance." And by that time they will be comparing notes with criminologists on Planet Simpleface, who are more and more addressing themselves to such topics as "The Influence of Nose-picking upon Absenteeism in the Second Grade."

RADICAL MONOTHEISM IN ACTION

He: "Why is single-malt Scotch to be preferred over a blend?"
She: "Because, stupid, God is One."

ONEUPSWOMANSHIP

Joan of Arc: "I hear voices telling me what to do. They come from God."
Robert de Baudricourt: "They come from your imagination."
Joan: "Of course. That is how the messages of God come to us."

—Bernard Shaw[15]

THE RISE—AND FALL?—OF THE NEW GNOSTICISM

As American Religionists, [George] Bush and his pneumatic supporters are devoutly sincere. Unwitting Gnostics, they follow the ancient heresy of believing that the Creation and the Fall were one and the same event. They therefore value the unborn over the born, the innocent and spiritual godlike fetus over the newborn babe who has fallen into the material world of poverty and sickness.

—Harold Bloom[16]

THE ROAD FROM ORTHODOXY, AND RETURN

I'm so skeptical I can hardly believe it.

—Chip Denman

THE SECRET

All lovers are secret lovers. They require vast privacy because their passion, so gorgeous and thrilling to each other, is incomprehensible to everyone else, a joke, even to their own children. No one can quite imagine the spark that lit the fire between one's parents; their desire seems improbable, like love between porcupines.

—Garrison Keillor[17]

THE SADNESS OF BEING ADJUSTED

The Tarkools are the most energetic people on Planet Simpleface. They move so fast that whenever they walk, they stumble over their future footsteps.
In this, the Tarkools contrast with the Hydrabosi, who move so slowly that their past footsteps keep tackling them.
A blessed alternative to both is the Twaddlebys, who have learned to move at just the right speed to avoid both these hazards. But sadly, unlike the Tarkools and the Hydrabosi, the Twaddlebys have never figured out where to go.

SHADOW BOXING

When I try to say "God," why does it come out "Ded"?

When I try to say "Devil," why does it come out "Govil"?
When I try to say "God/Devil," why does it come out "Spätleser 1989"?

SHOOTOUT AT THE NARTHEX DOOR

Parishioner: "Jesus is coming next October."
Pastor: "I don't expect that."
Parishioner: "Matthew 24:44: 'You also must be ready, for the Son of Man is coming at an unexpected hour.'"
Pastor: "But why October?"
Parishioner: "In September he has to clean out his desk."

SNIPPET FROM THE CONFESSIONS OF AN OLDTIME WRITER

I have always been terrified of editors—most especially, of myself when I was one of them.

THE SPOILER

It always makes me happy to see a woman wearing a wedding ring. It means there is someone to look after her.
But then it hits me: There's a good chance she's a battered wife.

THE STAGES OF HUMAN LIFE

As a lame duck president, you have a used up past, no future at all, and a present that is suspect (Rod McLeish).
Mr. McLeish thinks he is talking about presidents. What he is in fact describing is the human condition.

STILL TALKING

My father was a general practitioner—our family motto was, "A good epidemic means meat on the table." My mother could make anybody feel guilty—she used to get letters of apology from people she didn't even know. She was desperate to get me married. She used to say, "Sure he's a murderer. But he's a single murderer." I was dating a transvestite, and she said, "Marry him. You'll double your wardrobe." She was a very elegant woman. When a flying saucer landed on the lawn, she turned it over to see if it was Wedgwood.

—Joan Rivers[18]

SUPERMANSHIP

The basic Christmas gambit is to seem to be more truly Christmas than other people, to be top man for geniality, to be one up in general Christmas kindliness, to be so managingly unobtrusive in the background that background becomes foreground.

—Stephen Potter[19]

TRIAL AND TRIBULATION OF A PEDESTRIAN
(FOR EDWARD GOREY)

Clifford Jones was walking down the boulevard on a beautiful sunny day when he was suddenly and viciously attacked by Spuytenheuval Hemmish, who left him with a druytenyeuval blemish on the right cheek of his androflam.

TWO DEGREES OF DEGREE

L.H.D.: Doctor of Humane Letters
L.P.P.D.: Doctor of Poison Pen Letters

VEGETARIAN ON TRIAL

Isaac Bashevis Singer shied away from chicken soup—and chickens—and became a devoted vegetarian. From childhood on he had seen that might makes right, that man is stronger than chicken—man eats chicken, not vice versa. That bothered him, for there was no evidence that people were more important than chickens. When he lectured on life and literature there were often dinners in his honor, and sympathetic hosts served vegetarian meals. "So, in a very small way, I do a favor for the chickens," Singer said. "If I will ever get a monument, chickens will do it for me."

—Israel Shenker[20]

Dear Mr. Singer:
Where is your evidence that people are more important than vegetables?

—A.R.E.

THE VELVET NO

The art of the rejection slip, used to return unwanted manuscripts to writers, may have reached its apex with one cited by the British scholar Glyn Daniel in a collection of his columns, "Writing for Antiquity: An Anthology of Editorials From Antiquity" (Thames and Hudson).

We have never had a formal rejection slip or letter to send out week after week to the many contributors who kindly send in notes or articles for consideration, and for whose work we sadly cannot or gladly do not want to find space, but we are encouraged to draft one, inspired by that used by the editors of a Chinese economics journal, and referred to in the *Times Diary,* 9 July 1982:

"We have read your manuscript with boundless delight. If we were to publish your paper it would be impossible for us to publish any work of a lower standard. As it is unthinkable that, in the next thousand years, we shall see its equal, we are, to our regret, compelled to return your divine composition, and to beg you a thousand times to overlook our short sight and timidity."[21]

VIOLENT RESISTANCE IN THE LAND OF SATYAGRAHA

The Leftjab of the Punjab has challenged the Rightjab of Djibuti to a fifteen-round championship bout.

Clearly, the Rightjab of Djibuti retains the edge. Each and every left or right jab by the Leftjab of the Punjab will be met, not only by right and left jabs from the Rightjab of Djibuti, but also by the Rightjab's deadly JIBOOT.

WHEN SILENCE IS VIRTUE

> God sneezed.
> What could I say to him?
> —Henny Youngman

WHO'S IN CHARGE HERE?

The act of sex, gratifying as it may be, is God's joke on humanity. It is man's last but desperate stand at superintendency.

> —Bette Davis

IN THE END THERE IS NO SUBSTITUTE FOR BEING PRACTICAL

At the age of ninety-six [Roshi Yamamoto] was nearly blind, very feeble, and no longer able to teach or work in the monastery. He decided that he was only a burden to others, and that it was time for him to die. So he stopped eating. The younger monks, however, called to his attention the fact that it was not a convenient time for him to die, as it was January, and everyone would be uncomfortable at his funeral. Convinced by their reasoning that his death would be a burden to them, he agreed to resume eating. The monks were satisfied that they had won the argument, and that Yamamoto had abandoned the idea. But when it became warm again in the spring, the old master stopped eating, and died.

> —Conrad Hyers[22]

Notes

1. On the other hand, you might do better to forget this chapter entirely and turn instead to *The Nonsense Books of Edward Lear* (New York: New American Library, 1964).
2. William F. Fry, "Humor and Chaos," *Humor* 5 (1992): 219-32.
3. Conrad Hyers, *The Laughing Buddha* (Wakefield, N.H.: Longwood Academic, 1991), p. 103.
4. Nancy Jo Batman, *Yeah, But How Would She Look Beside the Go-Kart Trophy?* (St. Louis: Chalice Press, 1992), p. 29.
5. "Century Marks," *The Christian Century* 108 (1991): 1084.
6. Frederick Buechner, *The Clown in the Belfry* (San Francisco: HarperSanFrancisco, 1992), pp. 115-16.
7. *Excerpts From the Diaries of the Late God,* ed. Anthony Towne (New York: Harper & Row, 1968), p. 17.
8. Robert Graves, "In Broken Images," *Collected Poems* (Garden City, N.Y.: Doubleday, 1961), p. 104.

9. J. Peter Zane, "When They Can't Watch Another Patient Die," *New York Times,* 25 June 1992.
10. Joseph A. Coyle, in "Metropolitan Diary," *New York Times,* 19 Feb. 1992.
11. Gloria Steinem, "If Men Could Menstruate," *Ms.* (Oct. 1978): 25. I am indebted to Nancy A. Walker for this reference.
12. Lionel Tiger and Robin Fox, *The Imperial Animal* (New York: Holt, Rinehart and Winston, 1971), p. 23.
13. Ivor Richard, *We the British.*
14. Judith Martin, *Miss Manners' Guide to Excruciatingly Correct Behavior* (New York: Atheneum, 1982), p. 409.
15. Bernard Shaw, *Saint Joan,* Scene I.
16. Harold Bloom, "New Heyday of Gnostic Heresies," *New York Times,* 26 April 1992.
17. Garrison Keillor, "The Heart of the Matter," *New York Times,* 14 Feb. 1989.
18. Joan Rivers, "Get Thee to the Theatuh," *Columbia: The Magazine of Columbia University* 17, 3 (Spring 1992): 38.
19. Stephen Potter, *Supermanship.*
20. Israel Shenker, "The Man Who Talked Back to God: Isaac Bashevis Singer, 1904-91," the *New York Times Book Review,* 11 Aug. 1991, p. 11.
21. "The Velvet No," in "Noted With Pleasure," the *New York Times Book Review,* 9 Aug. 1992, p. 27.
22. Hyers, *Laughing Buddha,* pp. 156-57.

Selected Reading List

When I say "selected," I mean "selected"—which, when you think about it, or even when you don't, is hardly a profound statement. All I mean to say is that hundreds of alternative publications could be substituted or added here. My listing is a little idiomorphic. However, each entry has *some* bearing, though sometimes an oblique one, upon the argument of the book as a whole and in that sense is linkable to the other entries.

Abraham, William J. "Oh God, Poor God: The State of Contemporary Theology." *The American Scholar* 58 (1989): 557–63.

Adams, Cecil. *The Straight Dope: A Compendium of Human Knowledge.* Chicago: Chicago Review Press, 1984.

Aichele, George, Jr. *Theology as Comedy: Critical and Theoretical Implications.* Lanham, Md.: University Press of America, 1980.

Allen, Woody. *Without Feathers-Getting Even-Side Effects.* 1 vol. New York: Quality Paperback Book Club, 1989.

Almog, Shmuel, ed. *Antisemitism Through the Ages.* Translated by Nathan H. Reisner. Oxford: Pergamon Press, 1988.

Anshen, Ruth Nanda. *The Reality of the Devil: Evil in Man.* New York: Harper & Row, 1972.

Apte, Mahadev L. *Humor and Laughter: An Anthropological Approach.* Ithaca, N.Y.: Cornell University Press, 1985.

Aristides. "Merely Anecdotal." *The American Scholar* 61 (1992): 167–76.

———. "Toys in My Attic." *The American Scholar* 61 (1992): 7–16.

Avner, Ziv, ed. *Jewish Humor.* Tel Aviv: Papyrus Publishing House, 1986.

Baker, Robert A., ed. *A Stress Analysis of a Strapless Evening Gown and Other Essays for a Scientific Age.* New York: Prentice Hall Press, 1987.

Barson, Michael, ed. *Flywheel, Shyster, and Flywheel: The Marx Brothers' Lost Radio Show.* New York: Pantheon Books, 1988.

Batman, Nancy Jo. *Yeah, But How Would She Look Beside the Go-Kart Trophy?* St. Louis: Chalice Press, 1992.

Becker, Ernest. *The Denial of Death.* New York: Free Press, 1973.

———. *Escape From Evil.* New York: Free Press, 1975.

Beker, J. Christiaan. *Suffering and Hope: The Biblical Vision and the Human Predicament.* Philadelphia: Fortress Press, 1987.

Berger, Peter. *The Precarious Vision: A Sociologist Looks at Social Fiction and Christian Faith.* Garden City, N.Y.: Doubleday, 1961.

———. *A Rumour of Angels: Modern Sociology and the Rediscovery of the Supernatural.* Garden City, N.Y.: Doubleday, 1969.

Bermant, Chaim. *What's the Joke? A Study of Jewish Humor Through the Ages.* London: Weidenfeld and Nicolson, 1986.

Bierce, Ambrose. *The Devil's Dictionary.* New York: Dover Publications, 1958.

Birnbaum, David. *God and Evil: A Unified Theodicy/Theology/Philosophy.* Hoboken, N.J.: Ktav Publishing House, 1989.

Blue, Lionel. *To Heaven With Scribes and Pharisees.* New York: Oxford University Press, 1976.

Blyth, R. H. *Oriental Humor.* Tokyo: Hokuseido, 1959.

Bonfil, Robert. "The Devil and the Jews in the Christian Consciousness of the Middle Ages," in Almog, ed., *Antisemitism Through the Ages.*

Borge, Victor, and Sherman, Robert. *My Favorite Intermissions.* New York: Dorset Press, 1991.

Boyer, Paul, and Nissenbaum, Stephen. *Salem Possessed.* Cambridge, Mass.: Harvard University Press, 1974.

Brigham Young University Law Review 1992, 2—Special number: "Symposium on Humor and the Law."

Bruno de Jésus-Marie, ed. *Satan.* New York: Sheed and Ward, 1952.

Buber, Martin. *Good and Evil.* New York: Scribner, 1953.

Buechner, Frederick. *The Alphabet of Grace.* New York: Seabury Press, 1970.

———. *The Clown in the Belfry: Writings on Faith and Fiction.* San Francisco: HarperSanFrancisco, 1992.

———. *Telling the Truth: The Gospel as Tragedy, Comedy, and Fairy Tale.* San Francisco: Harper & Row, 1977.

Burnham, Sophy. *Angel Letters.* New York: Ballantine Books, 1991.

———. *A Book of Angels.* New York: Ballantine Books, 1990.

Camus, Albert. *The Rebel.* Translated by Anthony Bower. New York: Vintage, 1956.

Carmichael, Joel. *The Satanizing of the Jews: Origin and Development of Mystical Anti-Semitism.* New York: Fromm International, 1992.

Chapman, Anthony and Foot, Hugh, eds. *It's a Funny Thing, Humour.* Oxford: Pergamon Press, 1977.

Chopp, Rebecca S. *The Power to Speak: Feminism, Language, God.* New York: Crossroad, 1989.

Cobb, John B., Jr., and Ives, Christopher, eds. *The Emptying God: Buddhist-Jewish-Christian Conversation.* Maryknoll N.Y.: Orbis Books, 1990.

Cohen, Sarah Blacher, ed. *Comic Relief: Humor in Contemporary American Literature.* Detroit: Wayne State University Press, 1992.

———, ed. *Jewish Wry: Essays on Jewish Humor.* Bloomington, Ind.: Indiana University Press, 1987.

Coles, Robert. *The Spiritual Life of Children.* Boston: Houghton Mifflin, 1990.

Cosby, Bill. *Love and Marriage.* New York: Bantam Books, 1990.

Cox, Harvey. *The Feast of Fools: A Theological Essay on Festivity and Fantasy.* Cambridge, Mass.: Harvard University Press, 1969.

———. *Religion in the Secular City: Toward a Postmodern Theology.* New York: Simon and Schuster, 1984.

———. *The Secular City: Secularization and Urbanization in Theological Perspective,* rev. ed. New York: Macmillan, 1966.

Crossan, John Dominic. *The Dark Interval: Towards a Theology of Story.* Allen, Tx.: Argus/DLM Communications, 1975.

———. *Raid on the Articulate: Comic Eschatology in Jesus and Borges.* San Francisco: Harper & Row, 1976.

Dante Alighieri. *The Divine Comedy of Dante Alighieri,* 3 vols. Edited and translated by Allen Mandelbaum. New York: Bantam Books, 1982, 1984, 1986.

Davies, Christie. *Ethnic Humor Around the World: A Comparative Analysis.* Bloomington, Ind.: Indiana University Press, 1990.

Davies, Robertson. *The Rebel Angels.* New York: Viking Press, 1981.

Demos, John. *Entertaining Satan: Witchcraft and the Culture of Early New England.* New York: Oxford University Press, 1982.

Donnelly, Doris. "Divine Folly: Being Religious and the Exercise of Humor." *Theology Today* 48 (1992): 385–98.

The Door (bimonthly).

Downey, Michael, ed. *In Praise of the Irish.* New York: Continuum, 1985.

Domoulin, Heinrich. *A History of Zen Buddhism.* Translated by Paul Peachey. New York: Pantheon, 1963.

Dudden, Arthur Power, ed. *American Humor.* New York: Oxford University Press, 1987.

Durant, J., and Miller, C. J., eds. *Laughing Matters: A Serious Look at Humor.* New York: John Wiley, 1988.

Eckardt, Alice L., and Eckardt, A. Roy. *Long Night's Journey Into Day: A Revised Retrospective on the Holocaust.* Detroit: Wayne State University Press; Oxford: Pergamon Press, 1988.

Eckardt, A. Roy. *Black-Woman-Jew: Three Wars for Human Liberation.* Bloomington, Ind.: Indiana University Press, 1989.

———. *Collecting Myself: A Writer's Retrospective.* Edited by Alice L. Eckardt. Atlanta: Scholars Press, 1993.

———. "The Devil and Yom Kippur." *Midstream* 20 (Aug./Sept. 1974): 67–75.

———. "Divine Incongruity: Comedy and Tragedy in a Post-Holocaust World." *Theology Today* 48 (1992): 399–412.

———. *For Righteousness' Sake: Contemporary Moral Philosophies.* Bloomington, Ind.: Indiana University Press, 1987.

———. "Is There a Christian Laughter?" *Encounter* (Indianapolis) 53 (1992): 109–17.

———. *Jews and Christians: The Contemporary Meeting.* Bloomington, Ind.: Indiana University Press, 1986.

———. *No Longer Aliens, No Longer Strangers: Christian Faith and Ethics for Today.* Atlanta: Scholars Press, 1994.

———. *Reclaiming the Jesus of History: Christology Today.* Minneapolis, Minn.: Fortress Press, 1992.

———. *Sitting in the Earth and Laughing: A Handbook of Humor.* New Brunswick, N.J. and London: Transaction Publishers, 1992.

———. "Why Do You Search Among the Dead?" *Encounter* (Indianapolis) 51 (1990): 1–17.

———. *Your People, My People: The Meeting of Jews and Christians.* New York: Quadrangle/The New York Times Book Company, 1974.

Eco, Umberto. "Frames of Comic 'Freedom,'" in *Carnival!* Edited by Thomas A. Seboek, pp. 1–9. Berlin: Mouton, 1984.

Elliott, Bob, and Goulding, Ray. *From Approximately Coast to Coast It's The Bob and Ray Show.* New York: Atheneum, 1983.

———. *The New! Improved! Bob and Ray Book.* New York: McGraw Hill Book Company, 1986.

Erikson, Kai T. *Wayward Puritans.* New York: John Wiley, 1966.

Fackenheim, Emil L. *God's Presence in History: Jewish Affirmations and Philosophical Reflections.* New York: New York University Press, 1970.

———. *The Jewish Thought of Emil Fackenheim: A Reader.* Edited by Michael L. Morgan. Detroit: Wayne State University Press, 1987.

———. *Quest for Past and Future: Essays in Jewish Theology.* Boston: Beacon Press, 1970.

———. *What Is Judaism? An Interpretation for the Present Age.* New York: Summit Books, 1987.

Farley, Wendy. *Tragic Vision and Divine Compassion: A Contemporary Theodicy.* Louisville, Ky.: Westminster/John Knox Press, 1990.

Feinsilver, Lillian Mermin. *A Taste of Yiddish: A Warm and Humorous Guide to a Fascinating Language.* South Brunswick, N.J. and New York: A. S. Barnes, 1980.

Forsyth, Neil. *The Old Enemy: Satan & the Combat Myth.* Princeton: Princeton University Press, 1989.

Fred Allen's Letters. Edited by Joe McCarthy. New York: Pocket Books, 1966.

Freud, Sigmund. *Jokes and Their Relation to the Unconscious.* Translated by James Strachey. New York: Norton, 1960.

Friedlander, Albert H. *A Thread of Gold: Journeys Towards Reconciliation.* Translated by John Bowden. London: SCM Press; Philadelphia: Trinity Press International, 1990.

Frye, Roland M. *God, Man, and Satan: Patterns of Christian Thought and Life in Paradise Lost, Pilgrim's Progress, and the Great Theologians.* Princeton: Princeton University Press, 1960.

Fulkerson, Mary McClintock. "Sexism as Original Sin: Developing a Theacentric Discourse." *Journal of the American Academy of Religion* 59 (1991): 653-75.

Gall, Robert S. "Of/From Theology and Deconstruction." *Journal of the American Academy of Religion* 58 (1990): 413-37.

Galligan, Edward L. *The Comic Vision in Literature.* Athens, Ga.: University of Georgia Press, 1984.

Garrett, Susan R. *The Demise of the Devil: Magic and the Demonic in Luke's Writings.* Minneapolis, Minn.: Augsburg Fortress, 1989.

God: The Ultimate Autobiography. London: Pan Books, 1989.

Greeley, Andrew M. *The Devil You Say!: Man and His Personal Devils and Angels.* New York: Doubleday, 1974.

Green, Michael. *I Believe in Satan's Downfall.* London: Hodder & Stoughton, 1988.

Greenberg, Irving. *The Jewish Way: Living the Holidays.* New York: Summit Books, 1988.

Griswold, Wendy. "The Devil's Techniques: Cultural Legitimation and Social Change." *American Sociological Review* 48 (1983): 668-80.

Gritsch, Eric W. *Martin—God's Court Jester: Luther in Retrospect.* Philadelphia: Fortress Press, 1983.

Gurewitch, Morton. *Comedy: The Irrational Vision.* Ithaca, N.Y.: Cornell University Press, 1975.

Gutman, Yisrael, and Rothkirchen Livia, eds. *The Catastrophe of European Jewry: Antecedents-History-Reflections.* Jerusalem: Yad Vashem, 1976.

Gutiérrez, Gustavo. *The Power of the Poor in History.* Translated by Robert R. Barr. Maryknoll, N.Y.: Orbis Books, 1983.

Hall, Rich, and friends. *Unexplained Sniglets of the Universe.* New York: Macmillan, 1986.

Hampson, Daphne. *Theology and Feminism.* Oxford: Basil Blackwell, 1990.

Harris, Maria. "Religious Educators and the Comic Vision." *Religious Education* 75 (1980): 422-32.

Haynes, Stephen R. *Prospects for Post-Holocaust Theology.* Atlanta: Scholars Press, 1991.

Hoff, Benjamin. *The Tao of Pooh.* New York: Penguin Books, 1983.

———. *The Te of Piglet.* New York: E. P. Dutton, 1992.

Holland, N. N. *Laughing: A Psychology of Humor.* Ithaca, N.Y.: Cornell University Press, 1982.

Huizinga, John. *Homo Ludens: A Study of the Play Element in Culture.* Boston: Beacon Press, 1950.

Humor: International Journal of Humor Research (quarterly).

Hyers, Conrad. *And God Created Laughter: The Bible as Divine Comedy.* Atlanta: John Knox Press, 1987.

———. *The Comic Vision and the Christian Faith.* New York: Pilgrim Press, 1981.

———. *Holy Laughter.* New York: Seabury Press, 1969.

———. *The Laughing Buddha: Zen and the Comic Spirit,* rev. and exp. ed. Wakefield, N.H.: Longwood Academic, 1991.

Johnson, Robert A. *Ecstasy: Understanding the Psychology of Joy.* San Francisco: HarperSanFrancisco, 1989.

Jónsson, Jakob. *Humour and Irony in the New Testament: Illuminated by Parallels in Talmud and Midrash.* Reykjavík: Bókaútgafa Manningársjóds, 1965.

Jung, Carl G. "The Light With the Shadow." *Collected Works* 10: 218–26. Princeton: Princeton University Press, 1970.

———. "The Shadow." *Collected Works* 9: 3–7. Princeton: Princeton University Press, 1968.

Kaufman, Gloria, ed. *In Stitches: A Patchwork of Feminist Humor and Satire.* Bloomington, Ind.: Indiana University Press, 1991.

Kaufman, Gloria, and Blakely, Mary Kay. *Pulling Our Own Strings: Feminist Humor and Satire.* Bloomington, Ind.: Indiana University Press, 1980.

Keen, Sam. *To A Dancing God.* New York: Harper & Row, 1970.

Keillor, Garrison. *Lake Wobegon Days.* New York: Viking, 1985.

———. *Leaving Home.* New York-Penguin Books, 1989.

———. *We Are Still Married: Stories & Letters.* New York: Viking, 1989.

Kierkegaard, Søren. *Concluding Unscientific Postscript.* Translated by David F. Swenson. Princeton: Princeton University Press, 1941.

———. *Parables of Kierkegaard.* Edited by Thomas C. Oden. Princeton: Princeton University Press, 1978.

Klaits, Joseph. *Servants of Satan: The Age of the Witch Hunts.* Bloomington, Ind.: Indiana University Press, 1985.

Kundera, Milan. *The Book of Laughter and Forgetting.* Translated by Michael Henry Heim. New York: Penguin Books, 1981.

Lane, Belden. "Grace and the Grotesque." *The Christian Century.* 107 (1990): 1067–69.

————. "Merton as Zen Clown." *Theology Today* 46 (1989): 256–58.

Lattimore, Richmond. "Why the Devil Is the Devil." *Proceedings of the American Philosophical Society* 106 (1962): 427–29.

Laytner, Anson. *Arguing With God: A Jewish Tradition.* Northvale, N.J.: Jason Aronson, 1990.

Lear, Edward. *The Nonsense Books of Edward Lear.* New York: New American Library, 1964.

Lebowitz, Fran. *Social Studies.* New York: Pocket Books, 1982.

Levenson, Jon D. *Creation and the Persistence of Evil: The Jewish Drama of Divine Omnipotence.* San Francisco: Harper & Row, 1988.

Levin, Harry. *Playboys and Killjoys: An Essay on the Theory and Practice of Comedy.* New York and Oxford: Oxford University Press, 1988.

————. ed. *Veins of Humor.* Cambridge, Mass.: Harvard University Press, 1972.

Lewis, C. S. *A Grief Observed.* London: Faber, 1985.

————. *The Screwtape Letters.* London: Collins Fount, 1977.

————. *Surprised By Joy.* London: Fount, 1977.

L'Heureux, John. *Comedians.* New York: Viking Press, 1990.

Lipman, Steve. *Laughter in Hell: The Use of Humor during the Holocaust.* Northvale, N.J. and London: Jason Aronson, 1991.

McCann, Graham. *Woody Allen: New Yorker.* Cambridge: Polity Press/Basil Blackwell, 1990.

Maccoby, Hyam, ed. and trans. *The Day God Laughed: Sayings, Fables, and Entertainments of the Jewish Sages.* New York: St. Martin's Press, 1977.

McGloin, Joseph T. *I'll Die Laughing.* Chicago: Loyola University Press, 1990.

MacGregor, Geddes. *Angels: Ministers of Grace.* New York: Paragon House, 1988.

Mad (monthly).

Maduro, Otto, ed. *Judaism, Christianity, and Liberation: An Agenda for Dialogue.* Maryknoll, N.Y.: Orbis Books, 1991.

Manguel, Alberto, and Guadalupi, Gianni. *The Dictionary of Imaginary Places.* San Diego: Harcourt Brace Jovanovich, 1987.

Mann, Thomas. *Dr. Faustus.* New York: Knopf, 1948.

Marty, Martin E. "The Devil You Say: The Demonic Say I," in *Heterodoxy, Mystical Experience, Religious Dissent, and the Occult.* Edited by Richard Woods, pp. 101–04. Chicago: University of Chicago Press, 1975.

Marx, Groucho. *Memoirs of a Mangy Lover.* New York: Manor Books, 1963.

Marx, Groucho, and Anobile, Richard J. *The Marx Bros. Scrapbook.* New York: Darien House, 1976.

Mason, Jackie, with Ken Gross. *Jackie, Oy! Jackie Mason from Birth to Rebirth.* Boston: Little, Brown, 1988.

May, Rollo. *The Cry for Myth.* New York: W. W. Norton, 1991.

Merton, Thomas. *Honorable Reader: Reflections on My Work.* Edited by Robert E. Daggy. New York: Crossroad, 1991.

Metz, Johann Baptist, and Jossua, Jean-Pierre, eds. *Fundamental Theology: "You have sorrow now, but your hearts will rejoice."* London: Concilium, 1974.

Miedziam, Myriam. *Boys Will Be Boys: Breaking the Link Between Masculinity and Violence.* New York: Doubleday, 1991.

Moltmann, Jürgen. *The Way of Jesus Christ: Christology in Messianic Dimensions.* Translated by Margaret Kohl. San Francisco: HarperSanFrancisco, 1990.

Morreall, John, ed. *The Philosophy of Laughter and Humor.* Albany, N.Y.: State University of New York Press, 1987.

———. *Taking Laughter Seriously.* Albany, N.Y.: State University of New York Press, 1983.

Murray, Henry A. *Endeavors in Psychology: Selections from the Personology of Henry A. Murray.* Edited by Edwin S. Shneidman. New York: Harper & Row, 1981.

Nelson, Gertrud Mueller. *To Dance With God: Family Ritual and Community Celebration.* New York and Mahwah, N.J.: Paulist Press, 1986.

Nicholls, William. *Christian Antisemitism: A History of Hate.* Northvale, N.J. and London: Jason Aronson, 1993.

Niebuhr, H. Richard. *Faith on Earth: An Inquiry into the Structure of Human Faith.* Edited by Richard R. Niebuhr. New Haven, Conn. and London: Yale University Press, 1989.

———. *The Meaning of Revelation.* New York: Macmillan, 1941.

———. *Radical Monotheism and Western Culture.* New York: Harper & Brothers, 1960.

———. *The Responsible Self: An Essay in Christian Moral Philosophy.* Edited by Richard R. Niebuhr and James M. Gustafson. San Francisco: Harper & Row, 1978.

Niebuhr, Reinhold. *Beyond Tragedy.* New York: Scribner, 1937.

———. *Christianity and Power Politics.* New York: Scribner, 1940.

———. *Christian Realism and Political Problems.* New York: Scribner, 1953.

———. *Faith and History.* New York: Scribner, 1949.

———. "Humour and Faith," in *Discerning the Signs of the Times,* pp. 111–31. New York: Scribner, 1946.

———. *An Interpretation of Christian Ethics.* New York: Harper & Bros., 1935.

———. *Justice and Mercy.* Edited by Ursula M. Niebuhr. New York: Harper & Row, 1974.

———. *Man's Nature and His Communities.* New York: Scribner, 1965.

———. *The Nature and Destiny of Man,* 2 vols. New York: Scribner, 1941, 1943.

———. *The Self and the Dramas of History.* New York: Scribner, 1955.

———. *The Structure of Nations and Empires.* New York: Scribner, 1959.

Novak, William, and Waldoks, Moshe, eds. *The Big Book of Jewish Humor.* New York: Harper & Row, 1981.

———. *The Big Book of New American Humor: The Best of the Past 25 Years.* New York: HarperCollins, 1990.

Oberman, Heiko A. *Luther: Man Between God and the Devil.* Translated by Eileen Walliser-Schwarzbart. New York: Doubleday Image Books, 1992.

O'Brien, Edna. *Lantern Slides: Short Stories.* London: Weidenfeld and Nicolson, 1990.

O'Rourke, P. J. *Holiday in Hell.* New York: Atlantic Monthly Press, 1988.

Otto, Rudolf. *The Idea of the Holy.* Translated by John W. Harvey. New York: Oxford University Press, 1958.

Parker, Dorothy. *The Penguin Dorothy Parker.* London: Penguin, 1977.

Pekarske, Daniel T. "Santayana on Laughter and Prayer." *American Journal of Theology & Philosophy* 11 (1990): 143–52.

Peters, Ted. "The Selling of Satan in Popular Literature." *The Christian Century* 108 (1991): 458–62.

Plaskow, Judith. "Facing the Ambiguity of God." *Tikkun* 6, 5 (1991): 70, 96.

———. *Sex, Sin and Grace: Woman's Experience and the Theologies of Reinhold Niebuhr and Paul Tillich.* Washington, D.C.: University Press of America, 1980.

———. *Standing Again at Sinai: Judaism from a Feminist Perspective.* San Francisco: Harper & Row, 1991.

Podhoretz, Norman. "Speak of the Devil." *Commentary* 51 (April 1971): 6.

Polhemus, Robert M. *Comic Faith: The Great Tradition From Austen to Joyce.* Chicago: University of Chicago Press, 1981.

Rahner, Hugo. *Man at Play.* New York: Herder and Herder, 1967.

Randolph, Vance. *Pissing in the Snow and Other Ozark Folktales.* Urbana, Ill. and Chicago: University of Illinois Press, 1986.

The Random House Book of Humor for Children. Selected by Pamela Pollack. New York: Random House, 1988.

Raskin, Richard. *Life is Like a Glass of Tea: Studies of Classic Jewish Jokes.* Philadelphia: Jewish Publication Society, 1992.

Richler, Mordecai. *The Best of Modern Humour.* Harmondsworth, Middlesex: Penguin Books, 1984.

Rivers, Joan. *Still Talking.* New York: Random House, 1991.

Rosten, Leo. *Leo Rosten's Giant Book of Laughter.* New York: Bonanza Books, 1989.

Russell, Jeffrey Burton. *The Devil: Perceptions of Evil from Antiquity to Primitive Christianity.* Ithaca, N.Y. and London: Cornell University Press, 1987.

————. *Lucifer: The Devil in the Middle Ages.* Ithaca, N.Y. and London: Cornell University Press, 1984.

————. *Mephistopheles: The Devil in the Modern World.* Ithaca, N.Y. and London: Cornell University Press, 1990.

————. *The Prince of Darkness: Radical Evil and the Power of Good in History.* Ithaca, N.Y. and London: Cornell University Press, 1988.

————. *Satan: The Early Christian Tradition.* Ithaca, N.Y. and London: Cornell University Press, 1987.

Satan: The Hiss and Tell Memoirs. London: Pan Books, 1989.

Sartre, Jean-Paul. *The Devil and the Good Lord.* Translated by Kitty Black. New York: Vintage Books, 1960.

Sayward, John. *Perfect Fools: Folly for Christ's Sake in Catholic and Orthodox Spirituality.* Oxford: Oxford University Press, 1980.

Schiff, Stephen. "Edward Gorey and the Tao of Nonsense." *The New Yorker* (9 Nov. 1992): 84–94.

Schulweis, Harold M. *Evil and the Morality of God.* Cincinnati, Oh.: Hebrew Union College Press, 1984.

Schulz, Charles M. *And the Beagles and the Bunnies Shall Lie Down Together: The Theology in Peanuts.* Horsham, West Sussex: Ravette Books, 1984.

Shalit, Gene, ed. *Laughing Matters: A Celebration of American Humor.* New York: Ballantine Books, 1987.

Shenker, Israel. *Coat of Many Colors: Pages From Jewish Life.* Garden City, N.Y.: Doubleday, 1985.

————. "The Man Who Talked Back to God." *The New York Times Book Review* (11 Aug. 1991): 11.

Short, William J. "Restoring Eden: Medieval Legends of Saints and Animals." *Continuum* 2 (1992): 43–57.

Siegel, Lee. *Laughing Matters: Comic Tradition in India.* Chicago: University of Chicago Press, 1987.

Singer, June. *Boundaries of the Soul: The Practice of Jung's Psychology.* Garden City, N.Y.: Doubleday Anchor Books, 1977.

Sontag, Frederick. *The God of Evil: An Argument from the Existence of the Devil.* New York: Harper & Row, 1970.

Spalding, Henry E., comp. and ed. *Encyclopedia of Jewish Humor: From Biblical Times to the Modern Age.* New York: Jonathan David, 1969.

Spiegelman, Art. *Maus: A Survivor's Tale,* 2 vols. New York: Pantheon Books, 1986, 1991.

Stendahl, Krister. "Theology With Humor," "The Jewish Humor of Jesus," "Worship With Humor." Walter Pope Binns Lecture Series, 1987. Liberty, Mo.: William Jewel College, 1987.

Suzuki, D. T. *Zen Buddhism.* Garden City, N.Y.: Doubleday, 1956.

Swabey, Marie Collins. *Comic Laughter: A Philosophical Essay.* Hamden, Conn.: Archon Books, 1970.

Tannen, Deborah. *You Just Don't Understand: Women and Men in Conversation.* New York: Ballantine Books, 1990.

Taylor, James C. *A New Porcine History of Philosophy and Religion.* Nashville, Tenn.: Abingdon Press, 1992.

Thurber, James. *Collecting Himself: James Thurber on Writing and Writers, Humor and Himself.* Edited by Michael J. Rosen. London: Hamish Hamilton, 1989.

———. *Lances and Lanterns.* New York: Harper & Bros., 1961.

———. *The Thurber Carnival.* New York: Harper & Bros., 1945.

———. *Thurber on Crime.* Edited by Robert Lopresti. New York: Warner Books, 1991.

Tiger, Lionel, and Fox, Robin. *The Imperial Animal.* New York: Holt, Rinehart and Winston, 1971.

Tillich, Paul. *The Courage To Be.* New Haven, Conn.: Yale University Press, 1952.

———. *A History of Christian Thought: From Its Judaic and Hellenistic Origins to Existentialism.* Edited by Carl E. Braaten. New York: Simon and Schuster, 1968.

———. *The Interpretation of History.* New York: Scribner, 1936.

———. *Political Expectation.* Edited by James Luther Adams. New York: Harper & Row, 1971.

———. *The Protestant Era.* Translated by James Luther Adams. Chicago: University of Chicago Press, 1948.

———. "The Right to Hope." *The Christian Century* 107 (1990): 1064–67.

———. *Systematic Theology,* 3 vols. Chicago: University of Chicago Press, 1951, 1957, 1963.

Tinsley, E. J. *Christian Theology and the Frontiers of Tragedy.* Leeds: Leeds University Press, 1963.

Towne, Anthony, ed. *Excerpts From the Diaries of the Late God.* New York: Harper & Row, 1968.

Trachtenberg, Joshua. *The Devil and the Jews: The Medieval Conception of the Jew and Its Relation to Modern Anti-Semitism.* Cleveland, Oh. and New York: Meridian Books; Philadelphia: Jewish Publication Society of America, 1961 [1943].

Trillin, Calvin. *Enough's Enough (And Other Rules of Life).* New York: Ticknor & Fields, 1990.

———. *Uncivil Liberties.* New York: Penguin Books, 1987.

Ustinov, Peter. *The Old Man and Mr. Smith: A Fable.* New York: Arcade-Little Brown, 1990.

Via, Dan O., Jr. *Kerygma and Comedy in the New Testament.* Philadelphia: Fortress Press, 1975.

Vos, Nelvin. *For God's Sake Laugh!* Richmond, Va.: John Knox Press, 1967.

Walker, Alice. *Possessing the Secret of Joy.* San Diego: Harcourt Brace Jovanovich, 1992.

Walker, Nancy A. *A Very Serious Thing: Women's Humor and American Culture.* Minneapolis, Minn.: University of Minnesota Press, 1988.

Walker, Nancy, and Dresner, Zita, eds. *Redressing the Balance: American Women's Humor from the Colonies to the 1980s.* Jackson, Miss.: University of Mississippi Press, 1988.

Watts, Murray. *Bats in the Belfry.* Eastbourne, East Sussex: Minstrel, 1989.

————. *Rolling in the Aisles.* Eastbourne, East Sussex: Marc, 1987.

Wechsler, Robert, ed. *In A Fog: The Humorists' Guide to England.* Highland Park, N.J.: Catbird Press, 1989.

Welch, Sharon D. *A Feminist Ethic of Risk.* Minneapolis, Minn.: Fortress, 1990.

Welsford, Enid. *The Fool: His Literary and Social History.* Magnolia, Mass.: Peter Smith, n.d.

White, E. B. *Essays of E. B. White.* New York: Harper Colophon Books, 1979.

————. *Letters of E. B. White.* Edited by Dorothy Lobrano Guth. New York: Harper & Row, 1978.

————. *The Second Tree From the Corner.* New York: Harper & Row, 1989.

Wiesel, Elie. *The Trial of God (as it was held on February 25, 1649 in Shamgorod),* a play in three acts. Translated by Marion Wiesel. New York: Random House, 1979.

Wiesenthal, Simon. *Every Day Remembrance Day: A Chronicle of Jewish Martyrdom.* Philadelphia: American Interfaith Institute, 1992.

Williamson, Clark M. *A Guest in the House of Israel: Towards a Post-Holocaust Church Theology.* Louisville, Ky.: Westminster/John Knox, 1993.

Willimon, William W., comp. *And the Laugh Shall Be First: A Treasury of Religious Humor.* Nashville, Tenn.: Abingdon Press, 1986.

————. comp. *Last Laugh.* Nashville, Tenn.: Abingdon Press, 1991.

Willis, John Randolph. *Pleasures Forevermore: The Theology of C. S. Lewis.* Chicago: Loyola University Press, 1990.

Wilson, A. N. *C. S. Lewis: A Biography.* New York and London: W. W. Norton, 1990.

Wolpe, David. *The Healer of Shattered Hearts: A Jewish View of God.* New York: Holt, 1990.

Wood, Ralph C. *The Comedy of Redemption: Christian Faith and Comic Vision in Four American Novelists.* Notre Dame, Ind.: University of Notre Dame Press, 1988.

Wright, Nigel. *The Satan Syndrome.* Grand Rapids, Mich.: Zondervan, 1990.

Wyschogrod, Michael. *The Body of Faith: God in the People Israel.* San Francisco: Harper & Row, 1989.

Index